MANNO'S MANOR
The Story of Wolverton to 1838

Bryan Dunleavy

Magic Flute Publications

MANNO'S MANOR

Published by Magic Flute Publications 2013

ISBN 978-1-909054-05-9
Copyright © Bryan Dunleavy

Bryan Dunleavy has asserted his right under the Copyright, Designs
and Patents Act 1988 to be identified as the author of this work.
All rights reserved. No part of this publication may be reproduced,
stored in a retrieval system, or transmitted in any form or by any means,
electronic, mechanical, photocopying, recording or otherwise, without the
prior permission of the copyright owner.

Magic Flute Publications is an imprint of
Magic Flute Artworks Limited
231 Swanwick Lane
Southampton SO31 7GT

www.magicfluteartworks.com
www.magicflutepublications.co.uk

Illustrations © Bryan Dunleavy

A description of this book is available from the British Library

CONTENTS

PREFACE vii

ONE 1

Trackway, Waterway and Railway 1

TWO 11

Before the Manor 11

Bronze Age Settlement 14

Wolverton in the Roman Period 17

The Anglo-Saxon Settlement 22

Wolverton's First Village? 24

The Development of Anglian Society 28

The Situation in 1066 31

THREE 37

The Barons of Wolverton 37

The Barony 39

Life on the Manor 47

The Succession 51

The Third Baron 54

The End of the de Wolverton Line 59

William Vis de Lou and the Knights 60

FOUR 67

Town and Country 67

The Birth of the Town 72

A Child of Two Manors 76

Economic Development in the 13th and 14th Centuries 78

FIVE 91

Medieval Life in Wolverton 91

The Development of The Manor 91

The Open Fields 97

A Walk around the Manor in 1307 100

The Early Church in Wolverton 109

Population Growth 113

The Black Death and Wolverton 115

Social Change 117

SIX 121

The Rise of the Longuevilles 121

Wolverton in the 15th century................................... 130

Medieval Industry In Wolverton and Stony Stratford 131

Three Kings and Stony Stratford............................... 135

SEVEN 141

The Longueville Ascendancy 141

The End of Bradwell Priory...................................... 141

The Reformed Church 145

The Enclosures 147

Farms 155

Michael Hipwell's Will... 156

The Longueville's Last Century................................. 157

The Manor House 160

EIGHT 165

The 18th. Century and the Radcliffe Trust 165

A Brief Life of Doctor Radcliffe 169

Managing the Manor... 172

The Stony Stratford Fires 184

Clergy at Wolverton in the 18th Century 185

Parish Welfare 189

18th Century Buildings in Wolverton........................ 191

The Radcliffe Trust 195

NINE 199

Thomas Harrison and the Canal Age 199

Thomas Harrison and the Copper King 204

The Canal Comes to Wolverton 212

Wolverton House 216

TEN 221

Wolverton before the Age of Steam 221

Roads, Inns and the Coaching Trade 221

Trades in Stony Stratford 229

A New Church for Wolverton.................................... 234

Tucker's Girl 236
The Slow Decline of Farming 240
A Cock and Bull Story 243
Appendix I Wolverton at Domesday 247
Appendix II The Estates of the Barony 248
Appendix III Lords of the Manor 255
Appendix IV Vicars of Holy Trinity 256
Appendix V The Cock Inn 259
Appendix VI Money 265
Bibliography 267
Acknowledgements 272

List of Illustrations

The Canal Bridge at Wolverton 1819 .... page 1
Early Settlement at Wolverton .... page 16
Wolverton at Domesday .... page 32
Map of The Barony of Wolverton .... page 41
Landholdings in Buckinghamshire .... page 44
Barons of Wolverton: genealogical chart .... page 53
Barons of Wolverton 13th and 14th century chart .... page 58
Seal of William Vis de Lou .... page 61
Section of the 14th century "Gough" map .... page 81
Stony Stratford circa 1180 .... page 82
Stony Stratford circa 1220 .... page 84
Stony Stratford at the end of the 14th century .... page 86
The Manor in 1200 .... page 93
Wolverton's Open Fields .... page 98
Fields at Padbury showing Medieval strip farming .... page 100
Medieval Wolverton .... page 102
A Manor House c. 1200 .... page 105
Ploughing from the Luttrell Psalter .... page 106
Sheep Husbandry from the Luttrell Psalter .... page 108
Holy Trinity: The Medieval Church .... page 112
Longueville Genealogy, Part 1 .... page 125

Longueville Genealogy: Part II .... page 126

The Longueville Baronetcy .... page 158

The 1586 Manor House .... page 162

The Radcliffe Library .... page 166

The Radcliffe Infirmary .... page 167

The Radcliffe Observatory .... page 168

Dr. John Radcliffe .... page 169

Field Map after enclosure - west side .... page 178

Field map after enclosure east side .... page 179

Stony Stratford Great Fires .... page 184

A Page from the Churchwarden's Account Book .... page 190

Plan for the Durrant House .... page 193

Inventory of materials for the Durrant House .... page 194

A Portrait of Thomas Harrison .... page 200

Old Wolverton showing the Canal Locks in 1804 .... page 213

Working Barges on the Canal in the 1950s .... page 216

Wolverton House .... page 217

Wolverton House from the West .... page 218

Jeffreys map of 1776 .... page 223

Stony Stratford High Street: a view in the 1860s .... page 229

Stony Stratford Market Square in 1819 .... page 232

The New Holy Trinity .... page 235

A Map of Wolverton before the Railway .... page 241

PREFACE

In the early 1950s I came across a slim volume in Wolverton's Public library called *A Short History of Wolverton*. At the time my unformed mind was surprised. I did not think that Wolverton had a history; there were no castle ruins, no old churches and no ancient buildings, even in Old Wolverton, much more than a century and a half old. I did read the book, although I must confess that at the age of 11 it seemed rather dull, but it did stay with me and many years later I was able to find the book and read it properly.

The author was Francis Hyde, a man of my father's generation who grew up not 100 yards away from the house where I spent my own growing years in Wolverton. He went on to become an eminent Professor of Economic history at Liverpool University and his book remains the only book, as far as I am aware, written about the history of Wolverton by a professional historian. I never had the good fortune to meet Professor Hyde, but retracing his journey through Wolverton's history has been a rewarding one.

In the 65 years or so since he wrote his book much new information has come to light and this is my excuse for writing this history. The work undertaken by archaeologists in the Wolverton area over the last few decades is of enormous value in helping us to shape and in some respects reinterpret the history of the district. Some new documentary evidence has come to light, but for the most part what was there 70 years ago is still the same material that is available today; however, it has been possible to offer new interpretations of these documents in the light of archaeological discoveries.

Wolverton does not have a glamorous history. The people who lived and worked here over many centuries appear to have done so without the manor becoming the site of major battles or the birthplace of significant historical figures. People went through their timeless diurnal rituals, they were born, lived and died in this landscape and Wolverton may well have remained a provincial backwater were it not for the historical accident of a railway depot being sited on the edge of the manor. That major change and its consequences I will describe in the second projected volume of this history. Here I hope to describe the thousand years before 1838, when it was a manor much like any other in England. And because Wolverton was no more or less significant than a thousand other manors no attempt was made to record its history until there was a general growth of interest in the subject in the 18th century.

Browne Willis was probably the first local historian. He lived from 1682 to 1760 and his country seat was Whaddon Hall although he also built a large house at Water Hall in Bletchley, now the site of Bletchley Park. He was briefly a member of Parliament but in his mature years devoted his time and wealth to antiquarian interests. He published several books, the closest of which to our study is *The History of the Town, Hundred and Deanery of Buckingham*. This book appeared in 1755. The Reverend William Cole (1714-1782) served as rector at Bletchley between 1753 and 1767 left an important record in his notes and diaries about the area. He is highly regarded as an accurate antiquarian observer and has preserved for us some important nuggets of information, particularly about Wolverton's great house.

More ambitious work was undertaken in the 19th century, starting with the Lysons' brothers monumental (but never completed) *Magna Britannia* in 1811. In the mid-century George Lipscomb compiled, as only a Victorian could, *The History and Antiquities of the County of Buckingham* in 1847, a monumental work published in four volumes.

Following him, Oliver Ratcliff, an Olney printer, took it upon himself to print and publish *A History of the Newport Hundreds*. He rather unblushingly reprinted much of Lipscomb's work verbatim, but did add some material of his own. This he published in 1900, three years after the infant Sidney Frank Markham was born in Stony Stratford.

Sir Frank Markham, soldier, scholar, MP, became a dominant figure in North Bucks historical studies in his later years. He wrote and published a book on Stony Stratford's history in the 1940s, and then, once retired from his political life, turned his hand to a history of the North Bucks area he knew so well. This he published in his 70s just as North Bucks was beginning to transform itself into the new city of Milton Keynes.

My book keeps its focus on the manor of Wolverton. Inevitably that includes Stony Stratford. The manor did develop in interesting ways. Its position on the Watling Street by the River Ouse probably led to it being made the centre of a barony after 1066, and that in turn led to creating the circumstances for a town on the Watling Street. The manor was always a relatively wealthy one and even in straitened circumstances the last of the Longuevilles was able to sell the manor for £40,000. The untimely death of the purchaser, Dr. Radcliffe, only one year later led to the estate being under the control of a committee rather than an individual. As a result the estate developed under a group of distinguished men who had no personal interest in the estate which probably put it under rather benign if unadventurous management. The sale of a corner of the estate to the new railway company in the 1830s transformed Wolverton in ways which no one could have imagined at the time. And it is here that this volume ends.

The first baron of Wolverton was a Breton soldier called Maigno in the Domesday Book, which is usually written as Mainou or Manno in a modern form. This may or may not be close to how the name was pronounced. I have seen one document where it is written as Mayny. I have chosen to call him Manno and this is the form I will use in the book, largely as a convenience for the modern reader.

I have applied a similar rule with the Longueville name. It does appear under variant spellings but this version will be used throughout the book.

This book attempt to cover a huge swathe of time and because of the almost complete absence of any information about Wolverton itself certain periods I have had to depend on our knowledge of England's wider history or to draw parallels with similar communities elsewhere. There is also the issue of time itself. It is often tempting to dismiss a century with a few sentences because we have so little to go on. What we summarily term the Middle Ages extended 1000 years in time, 30 generations. I have tried to keep this in mind throughout the book

ONE

TRACKWAY, WATERWAY AND RAILWAY

In the early 19th century the travel writer and illustrator John Hassell followed the progress of the new Grand Junction canal through Wolverton. This what he encountered:

> Passing Stone-bridge-house, by a very pleasant road, shaded with an abundance of very lofty trees, we come to the village of Wolverton. The country here burst upon us with peculiar beauty.[1]

This moment of observation had already been preceded by the development of the canal itself, twenty years before - a huge step forward in transportation and a mere glimmer of the change that was to come. Only 100 years earlier the first turnpike act had triggered a century of road improvement which in turn led to speedier travel and communications. Prior to that there was a long period of gradual, perhaps even imperceptible change, punctuated by a few seminal events such as the enclosure of the manor in the 17th century and the establishment of a market in Stony Stratford at the end of the 12th century.

The canal bridge at Wolverton in 1819

Manno's Manor

This engraving, which we can date before 1819, illustrates some features of the Wolverton landscape that we can still identify: the canal, the bridge by The Galleon, the turn on the Old Wolverton road and Cosgrove Hall in the distance. It may be the closest visual representation we have of Wolverton as an uncrowded landscape. Yet in the early 19th century the canal was novel. This new man-made feature of the landscape, in itself a radical transformation, was a pivotal point between the pre-nineteenth century world of timeless agricultural practice and an emerging world of technology. At our distance of 200 years this scene has the charm of a Constable painting (with which it is contemporary) and speaks to us of a time when activity was measured in days and weeks rather than minutes and hours but will I hope, provide us with a picture of a Wolverton which had already come a long way over 1,000 years. It represents Wolverton at the closing of this volume, a Wolverton adapting to its first introduction to industrial progress.

The engraving also, with similar subject matter to Constable's *Hay Wain*, offers us a useful glimpse into that world of 200 years past. There is a vast social differential between the large hall at Cosgrove and the simple cottages beside the canal. The wharf cottage on the right betrays its medieval vernacular antecedents with low walls and a steep roof and appears to be no more than a parlour with a sleeping loft above it. The thatched roofs appear to be universal and give a context to the Slated Row cottages erected a decade later, which must have appeared highly advanced to Wolverton natives. Horses, we are reminded, are the only means of land transport, and the barge, waiting to go over the iron trunk, represents the beginning of a new age.

It appears very old and quaint to us today but the picture does show us elements of a society in transition, and perhaps it is worth underscoring the point that society is always susceptible to change. We can merely note that change in the past came about at a slower pace than we are accustomed to in our present time.

At the time of writing this book people are confronting the prospect that High Street shopping may eventually disappear, and may be regarded by future historians as a 19th and 20th century phenomenon. For a few generations this was the way goods were passed from manufacturer to consumer and most people living through this period would not have given

Trackway, Waterway and Railway

the matter a second thought. Was it not always so? The short answer is no. Economies have always used different models adapted to particular social and political circumstances as well as to geography and technology. The High Street means of distribution evolved from a combination of industrial development and advanced distribution methods. Today ordering of goods and services can be accomplished through a computer and distribution can be speedily organised in the form of the delivery of a packet to your door.[2] No wonder village and small town shops are disappearing. The point of this preamble is to establish the fact that human society is always in a state of change. Change today is more dramatic and sudden and therefore more noticeable, whereas change in the past moved at a more glacial pace. In the present age a product can become obsolete within a decade and fields and towns can lose all sense of past identity within a generation. Places change. They are subject to development. Familiar monuments or landmarks disappear. The landscape is all too easily modified. This has been spectacularly apparent within the lifetime of many who grew up in the Milton Keynes area, although this rapid development has not been confined to this part of England. For these reasons alone it is worth trying to capture the history of the area while memory can still draw upon images of the recent past. Seckloe, the ancient Saxon meeting place, is now a fenced-off mound in the shopping centre of Milton Keynes. It is there; it has been preserved. But the surrounding development can in no way convey what it was for 1,000 years, and within recent memory, a high point at the edge of an unpopulated Bradwell Common with ancient trackways leading to it.

The place that has carried the name of Wolverton for over 1300 years is the subject of this history. Change has been a feature of its existence and those changes make up its history. Recent changes have been the more noticeable. Those growing up in the town in 1950 will be able to register dramatic changes. Their counterpart of 1850 might find little that they could identify. Anyone walking the lanes and trackways in 1750 might find the changes hard to understand and that landscape, which by that time had been enclosed in fields for 100 years, might be equally unrecognisable to a peasant tilling the fields in 1066. It is nonetheless the same place. Its history is the accumulating factor of interest and it is the expectation of these pages to trace that history from the earliest records.

Manno's Manor

There have been significant changes: the departure of the Romans in 400AD and the evolution of an Anglian kingdom, the Norman Conquest in 1066, the emergence of Stony Stratford in the 12th century, the land enclosure of the 16th and 17th centuries, the loss of a resident lord of the manor in the 18th century, the canal development at the end of the 18th century, the introduction of the railway in 1838 and the creation of Milton Keynes in 1970. Each of these triggers was pulled by external forces; none originated in Wolverton, but each one shaped the area. History is often large, and great movements can have big consequences for a local population remote from the centre. Most of these events affected everybody. The Roman abandonment of this island had a universal impact on the farming and the economic management of the country, as did the Norman Conquest 600 years later. Land enclosures were part of a country-wide trend as indeed were the cutting of canals. The railway enterprise was somewhat different in that the new workshop was quite specific to Wolverton, which then became more than an isolated railway station. While the industrial revolution affected everybody, the railways works brought this revolution to Wolverton's doorstep. It was the most radical change to come to Wolverton since the land enclosure and in my view enabled the greater change of Milton Keynes a century and a half later.

This volume is not going to be about the railway, but I feel I have to mention it first because it does offer a both and end point and a starting point for this history. Were it not for the railway development of the 19th century its history might have been similar to neighbouring Calverton, an equivalent manor bisected only by the Watling Street. For this reason alone Wolverton has a peculiar history.

The railway town of Wolverton as a railway town was an accident rather than the consequence of considered planning. The ancient village might have easily found its way into the 21st century like its namesake in Hampshire – a scattered and small population near to a small market town; however, decisions made in 1837, the year the young Victoria became queen, permanently and dramatically transformed a quiet rural area in the northern part of Buckinghamshire. The Manor of Wolverton, some 2,500 acres defined by the natural boundaries of the River Ouse and Bradwell Brook and the ancient line of the Watling Street, which had been an entity for more than 1.000 years was to change.

4

Trackway, Waterway and Railway

The impetus for this change began with the desire of Birmingham and London businessmen to link the two cities by rail. Discussions began in the 1820s and, after a long incubation period, the venture was finally approved by Act of Parliament in 1833. Wolverton was not in the minds of the promoters of the railway at that date and I doubt if anyone in North Buckinghamshire was paying much attention. The estate was not even close to a direct route between the two cities and the prospect of the new railway having any future impact on the Wolverton Manor was then remote. Two possible routes were proposed for the projected line – one which went through Oxford and Banbury and another through Aylesbury and Buckingham. By 1830 the eastern route was the preferred choice and a report from Richard Creed, the Board Secretary, appears to confirm this.

> Certainly the fertile vale of Aylesbury with its wide expanse of level ground, affords great inducement to look at it - Mr. R. Stephenson having besides called my attention to this point. I proceeded thence on the road to Buckingham, by the high grounds of Whitchurch, Wing and Winslow. extended my observations   sufficiently to the westward to ascertain where the levels   most favourable for our purposes were to be found.

> Having examined the ground on both banks of the Ouse west of Buckingham, and satisfied myself as to the direction that the line should take, I followed it to the town of Brackley.[3]

Ironically, the new and somewhat controversial plans for a high-speed rail line between London and Birmingham are not too far from the proposed route of 1830.

The original planned route from London to Birmingham would have taken the line closer to Buckingham and had this proceeded no line would have come close to the old village of Wolverton or the coaching town of Stony Stratford, but the Duke of Buckingham, then a powerful influence in Parliament, wished to preserve the 18th century peace and quiet of his Stowe estates and successfully deterred the directors from pursuing the matter further. So they fell back on an alternative survey undertaken by Robert Stephenson, which took the rail line north to Leighton Buzzard and through the eastern edge of the Wolverton estate. Wolverton was then, as

Manno's Manor

it had been since Domesday, a farming area which supported a small rural population.

The railway line which bordered Wolverton had been staked out by January 1834 but no decisions had been made about stations at that early stage. In the second week of October 1836 Edward Bury and Robert Stephenson were out on the line to determine locations for possible stations. At Wolverton, Bury pointed out the advantages of the site for a repair shop. It was at the side of the Grand Junction Canal which would be a considerable advantage in bringing in heavy materials and was also on a good cross country road but two miles from the coaching town of Stony Stratford. At 52½ miles from London and 60 miles from the terminus at Birmingham it was probably the best site for such a depot. The two men agreed and negotiations re-opened with the Radcliffe Trust for more land.[4]

And so the directors began to focus their attention upon Wolverton. It was by no means a bad choice. It was located roughly half-way between the two termini of the new railway and it had canal and road access. An engine repair shop was a necessity for those early steam engines whose boilers quickly scaled up. The depot maintained as many as 30 engines at Wolverton which would replace those which had done a fifty mile stint. I am sure that the directors were not thinking much beyond this when plans were first laid for Wolverton; in fact, Phillip Hardwick, the company architect, recommended that they keep the wooden shacks which had been erected for the navvies as temporary accommodation for the new work force. But some sort of plan did emerge for a large workshop surrounded on three sides by houses for the incoming workers. The layout of the "new town" was largely determined by the limits of the available space and the greedy consumption of most of that space by the workshop. Planning and design was given minimal attention and probably left to the builders. No architect, with the possible exception of Phillip Hardwick, who was asked to give a progress report, was involved in the design and construction of housing. The engine shed, however, was entrusted to an architect, although Edward Bury was not always in accord with the architect's design. In contrast, Swindon, Crewe and Derby each obtained the services of an architect to develop their new railway towns.

The relative lateness of the Wolverton decision is confirmed by the eventual purchase of an additional 8 acres for a station. The Board had

Trackway, Waterway and Railway

already purchased 27 acres at £60 an acre for the construction of the line and embankments but it was only in June of 1837, just over a year before the line was to be opened, that agreement was reached with The Radcliffe Trust, owners of the Wolverton Manor, for the sale which would mark the beginning of the new town. They had to pay a high price for it - £1,600, or £200 an acre at a time when £5 an acre would have been a good price for agricultural land.

It was not long before the inadequacies of this decision became apparent and in 1840 the railway company purchased a further 13 ½ acres to the south of the original plot for the creation of new houses and a station and refreshment rooms.

The new inhabitants were a mixed group, coming from all parts of England, Wales, Scotland and Ireland. They brought with them different religious allegiances and different cultural practices. The only thing that bound them was their common purpose. Not all stayed. George Weight, the first incumbent of St George's was to complain about the high turnover in his congregation during that first decade. The decade was one of great industrial expansion and families might easily have been tempted back to their roots once work commensurate with their skills became available. Those first years may well have been insecure. Although the railways were an extraordinary phenomenon for the time, it cannot have been obvious to many, even to those working in the new industry, that they could have a lifetime's employment and that this would extend to their sons and grandsons.

Wolverton was the first company built railway town. New Swindon and Crewe, coming as they did a few years later, had the advantage of learning from the Wolverton experience and were able to plan with a little more forethought. Indeed, Brunel was known to have visited Wolverton prior to the layout of Swindon. Wolverton's genesis was an ad hoc creation and its subsequent development was hampered by the legacy of those early decisions. No one was particularly to blame for this. Nobody could have foreseen the social ramifications of the development of a railway line that was simply intended to improve communications between the mercantile centre of London and the manufacturing centre of Birmingham. The Radcliffe Trustees for their part were guardians of an older heritage; the arrival of the railway proved to be a disruption, which they sometimes

Manno's Manor

struggled to accommodate. Wolverton's development was squeezed between the railway's desire to expand its mercantile enterprise and the Trustees' commitment to their tenants and their charitable interests. Had both parties been able to consider the impact and ramifications before they entered into a relationship in 1837, the history of Wolverton may well have been different. Much of Wolverton's 19th century development was set against the background of these two disparate interests.

The railway changed everything for Wolverton. It might well have continued its slow evolution from a Domesday manor. Who knows? But nothing starts entirely from scratch. Wolverton was to grow as a new town with red brick, terraced housing, but many of the people who came there, especially those who moved from North Buckinghamshire villages, arrived with their own set of values and experiences that had no connection with the railways or industry. The old and the new entered into a dynamic interplay that perhaps cannot be properly understood unless we examine Wolverton's past history.

The writer, Sidney Smith, visiting Wolverton in 1851, when it was beginning its second decade, made this observation about the character of life in Wolverton:

> When work is ended, Wolverton is a pure republic — equality reigns. There are no rich men or men of station: all are gentlemen.[5]

Smith, perceptively, saw the beginnings of a new culture in Wolverton. What he encountered in 1851 was genuinely new and no longer a world where peasants could be governed by the lord of the manor. Wolverton's new population were literate, independent-minded mechanics. Their rulers were a board of directors, not an individual with hereditary rights. What he discerned was the beginnings of a culture of community organisation, which later found its expression in Bands, Orchestras, Horticultural Societies, Sporting Clubs, Working Men's Clubs and Charitable organisations. This tendency evolved in the twentieth century into voting patterns, where the rising Labour Party could count on strong support from Wolverton voters. 1838 marks a break with the notion of gradual evolution spiked with occasional change. During the 1,000 years that preceded the "pure republic" of Sidney Smith's description it was a far from equal society. There was change and there were events but the change

Trackway, Waterway and Rail

was gradual and organic. An agricultural labourer of earlier centuries mig, reasonably expect his grandson to be doing the same work at the same pace and with the same tools. How much and how far this really changed, we shall see. The purpose of this volume is to survey the history of the area known as Wolverton before it sprang into being as the 19th century industrial town we can partly recognise today.

The old phrase "time out of mind" has dropped out of the language in recent years because our ever changing world has made the expression redundant but it could have been applied by Hassell to the attractive view he encountered before 1819. He was of John Constable's generation and Constable's much admired paintings became popular because there was a growing sense that the new industrial age was taking away a landscape that had been unaltered from time immemorial. That was part of the romantic cast of mind of the Constables and Wordsworths who tended to elevate the rural way of life above that which it was. The peasants of earlier ages who tilled the soil, broke the land, and fashioned their implements and houses and clothing by hand probably did not have time to reflect on the visual joys of the landscape. Their lives were, to quote a later writer, "nasty, brutish and short."[6]

Even as late as 1970 it was still possible to reconstruct the pre-industrial manor in one's imagination. Urban and industrial development in Wolverton and Stony Stratford had eaten away some farmland, but the four larger farms had survived for at least three centuries of record. Today, the leap of imagination is more difficult. Field names are preserved in recent housing developments, such as Greenleys and Fuller's Slade, figures from Wolverton's historical past can be discovered in street names, like Longville and Hamon, or the recent industrial past like McConnell and McCorquodale; however, the imaginative effort to reconstruct an earlier Wolverton is hard. When Professor Hyde wrote his *Short History of Wolverton* nearly 70 years ago it may have been easier to approach the distant past.

70 years ago there were very few remnants of medieval Wolverton. The old manor house was lost in the 18th century and was followed by the church at the outset of the 19th century. Stony Stratford held on to a few late medieval buildings after the destructive fires of the 18th century. Wolverton's ancient past is now held in surviving documents, in the

Manno's Manor

excellent archaeological work of the past 40 or 50 years, and in many external sources which can inform our understanding.

The manor has vanished. It was an economic construct that served its society through a long period when agriculture was the engine of the economy. Its foundations were weakened during the industrial revolution and it was obliterated in the post-industrial age. This history will try to recapture it.

---

1 J Hassell. Tour of the Grand Junction. Islington, 1819. p74-5
2 As an interesting aside, the very recent city of Milton Keynes has an economy that is given over almost entirely to warehousing and the distribution of goods.
3 Report to the Board of the London & Birmingham Railway. 4th July 1831
4 Harry Jack. Locomotives of the LNWR Southern Division. RCTS 2001. p. 26.
5 Sidney Smith. Rides on Railways. 1851
6 Thomas Hobbes. Leviathan. 1651.

TWO

BEFORE THE MANOR

Just over 900 years ago the place we know as Wolverton made its first appearance in a document.

In 1086, three years before his death, King William, ordered the remarkable land survey which has come down to us as the Domesday Book, so-called in its day because its thoroughness indeed resembled the "day of judgement" – a final reckoning. William's immediate purpose was to provide a vehicle for the settlement of land disputes and to determine taxation levels. Later generations, and ourselves with this particular reference, possess the first detailed assessment and description of the Manor of Wolverton and it is from here that we can begin to tell the story of the manor of Wolverton from a documented source.

Wolverton was therefore a recognised place at this date. The Manor of Wolverton had become an entity in Anglo-Saxon times sometime in the 9th century. according to most opinion and evidence, The natural boundaries of the River Great Ouse and the stream that runs down from Loughton and is known as Bradwell Brook defined it to the north and east. The green highway that cuts a straight track from London to Wroxeter, known as the Watling Street, was the western boundary, dividing Wolverton from Calverton as it divides many manors on a south-western and north-eastern line along its progress. We do not know when this road was built but it is estimated at some time during the first century of Roman occupation. We can assert with some confidence that the presence of this road was judged to be a boundary when the Saxons began to develop their legal territories. The southern boundary of the manor was a line from Two Mile Ash to Bradwell. At one time this was marked by a footpath or cart track, although this has now been covered by recent development. This track used to mark the boundary of Bradwell Abbey parish.

The total area was about 2,500 acres of largely productive land, presumably cleared over many centuries, but sufficient to make the owners prosperous. The year 1086, when King William ordered his survey, offers a foothold for documented information about the manor. It had a very high assessment, which at 20 hides made it the richest in North

Manno's Manor

Buckinghamshire and it is perhaps no surprise that Manno identified the manor for himself. Even at this stage the land was not used to its full potential. The commissioners note that there was land for 20 ploughs, although only 15 were in use. Manno held approximately half the manor for his own demesne and the rest was available to 32 villagers and 8 smallholders. The two mills were the predecessors of the two that were still operating there in the 19th century. This should lead us to infer that quite a large part of the manor was under cultivation, even though part of this high assessment might be attributed to commercial activity on the Watling Street as we shall consider in Chapter 4. Much of the land on four sides of the manor must have been under cultivation, leaving perhaps only the higher land in the middle as commons.

Archaeological activity in recent times has established proof of early settlement across the manor. A hoard of flint tools, indicative of a Neolithic settlement, on higher ground at Hodge Lea has been discovered, although only the broadest interpretation can be drawn from this. More detailed investigations were undertaken at Wolverton Turn, on the south side of the Stratford Road, which revealed a Bronze Age settlement and a later Saxon village, although the authors of the report are careful to note that there is no evidence for continuity. It does show at least, that the site was chosen at different periods for settlement.

In addition, there is the revelatory discovery at Bancroft of a prosperous Villa from the Roman occupation period and evidence of another villa on the site now known as Manor Farm. Both sites were based on good arable land with easy access to a good water supply. The Bronze Age site at Wolverton Turn may be a little harder to understand. They would have had to dig wells for a water supply and the lie of the land, although higher, is not especially defensible. It is possible (and this is one suggestion from the archaeologists) that these settlers were primarily engaged in animal husbandry[1] and the higher ground, being less susceptible to becoming waterlogged, was more suited to their purposes. The fact that it was occupied in both the Bronze Age and in the early Saxon period does suggest that it had attractions. Later in the 9th century the village, for no obvious reason, moved to a new site to the north west. This later site is known as the medieval village of Wolverton.

Before the Manor

2000 years ago we would have encountered a different landscape in Wolverton with much more wooded terrain; however, it was not as overgrown as a former generation of historians believed. W.G. Hoskins, writing 60 years ago, was able to draw this picture of medieval England:

> From rising ground England must have seemed one great forest before the fifteenth century, an almost unbroken sea of tree-tops with a thin blue spiral of smoke rising here and there at long intervals. Even after twenty generations of hacking at the waste, the frontiers of cultivation were rarely far away from the homesteads.[2]

The notion that the country became overgrown with forest after the end of the Roman occupation turns out, on the basis of recent scientific evidence, not to have been the case. Land that had been cleared for farming continued to be used. If anything, the process of land clearance continued over these centuries. Warlike activities could interrupt this development, but it could not arrest it. Land that had been cleared remained largely clear, even if it was uncultivated. The march of the forest was not inexorable. Cleared land, even if uncultivated, was probably used by animals for grazing and foraging. The Wolverton landscape during the Roman period certainly had cleared land stretching back from the river banks and it is possible that some of the higher ground had been partially cleared in Bronze Age and Neolithic periods. The Calverton Weald, as the name suggests, must have been wooded, and this may have extended across the Watling Street. The word "slade" preserved in the name Fuller's Slade, tells us that the land was cleared from woodland at one time. Equally, the field names of the *furzes* and *shrub* or *bush* fields tell us that this higher land in the manor was only late brought under cultivation.

The relatively few people who populated this island had to do everything by hand. Clearing the land, claiming the "waste" was a slow process, tree by tree, stump by stump and root by root, until there was sufficient land for the rather primitive plough board to turn over. The process took several generations rather than countable numbers of years.

From what we know from the work of archaeologists, particularly in the last century, population numbers were very small indeed, and recent DNA studies have tended to confirm the work of archaeologists who theorise that the native British come from a very small migration – the

Manno's Manor

descendants of "Jasmine".[3] Such groups of people as there were, were essentially families, each farming at some distance on pieces of land that could be easily cleared and coming together on occasion at certain significant places – Stonehenge being the most spectacular example of such a place.

Two thousand years ago, if the accounts of the resistance met by Julius Caesar's invasions of 55 and 54BC are to be taken at face value, the British people has organised themselves into tribal units of some size and strength. However, even at this time we were a long way from the concept of a village. The Celtic way was to settle more-or-less on the spot where one grew one's crops, sometimes in clusters for defensive purposes, but mostly in a scattered way. The village, as we now understand it, defined by a manorial tract of land, was a later invention and a development over centuries.

The population of the island was still very small and fluctuated according to the scarcity or abundance of food. People lived at subsistence level. Food storage could see people through the winter months, just about, but a poor harvest could put the population at risk and a succession of poor crop years could lead to famine. Life was very hard for early inhabitants. Only during an interlude such as the Roman occupation, which had an economy built upon surpluses, could the population increase. Once that era was over, the natives and the settlers in this country returned to subsistence livelihoods. There have been estimates of between two and five million on the island during the Roman occupation, which fell off to between 1.5 and 2.5 million by the time of the Norman Conquest. There was significant population growth in the following centuries, up to 5 million in 1349, the year of the Black Death. As much as 40% of the population was lost in the plague years and the population did not again reach its pre-plague level until 1700. Regardless of whether you take the upper or lower limit of these figures the numbers are minimal compared to that which we are accustomed to today, but this also meant that was less demand on resources, so timber, for example, was plentiful.

Bronze Age Settlement

Over the entire period covered in this book, the rural population on Wolverton manor was small, and were it not for the development of a town

Before the Manor

at Stony Stratford in the 13th century, may have remained so. But from the time farming was invented, so to speak, there have always been people on this land.

Wolverton Turn is the name given to the area just south of the bend in the Old Wolverton Road beside Wolverton Park House and the junction with the road built in 1844. It was partially excavated in 1972 with a more thorough study undertaken in 1994. The various findings, summarised in a paper published in 2007,[4] enable us to construct a picture of a settlement over several centuries up to the middle Saxon period.

Initially two ring ditches were excavated in 1972 which proved to be the remains of burial barrows for the community. There they discovered pottery fragments and evidence of burials and cremations from the period known as the Bronze Age (2100-750 BC). The last excavation in 1994 revealed evidence of post holes in the form of circular structures together with more fragments of pottery and flintwork. The authors of the report are properly cautious about their findings:

> Given the paucity of dating evidence, it is dangerous to ascribe too positive an interpretation to these features, but the probability must be that most or all of them can be associated as a Bronze Age settlement. Even if some of the features represent no more than tree-clearance, it seems mainly to have been Bronze Age tree-clearance. The consistent patterning of post holes suggesting irregularly circular structures also points towards a Bronze Age date, and the lack of positive dating of such features is (unfortunately) fairly normal. The existence of buried soil could also indicate agriculture.[5]

There is evidence of later settlement, which I will come to, but the importance of these discoveries is to offer us an historical continuity with our past and to confirm what we might intuitively expect, that the Wolverton area was populated from the earliest times. This is not to suggest that there was continuity of settlement at Wolverton Turn. There may have been, but the archaeologists are careful not to draw this conclusion from their findings. There are some artefacts to be found from the Roman period, but in comparison with other parts of the country there are relatively few. What Roman period pottery they did find dated to the later Roman occupation rather than the earlier, and Preston is of the view that "the absence of solid evidence has led to the omission of a true Roman phase from the site chronology."[6]

The group living here was probably a few families of close kinship. It is likely that they found mates outside of the family group. Their way of living, which may appear primitive to us now, was probably quite sophisticated in terms of social organisation and as dwellers in the Bronze Age they would have had access to tools which could only be manufactured from the raw materials of mining - in itself a process derived from complex knowledge, decision making and social organisation. As this report says, the evidence from the site is fragmentary and a complete picture cannot be drawn, but it does tell us that some of our forebears were living here 3000 years ago.

This may be a banal conclusion but it serves to note that the Wolverton manor did not spring fully formed into life in the 9th century and that these parts have a long history of settlement.

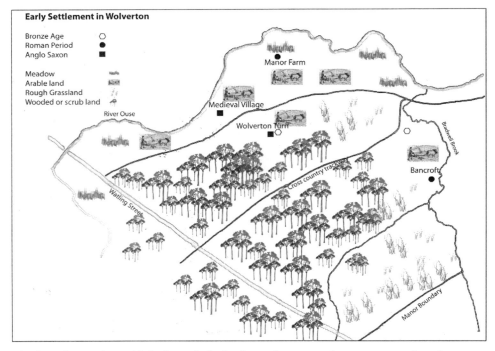

In the early periods it is likely that only the land near the rivers and streams was under cultivation.

Before the Manor

Wolverton in the Roman Period

The prime discovery of recent years was the archaeological work at Bancroft. The field, sloping down to Bradwell Brook, was known only as a field to those of us growing up in Wolverton in the last century and we had little inkling that the dust of 1400 years covered such an extensive development. After enclosure this field acquired the name of Bancroft Close and this name has now been applied to the Romano-British settlement discovered in 1971. Excavations undertaken between 1973 and 1978 and further investigations between 1982 and 1986, revealed a complex of buildings.

The discovery was remarkable, although consistent with other archaeological remains from the Roman occupation. It represented a style of living and farm organisation imported from the Mediterranean but not apparently one which maintained its appeal after the Romans left.

The first house was 28 x 12 metres in size and was south facing. The placement is entirely consistent with other villa-type farm buildings of the period. They tend to select a rather special type of site: a valley-slope facing south or east, not too high up, with shelter from the wind, exposure to the sun, and water close at hand[7].

The archaeologists discovered limestone foundations and post holes inside the building to support the roof and interior partitions. The roof covering was probably thatch and the walls were likely to have been "wattle and daub". The wattles were made by interleaving thin branches into a kind of lattice. Once the lattice was in place the wall was daubed with a mixture of sand, earth and straw mixed with a binder. The mixture dried quite hard and was often sealed with whitewash, It was an effective wall-making material, although it had no structural strength. The plan of this building had a large living area with two small rooms, probably for sleeping, at the west end. The north side had a corridor. Later in the second century a bath suite was added, which had two heated rooms and a cold room. Roman technology is apparent in the design.

The team found a cobbled farmyard and additional farm buildings and two large circular stone buildings, which were living quarters for the farm workers.

Manno's Manor

Much of this is consistent with what we already know. Circular or round buildings are easier to build and roof and tend to be warmer in the winter. It is possible that each of these buildings accommodated several families.

The archaeologists also found evidence of an even earlier settlement on the hilltop above Brook Field which was later used as a place to cremate their dead. By the second century AD funeral customs had changed and this site was now used to bury the dead. These farmers now built a Mausoleum – an underground burial vault under a central tower some 10 metres high. This was surrounded by a verandah with columns. There may also have been a water mill beside the brook.

It is probably impossible to tell how much land was under cultivation. Did they farm on both sides of the brook or just on the north side? How many acres were required to support the villa families? Was the villa a centre for outlying farming operations? While our understanding of Roman Britain is increasing, we still do not have sufficient information to answer these questions.

In or about AD 170 the farm was destroyed by a serious fire and that it was thereupon abandoned. The archaeologists present this as a fact but don't explain why. And we don't know. Speculation might include a raid from a neighbouring tribe which destroyed the villa, or that the destruction and abandonment of this farm may have been due to a slave revolt. Slave labour was integral to the economy of the Roman Empire and practices were no different in Britain. For most slaves the deal was food and shelter and clothing in exchange for work. With a reasonable master I suppose this was just about bearable but situations arose where the conditions became intolerable and there were slave revolts. This may have been one such. The slaves rose up against their master, killed him and his family, burned the house and retreated into the waste lands and into outlawry. They may subsequently have been caught and executed.

This is only a theory, but it would explain the complete abandonment of the farm for almost 100 years. Had it been an accidental fire, a kitchen fire perhaps, surely it would have been rebuilt. Even after a raid, there would have been survivors who could have rebuilt the farm. A slave revolt was likely to be final, because not only was no-one left from the organising family but also the workforce, upon which the farm depended

Before the Manor

had left too. 170AD was a period at the height of the first wave of Roman prosperity, which still had another 60 years to run, before economic decline set in, and it can hardly be argued that it was uneconomic to rebuild the farm.

Whatever the reason, it did fall into disuse. A hundred years after this another family decided to settle here and they built another house partly over the remains of the original. This house was 31 x 10 metres and built entirely of stone and had the luxury of a concrete floor. The house had three large rooms with a bath suite at the south end.

In both cases advanced Roman technology was used – in the first case more obviously the baths, but in the second, with the use of concrete, stone building, mosaics and painted decoration of the walls, and an efficient heating system for the baths and the house.

Scholars are revising their view about Roman settlement. At one time it was thought to be predominantly urban with villas fairly close to a major centre, but more recent discoveries reveal a definite preference for country living and a decline in the public administration functions of the towns, particularly after the economic separation from Roman trade in the third century. Wealthy families tended to build their villas large enough to contain their household and their necessary administrative functions without recourse to the forums and public buildings of the towns. These fell into decay.

The second Bancroft villa appears to fit into the model of the second Romano-British economy, which depended less on imported goods from the Mediterranean and more upon locally produced goods. It is in these years that beer replaces wine, that butter and lard replace olive oil and tallow candles replace oil lamps. The villa was at the centre of its own economy and owed very little to its Mediterranean connection in the fourth century. It must have been entirely self-sufficient. North Buckinghamshire remained distinctly rural until the nineteenth century and throughout that period one would have to go a long distance to find a town of any size. Settlements were known along the Watling Street at Magiovinto (Fenny Stratford) and Lactodoro (Towcester), and possibly Old Stratford, although there is no hard evidence for the latter. It is more likely that these villas represented the economic model for the organisation of agriculture. Whoever built the villa clearly had the resources and power to

Manno's Manor

do so and there were probably a number of families engaged in and drawing their livelihood from the farm. The villa owner clearly lived in some style and directed operations and probably arranged for the produce to be sold at market – although where these markets might have been we don't yet know. We might judge that Newport (new market) emerged during the Anglo-Saxon period as a new place for trading and infer that there were other such places in the district before this.

The extent of the farm is unknown. There are instances of villas of this period having 1000 acres under their control but 300 acres would have provided a prosperous economic unit. Given the location of Bancroft it is arguable that all of those south facing slopes leading to Bradwell Brook could have been cleared for cultivation as well as those on the other side of the stream.

But if Bancroft is the prime example of a villa settlement in the area, it was not the only one, as evidence has been unearthed near the site of Manor Farm and in neighbouring Cosgrove and Haversham.

On the eve of the Roman Conquest the population of Britain has been estimated at no more than 400,000 so one can infer from this that huge areas of the country were unpopulated and certainly under populated. Even at the end of the Roman rule 400 years later, the population has been estimated at between 600,000 and 1.5 million. Even if we take the higher figure, this is a very low population density, almost unimaginable to us today. If we use the population figure for rural Wolverton in 1801, which was 238 out of a total population of 8 million for the country and pro-rate that to the estimated figure of 1.5 million in 400 AD, that would amount to a population of about 40 people supported by the Wolverton lands.

Historians have speculated that the population may have declined after this Romano-British peak, and it certainly did not rise, despite immigration. There was apparently no growth in population until the reigns of the Norman Kings.

This Bancroft settlement was abandoned in the late 4th century AD, a date that is quite consistent with the general collapse of the Romano-British economy in the later years of that century, although the archaeologists have found evidence of occupation of sorts in the early 5th century. Its demise marks the end of an era across Britannia and was not simply a local phenomenon. Bancroft and other villas fell into disuse, not

Before the Manor

because the native Britons lacked the knowledge or skills to maintain them but because the economy which supported such palatial houses was no longer sustainable. Just as the grand mansions built by the wealthy of the 18th and 19th centuries became redundant in the 20th century, so did these spacious Romano-British villas suffer the same fate in the 5th century. Archaeological evidence supports this view. The villa was occupied for a period after the end of the Roman administration but a building of this size required production surpluses to maintain it and an administrative system to support taxation. In a subsistence economy the villa made no sense. The economy upon which they depended had collapsed, and they disappeared with it just as quickly.

Some current opinion has it that the Britons left behind by the Romans abandoned the Villa economy, not because they lacked the technical know-how, but because they preferred to revert to their own agricultural practices. A topical comparison has been made to the situation in Afghanistan, where western powers impose a model of social and economic organisation upon the populace from the top, only to discover that it is immediately be abandoned once the external ruling power leaves.[8]

Each of these viewpoints may carry some weight but the governing factor must have been the need for survival after the sudden exodus of the Roman government after almost 400 years. People had no choice but to organise themselves by families and kinship groups with looser ties to a wider community. With the overnight arrival of self government each of these units became smaller and weaker and less able to do much more than take care of their immediate needs.

The door was open. The newer settlers, from Ireland, Scotland and the northern shores of the European continent, including those Germanic-speaking peoples loosely bundled as Angles, Saxons and Jutes, began to arrive, and the natives may have noticed little difference in the lifestyle of their new neighbours. As they began to arrive in numbers over the next 70 years they eventually had a more lasting impact on language and social and political organisation than their Roman predecessors. When civilizations collapse they do so in an absolute fashion. An object lesson perhaps. The Roman occupation made surprisingly little difference.

Manno's Manor

The Anglo-Saxon Settlement

We now enter an unusual period in the history of these islands. They became, in a very real sense, vacant. The gradual, and in the end, complete withdrawal of the Romans at the end of the fourth century left Britain without government and with no central or even regional authority to fill the vacuum. The immediate response of the native inhabitants must have been to get on with their lives. What they did not do, were unable to do, was replace the complex machinery of Roman government and through it have the capacity to resist new settlements. These new settlements did not begin immediately. It was a good twenty years before the first boats beached on the eastern shores. As Robin Fleming remarks in her recent book,

> By 420 Britain's villas had been abandoned. Its towns were mostly empty, its organised industries dead, its connections with the larger Roman world severed: and all with hardly an Angle or a Saxon in sight."[9]

Until quite recently historians have presented the Anglo-Saxon settlements of the 5th century as an invasion. They drew upon the witness of Bede, who, writing in the 8th century, famously distinguished the earliest Germanic settlers as Angles, Saxons and Jutes. The Jutes, thought to be from Jutland, made their new home in Kent, the Isle of Wight and parts of Hampshire. The Saxons took over the south of England and the Angles settled in the east and gradually filled central and northern England. In the absence of any other information this version of events was accepted for over 1000 years. But, as archaeologists have recently uncovered more and more information, a very different narrative has emerged.

To begin with the new arrivals were not simply Germanic people with full blown tribal identities; they also included the Franks, the Irish, and Norsemen. And there is now considerable doubt as to whether the new arrivals even came with tribal affiliations. They came in small numbers, probably small extended families - enough to fill a boat and no more. There is no evidence from early burials that they were from a military caste and the conclusion now is that they were simple farmers looking for land to settle upon. The fact that Britain was "open" made the new settlement relatively painless. There was no need for armed conflict or to force people off their land. In the early years there was plenty of available land and if the

Before the Manor

newcomers wished to clear waste land then there was no authority to prevent them. Later in the century that trickle became a flood, leading to the eventual dominance of the Germanic culture and language, but in the early years this was not evident.

The presently accepted view of the history of this period is that movement of peoples from the eastern shores of Europe was never a planned invasion as such but more along the lines of a gradual settlement over many years. The settlement of North America from the 16th to 19th centuries provides a better comparative model than the image of marauding and conquering tribes. There, the European immigrants farmed in proximity to the natives in a warily respectful manner. There was, after all, enough land to share and it was surely easier to take over unoccupied land than to fight over land that was already in use. There were disputes and occasionally whole colonies were wiped out but for the most part co-existence prevailed. Our imagination has been nourished by Hollywood depictions of the 19th century battles against the plains indian, where there was a vital clash of cultures between the nomadic, hunting lifestyle of the indigenous people and the mechanised, farming, land-owning habits of the new settlers, and we have overlooked the earlier settlement of the eastern and central parts of the United States and Canada, which was largely peaceful.

These new settlers, coming close upon the departure of the Roman authorities, entered a governing void which meant that newcomers could come to these shores, find unused or abandoned land and establish themselves without too much trouble. These new settlers did not occupy an established villa or nearby Celtic settlements because they were already in use. And from what we have learned from archaeological discoveries in the Wolverton area in recent times, that narrative does fit the facts. The archaeological evidence from Bancroft, described earlier, shows that there were squatters living within the villa in the early 5th century. This may not have continued for very long but it may suggest to us that indigenous Britons were continuing to farm this cleared land. The same might also be true of the Grange at Manor Farm, Wolverton. For while the economy had collapsed and the old towns and villas no longer required, people still had to eat and it is a reasonable conjecture that farming continued in some form or other. If the natives occupied the pre-existing farms that we know

Manno's Manor

about, this surely steers one to the view that the new settlers, coming in from the east coast, would occupy some vacant land.

In Wolverton this could be found. The land at Wolverton Turn was already a clearing of sorts and even if it had been long abandoned, it would not have reverted to dense woodland. It may have been the only place to settle in these parts. We can therefore allow ourselves to imagine the native Britons farming in the Bancroft and Manor Farm areas. They may not have been farming on the organised scale of the villa owners of the previous century but they must have had sufficient resources to farm at a subsistence level. Earlier buildings were abandoned and eventually forgotten, but the land and its cultivation remained.

We might also assume that the native Britons, with fewer demands on their labour, being no longer under pressure to pay taxes, for example, may have been quite content to farm the south east and northern parts of the manor and were not much interested in the higher ground. With no great increase in population there was no pressure to open up new land.

The new arrivals changed this pattern, and if, as seems evident, they did settle at Wolverton Turn, then it is unlikely that the natives would be overly concerned and the two cultures could coexist. The archaeological evidence from across the country does support this idea. Evidence of shared burial sites and even shared cultural practices has been unearthed at various sites across the country, and, over generations, confirmation of the cultural fusing that one might expect as people inter-married between the two racial groups.

Wolverton's First Village?

At Wolverton Turn, at least two Saxon structures have been identified: a Grubenhaus based on a rectangular plan of 3 x 4 m and another post built structure of 3 x 5m. The Grubenhaus, was an imported Saxon structure which was partially dug into the ground with low walls and a roof supported by centre posts. The archaeologists are certain about the description of this building but questions remain about the second structure.

Some animal remains have been radiocarbon dated: a horse metacarpal and a pig skull to between 680 and 890, a cattle carpal to 420-620 AD and a sheep or goat metacarpal to 430-610 AD. Settlement

Before the Manor

during these years was probably continuous. Two surprising findings were the relatively higher percentage of horse and sheep in comparison to equivalent Saxon period excavations across the country. One suggestion is that it may have been an equine breeding centre. The relatively high incidence of sheep may be explained as an early area for sheep farming. Another observation they made was that the number of cattle remains was unusually low compared to the normal incidence again suggesting that sheep husbandry was preferred by this settlement.

The radiocarbon dating is within the period but it does not tell us whether this was an early or later settlement. One would guess later. If the early settlers who arrived after 420 AD found land in East Anglia then there was no compulsion to move further westwards. So it is probably at the height of the influx of new settlers, between 470 and 520 that Wolverton was first settled by the newcomers. Who were they?

A neat answer would be to imagine them as Wulfhere's people, after Wulfhere, who gave his name to the manor, but we cannot be sure of this. We can accept that the Germanic settlers, probably Anglian in origin, came to Wolverton at the end of the 5th or beginning of the 6th century. They may only have been one family or an extended family at most, but as newcomers they were in no position to be dominant and there must have been a period where they co-existed with the native Britons in the area. Within a generation or two, as evidenced by studies of burial sites, social stratification emerged. Higher status individuals might marry their sons and daughters to those of equal status some distance away and thus additional wealth and status would accrue to these people. As social organisation became more complex the more powerful graduated to the status of a lord or chief. Such a one may have been Wulfhere, who had sufficient resources to maintain an enclosure for his family and animals and whose farm was a recognised centre for meetings, judgements and the paying of taxes.

It is now believed that the Anglo-Saxon place names ending with ham are the primary settlements and the ingas names came later. Thus in our area Boca's Ham (Buckingham) and Passa's Ham (Passenham) are likely to be older settlements. Passenham's location at an easy river crossing suggests a natural and ancient location. So far from being indicative of primary settlement, the *-ingas* names as a whole belong to secondary places of

Manno's Manor

colonizing activity.[10] We could therefore surmise that the first settlement at Wolverton Turn was a *ham* (and a name now lost in history)[11] and it was the later Wulfhere who gave his name to the settlement which relocated a little further north. Many of these early Saxon settlements may have developed into later villages and therefore their very existence has been obliterated. Some, however, apparently like the one at Wolverton Turn, moved. There are no available explanations for this but from the archaeological evidence it appears that there was no activity there after the 9th century.

If we use this observation to construct our theory, Wulfhere may not have been amongst the early arrivals. Only after the Wolverton society became larger, more complex did it need a high status individual to act as a chief. This was probably a man called Wulfhere and his name stuck to the settlement. His name was never written down and all we can do is infer from the name of the place. Wolverton derives its name from a man called Wulfhere, and his name is all we know about him. Wulfhere, derived from wolf and the Saxon word *here*[12] *(pronounced "hair-uh"*, meaning raiding party), was not an uncommon name. The Saxons admired the wolf for its predatory skills and its ability to hunt in packs, and Wulfhere, loosely translated as Wolf Raider, could easily be applied to a leader of a militant group. This Wulfhere was not his more famous namesake who became a Mercian king, but one of several of that name who have given their name to the various Wolvertons found in parts of England.

We can only assume that he was a small chieftan and indeed most of the village names in the area draw their name from one man or another who was probably the leading figure. Loughton – Lucca's tun, Calverton – Calver's tun, Haversham – Haver's ham. Other places in the area derive names from descriptions of the location Stanton – Stan (stone) tun, Bradwell – Brade (broad or wide) well.

A tun (from which we later derive the word town) was a fenced enclosure. A ham was a homestead (home). Ing derives from ingas meaning people.

Thus the name Wolverton comes from three elements: Wulfhere + ingas + tun – Wulfhere's peoples' farm enclosure. At times it was written down as Wolvrington or Wolcerston but over time the pronunciation and

Before the Manor

spelling settled on Wolverton, as it has now remained for hundreds of years.

In reality, Wulfhere's *ingtun* might be visualised as a hall of some sort for Wulfhere and his (extended) family, possibly some outbuildings, and an enclosure, partly for protection against raids and partly to keep livestock. It is possible, although there is no archaeological evidence to support this, that Wulfhere's *ingtun* was built on the overlook where Manno le Breton later built his castle for no other reason than it was a defensible site. The *ing tun* was a place where people later came to pay their taxes or tithes or tributes, and was therefore an administrative centre of sorts. It was not a village in any sense that we would later understand it and sometimes a parish might have several such centres, an ing tun for the local lord, a centre for the church, and perhaps another centre for the king's taxes to be paid. Wulfhere and his successors, we might speculate, governed a population of upwards of 40 people. Whether or not he had alliances with neighbouring lords we do not know. History has nothing to say about Wulfhere, other than to recognise his name in the place name.

The settlers in East Anglia were Engles or Angles and their increasing spread and dominance eventually gave us the name England. Those who settled in Wolverton descended from these Angles and either represent a descent of several generations from the first coastal settlers or may even have been more recent arrivals from the continent who had to penetrate deep inland to find a place to farm. It is quite right to speculate on a sixth century rather than on a fifth century settlement for Wolverton.

As I have written earlier, most recent scholarship tends to the view that the Celtic people stayed where they were and integrated with the arriving Angles. The conclusions drawn by 19th century historians that they were driven westwards was based upon surviving place names and linguistic inheritance. The apparent dominance of the English language and English place names in the east, they argued, compared to the survival in the west of Celtic words like *avon* and *tor*, was sufficient evidence for a wholesale migration, leaving empty farms for occupation by the invaders. Recent DNA studies, in particular those undertaken by Bryan Sykes, taken together with archaeological evidence supports the modern view.[13] They find significant Celtic strains in abundance in south eastern England as well as the predicted Anglo Saxon blood inheritance, which rather puts it at

Manno's Manor

odds with a theory of armed invasion and the forcible displacement of tribes.

The Development of Anglian Society

The Angles and Saxons, when they came, had a different approach to social organisation and were not interested in using what were then the overgrown and ruined buildings that were remnants of villas and towns. It was easier for them to construct their own settlements, rather than reclaim pre-existing buildings. It was not ignorance, as has sometimes been claimed by earlier historians, but simply a preference for a different kind of social structure. They showed no interest in the underfloor heating systems they found in the villas or even the planning of towns. Places like Silchester were gradually abandoned. The Romans, and by extension the Romano-British, were bound together by the concept of Rome, a centralised state that administered laws and justice. The Germanic people were bound by personal allegiance. Men swore oaths to their leaders and their honour and social standing demanded that they live up to their sworn obligations, or, in some cases, die for them. The result was a tribal society where kinship was supreme and remote authority mattered little. Laws and customs were locally administered.

However it was not simply the intrusion of the Anglo-Saxons that brought about this change. The invasion of the Germanic tribes was not an apocalyptic event, but a slow and spasmodic dribble of settlement which became a spate at the end of the fifth century. As I have discussed in the previous section, there is increasing evidence which suggests that the new arrivals integrated into the pre-existing farming structures. And these were not Roman for it now seems true to say that once the Romans left in 400AD the native peoples saw no reason to continue with the Roman market towns and villa farming economies, which were imported Mediterranean concepts, and instead reverted to their customary practices. 19th Century historians struggled with this apparent abandonment of civilization, and concluded that only a deeply primitive people could abandon the obvious benefits of paved roads and streets and water and sewage systems. Perhaps in the 21st century we can take a broader view.

Laycock's[14] works draws greatly upon archaeological evidence which has been newly available to historians over the last 50 years. Hitherto,

Before the Manor

historians relied almost totally on a few surviving written sources, which were either written by the Roman occupiers or by chroniclers writing hundreds of years after the events. Archaeological evidence has brought some balance to these sources and it now appears probable that some warring Celtic leaders brought in Germanic tribes to reinforce themselves against hostile kingdoms. In a pattern that has been repeated through history, these temporary adventurers settled and with this toehold invited their kin to join them. In time this new resident population rooted their language and some of their customs in the British living experience.

The story of the development of Anglo-Saxon England is the gradual development of a larger society, from extended family groups to small tribe, to regional kingdoms and eventually, after about 400 years, into a unified kingdom. As the pioneer settlers put down roots they held status in the community, particularly over those whom they "invited" later. Gradually the higher status individuals or families were able to exercise more power over their communities. Exceptional leaders could control tribes and eventually kingdoms. This gradual increase in the size and power of kingdoms brought with it more consistency and centralisation of laws and taxes. Land made this possible. Grants of territory made by the king and powerful nobles to their men resulted in further subdivisions amongst heirs or family members. The trade-off being made for food-rent and military service. It was not quite the more formalised feudal system imposed by William I but it was developing in that direction.

This is the general picture. In the case of Wolverton or North Buckinghamshire there is little to draw upon to localise this period of transition, from a society of warlords competing for power and the eventual emergence of larger kingdoms. When the picture does clarify, by the 7th century, the Wolverton area is considered to be an outlying part of the Mercian kingdom.

Alfred of Wessex is credited with establishing the shire system of governance and the boundaries of the southern shires generally reflect the divisions of tribal authority – Kent, Sussex, Hampshire, Dorset and Somerset. Mercia developed shires somewhat later, being content to define their taxation system through *regio*, or provincial regions, based upon tribal dominance. Thus Oxfordshire and Buckinghamshire was the province of the Cilternsaeten and the Tribal Hidage, a late 10th century document,

29

Manno's Manor

assigns 4,000 hides to the Cilternsaeten. The jurisdiction of the Cilternsaeten covered the swath of countryside from Abingdon and Dorchester on the River Thames to the River Ouse in the North West - the North Buckinghamshire area later defined by the Newport Hundreds.

Buckinghamshire probably emerged as an administrative unit in the late 10th century and took its name from Bocca's Ham where a castle or *burh* was built to defend this part of the country against Danish incursions. Buckinghamshire itself is a curious construction with three distinct regions - the Chilterns in the south, the vale of Aylesbury in the middle and North Buckinghamshire. Topographically, North Bucks had more in common with Bedfordshire than with the south. Even today, there is little to connect those living in the north to the south, not even a motorway. As the administrative structure of the county became more settled, Aylesbury proved to be a more central place for shire courts and although Buckingham gave its name to the county it was never in any sense a county town.

Gradually the land was divided into manageable units, based upon the hide, a Germanic measure of land area used for tax purposes. A hide was considered to be the amount of land that could support one family and was about 120 acres. It was not a precise measure and areas of infertile soil might cover larger territory. These units were then grouped into areas of 5, 10 or 20 hides and through this the manorial system was born. Wolverton was a rather wealthy manor at 20 hides, consisting as it did of good arable land and good pasture. Neighbouring Loughton was assessed at 10 hides and was divided into two manors. Calverton was valued at 10 hides and Bradwell and Stantonbury were both small manors of 5 hides each.

When detailed records of taxation first appear in the eleventh century almost all of Wessex and Mercia was divided into villages of five hides or some multiple of that number. The incidence of these round numbers would suggest that the measurements were not precise; however, there is enough to suggest that these numbers were grounded in some sort of reality.

So it is here that the village begins to emerge and why virtually all place names in England have an Anglo-Saxon origin, even where Celtic names have been "anglicized".

Before the Manor

The trend towards larger power units was not entirely benign. Sir Frank Stenton has observed that:

> The central course of Old English social development may be described as a process whereby a peasantry, at first composed essentially of free men, acknowledging no lord below the king, gradually lost economic and personal independence.[15]

This must have been the development during the centuries between the first settlement and the time of the Conquest. A relatively simple society, such as the few families who settled in Wolverton in the 6th century had grown more hierarchical. The interposition of other lords, thanes and earls, meant that many had to give up their free status in exchange for their lord's protection and security. For some it was not entirely a bad bargain. It meant that they had customary rights over certain strips of land and the quid pro pro was some service to the lord. At the bottom end of the social scale, for those too poor to bargain for a better choice, it meant slavery – a return to the economic subjugation of Roman times. In fact 10 slaves were recorded in Wolverton in 1086, and for this read ten families, possibly one-quarter of the population. What their function was we do not know but it was presumably doing work for one or more of the thanes, who, in turn, provided food, shelter and clothing for the slaves.

The Situation in 1066

In the 11th century we come to a period of less obscurity. Once again we are limited to inferences that can be drawn from the survey of 1086 and were it not for this we might know almost nothing about the men and women who held rights to land. Even so we have only a few scraps of information, but we do have some names and we can attempt to put together some kind of picture of the society that preceded the invasion.

The Wolverton Manor was split between three thanes, Godwin, Thori and Aelfric. Godwin had 10 hides, half the assessment of the manor; Thori, one of King Edward's guards, had 7 ½ hides, almost the other half of the manor. The third man Aelfric only held 2 ½ hides. He is described as Queen Edith's man and he is clearly the junior of the three in status. He may also have been junior in terms of age and might possibly have received his land as part of a subdivision. Where his land might be cannot be determined. It could have been the land contiguous to the Loughton

Manno's Manor

Manor, possibly including that part of the manor which later became the land of Bradwell Priory.

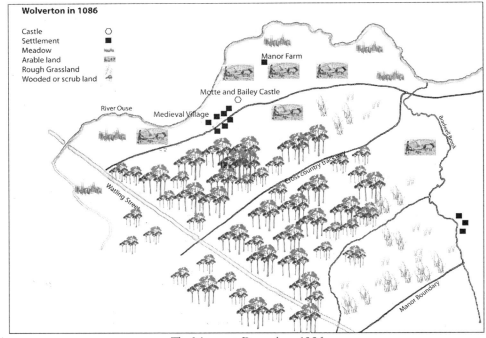

The Manor at Domesday - 1086

The three thanes were well-connected. Godwin served King Harold; Thori was one of King Edward's housecarles and Aelfric was a guard for Queen Edith. Aelfric does not appear anywhere else in Domesday, so his 2½ hides was a relatively small holding, although sufficient to maintain himself as a fighting man. Godwin's 10 hides, or 1200 acres, also appears to be the limit of his landholdings, but Thori owned the Manor of Thornborough and a few other parcels which gave him about 2,800 acres.[16] This would make Thori the richest and most powerful of the three and leads me to believe that he held the capital part of the Wolverton Manor.

The significant phrase "they could sell to whom they would" meant that their rights to the land were not tied to service as was customary after the conquest. In other words it was understood that they had free title. This should lead us to the conclusion that much had changed since the time of Wulfhere. From the dominance of a single lord, there were three thanes

Before the Manor

(not necessarily of equal rank) who had control over the resources of the manor.

Another factor to take into account is that much of the manor would have been common land, particularly the higher land which was largely scrub land. Those fields which were later named furzes and shrub (scrub) fields at the southern end of Wolverton were most likely the common grazing lands until enclosure. The hidage may not have assessed this land at all. As I have already observed, the hide was not an exact measurement. It represented the amount of land that could support one family, so the boundaries of a hide were elastic depending on the quality of the soil. To give some idea of what a variable concept this was, the Manor of Hanslope which included Castlethorpe) was only assessed at 10 hides, even though it encompassed over twice the area of Wolverton Manor.

Each generation might witness the rise in the fortunes of some and the decline of other families. Higher status individuals and families emerged to direct the activities of others. Laws and customs were adopted and the mechanisms to implement them. Anglo-Saxon society of the 9th and 10th centuries was very different from its beginnings in the 5th and 6th centuries.

Aelfric and Godwin appear to have been small fry. Thori, with his holdings at Thornborough was somewhat richer. They are dwarfed, however, by Burgred of Olney, who in addition to his Olney and Lavendon Manors had substantial holdings in Northamptonshire and Bedfordshire. There were also small pockets of land in North Buckinghamshire held by some powerful figures such as Wulfward White and Countess Judith. We can safely say that no major players had holdings in Wolverton or had any wider influence. Whatever the subdivisions (and many manors were sometimes shared by 8 to 10 thanes) it is clear from Domesday that the manor as a concept was fully realised and when Manno took over he was able to assume this as an entity. It is quite possible that the three thanes were related. There again, parts of the manor may have been subdivided between, say, two sons, and then sold off by one who had no heirs. The possibilities are endless and these are complete speculations. However this developed there must have been some mechanism for administering justice and the manor court must have encompassed the lands of all three thanes. One or all of them may have been party to judicial decisions but there

Manno's Manor

would only have been one court. One manor, one court. Beyond that was the hundred court, which in the case of Wolverton was at Seckloe Hill. Here disputes between thanes which crossed manorial borders could be resolved and matters in the larger community interest could be addressed. The king's taxes or geld could also be raised at these assemblies. In sum, Anglo Saxon society was highly organised and, within that sophisticated level of organisation lay its a sense was its vulnerability, because an adventurer like William could successfully invade, cut of the head of this social organisation, and the whole of society could continue to function much as before.

But life and farming did not start in 1086 and the Normans took over a functioning society and economy, so it is safe to assume that when Mainno le Breton appropriated the manor from three Saxon thanes he acquired a manor which was being farmed according to traditional practices. For the average peasant, besides the temporary disruption and ravages of conquest, life would have continued much as before, but instead of paying their taxes and customary service to Saxon masters, they were now subject to Norman control

Before the Manor

1 The report suggests that large amount of horse bones and other domestic animals found.
2 W G Hoskins. The Making of the English Landscape. 1955
3 Brian Sykes. Blood of the Isles. Bantam Press, 2006.
4 Steve Preston et al. Bronze Age Occupation and Saxon Features at the Wolverton Turn Enclosure, near Stony Stratford, Milton Keynes. Records of Buckinghamshire 2007.
5 Steve Preston et al. Bronze Age Occupation and Saxon Features at the Wolverton Turn Enclosure, near Stony Stratford, Milton Keynes. Records of Buckinghamshire 2007. p.88
6 ibid. p. 15
7 Christopher Dyer Making a Living in the Middle Ages.Yale University Press: 2002.
8 Stuart Laycock. Britannia - The Failed State: Tribal Conflict and the end of Roman Britain. The History Press, 2008.
9 Robin Fleming. Britain After Rome. Penguin: 2011. p.29
10 J N L Myres. the English Settlements. Oxford, 1986, p. 40.
11 One wonders, for example, if the curiously named copse at Wolverton Turn "The Happy Morn" was not a corrupted version of a ancient Celtic name.
12 The Anglo-Saxons had two words for army (we now use the French word) – *fyrd* and *here*. In the Anglo-Saxon Chronicle the *fyrd* is generally used to describe the defending militia (by this time the native English) and the *here* ascribed to the invading Norsemen. However in early Saxon times a raiding warrior would be seen as virtuous and we may conclude that Wulfhere was indeed a successful military leader.
13 Bryan Sykes. The Blood of the Isles. Bantam Press, 2006.
14 op cit.
15 Sir Frank Stenton. Anglo Saxon England. Oxford University Press, 1970.
16 While it is possible that this Thori is another man entirely, I would deduce from the fact that Manno acquired both the Wolverton and the Thornborough manors that this was the same man.

THREE

THE BARONS OF WOLVERTON

Through a combination of determination, leadership, tactical imagination, luck and statesmanship, Duke William of Normandy made 1066 one of the pivotal events in English history and transformed the nation that was to develop from this historic moment. Wolverton was at the periphery, being neither directly affected by the invasion nor by William's foray into Buckinghamshire. No doubt Wolverton's thanes and some of their men were involved in the fighting of that year and we do not know what happened to them. Nobody could have anticipated, even in those uncertain times, the aftermath of the new Norman rule which would disinherit the ruling thanes and their families and make Wolverton a centre of increased importance. This was solely due to the man who established the seat of his barony there, Manno the Breton.

William attracted quite a large contingent from Brittany to his English enterprises and most were rewarded. Some were quite powerful and were compensated with huge estates. One of them, Ralph, was created Earl of East Anglia shortly after the invasion and I will return to him later. Manno, judging by the fact that we know little about him, was in the second rank of tenants-in-chief.

Of his person and his origins we know nothing. We do not even know very much about his life, but we do, from the Domesday Survey of 1086, know quite a lot about his landholdings. From this we can draw certain inferences about his importance and learn something about the first baron of Wolverton and the founder of a family which was to prosper here for about 300 years.

I am perhaps too extravagant in saying that we learn something. We actually know the scantiest of detail: his name, that he came from Brittany, and that he had an heir. Anything else is a matter for conjecture. There is much more that we do not know. We have no information about his year of birth, where he came from in Brittany, his parentage, nor his wife and family. We can only guess at the year of his death. Yet this man was one of the 150 or so most important men in England after the Norman Conquest

Manno's Manor

and all we know for certain is the list of landholdings he acquired after 1066.

One of Manno's first acts must have been to build a castle and for this he chose a promontory overlooking the Ouse Valley to the north and west. This first castle was a motte and bailey type. The raised earthwork, the motte, is still visible and the probable outline of the bailey has been determined by an archaeological assessment. I will describe this in Chapter 5. The surrounding moat was filled in during the construction of the new Holy Trinity church in the 19th century. All that remains today is a bushy mound where the keep may have stood. Most of these early castles were wooden fortresses; later, some barons and earls built themselves stone strongholds. We must assume that Manno and his successors never felt under sufficient threat to resort to stronger fortifications.

Outside of Wolverton there were events that threatened the stability of the new monarchy, but Manno seems to have kept his head down, a characteristic he passed on to his descendants who were content to administer their estates and not to risk what they held by contending for an even greater share. Greed does not appear to have been a characteristic of this family.

From the blank page that is Manno's life it is possible to infer that at the time of the conquest he was in his twenties at least and that he might have been born circa 1040. He must have had some status in Brittany to be able to bring a force of men to support William in his invasion. His rewards would suggest that he was a significant player in the battles to establish William's supremacy. It is possible too that he was a younger son of a Breton lord, and with no prospect of an inheritance, had the motivation to join the invading force with the future promise of land. He did not, for example, share the privilege of some Breton lords who held land in both countries, and this may explain why he remained loyal to William. He had gained everything through the Conquest and disloyalty could cost him everything.

He was not in the same rank as the magnates close to William who were given huge landholdings. The Domesday Book, which is quite careful about precedence, ranks him 43rd in the Buckinghamshire record of tenants-in-chief. In Leicestershire he ranks 37th , In Hertfordshire 39th and

The Barons of Wolverton

in Northamptonshire 54th. He does not appear as a witness in any of the documents of either William or his sons William Rufus and Henry which would suggest that he was never close to the king and that we are right to place him in the second rank of barons. He could be depended upon for his feudal obligations and since there is no record of any default, he most likely was. William worked closely with a handful of men who were his trusted advisors and supporters. As for the rest, lesser barons like Manno, he apparently met with them three times a year – at Easter, Michelmas and Christmas, using the Saxon institution of the *witan gemot*, or great council. Stenton says that there is little evidence that any decisions were made at these meetings but it was an opportunity for William to seek reaffirmation of loyalty and possibly deal with personal grievances.[1] It has been written that William was mistrustful of the Bretons, so one suspects that Manno, as an intelligent man, correctly assessed the situation and decided to get on with managing and building his estates. This does not make glittering history but the end result was that he provided a firm foundation for the Wolverton barony. One is tempted to observe that he may have set the tone for 1,000 years of relatively peaceful history on the Wolverton Manor.

The Barony

After the Conquest he was given quite extensive landholdings in Leicestershire, Northamptonshire, Hertfordshire and Buckinghamshire – mostly in the last-named County. We do not know precisely when this happened and these transactions may have been spread over several years. When all was settled by 1086 (or perhaps as early as 1075) he held sway altogether over 127 hides and taking as a rough guide a hide to be about 120 acres, this gave him total landholdings of over 15,000 acres. The most valuable portion was the Manor of Wolverton, which was valued at £20 and this high value may have been one the reasons that he chose to settle there. Nor should the roads be ignored as an influence. The Watling Street, even though a green trackway, may still have been one of the fastest routes to move armed horsemen. A good part of his landholdings were also in North Buckinghamshire, so the location may also have been practical for administrative purposes.

Manno's Manor

Not too far away, he held the manors of Loughton, Stoke Hammond, Wicken, Thornborough and Padbury, which amounted to well over half of this land. Beyond that he held the manor of Ellesborough near Aylesbury some scattered small manors at Aston Sandford, Chalfont St Giles, Drayton Beauchamp, Helsthorpe and Lamport. Neither Helsthorpe nor Lamport are recognised as places today. Helsthorpe preserves its name as a farmhouse near Wingrave and Lamport, probably part of Water Stratford, just outside Buckingham, ceased to exist in name long ago.

Manno also held a sizeable but not overly valuable manor at Lutterworth and two small manors at Misterton and Catthorpe in Leicestershire. The Lutterworth Manor supported 6 villagers and 7 smallholders and 12 of these were Freemen, that is they were able to work the land without any obligation of service. It appears that the lord's demesne was operated by 2 male slaves and 1 female slave. The value of this manor was £7, some of which was owed to the King, so it may not have been a great source of revenue for Manno. The same could be said for Misterton and Catthorpe which were only valued at 20s each. What is noteworthy is that these manors were first held by Earl Ralph, the Breton lord who was appointed Earl of East Anglia, in 1066. He died a few years after the invasion and his son, also Ralph, became earl, and for reasons which are not clear joined a rebellion against William in 1075. He lost and fled to Brittany, never to return. Needless to add his estates were forfeit, and these manors granted to Manno, who presumably stayed loyal. Thus we might date Manno's acquisition of these manors to sometime after 1075. These exact connection of these properties with the Wolverton barony is difficult to pin down. There are surviving deeds of land transactions in the Market Harborough area in the first half of the 14th century so it might be fair to assume that the Lutterworth, Misterton and Catthorpe manors had been granted to followers and had passed out of the family by that time.

He also held some Northamptonshire properties. There was one hide held from the King at Thenford, near Banbury, 3 virgates at Wicken and something over 4 hides at Maidwell, north of Northampton. Each was valued at £2. Each manor was worked by slaves, a mode of operation which may have become obsolete by the end of the 11th century. Thenford never features in later documents although both Wicken (Wick Hamon) and

40

The Barons of Wolverton

Manno's Manor

Maidwell play their part in subsequent transactions.The last piece of land, "the third part of ½ hide in Dunsley", which is part of Tring, was valued at only 12d and provided sufficient land for 1 ox.

The core of the barony was made up of the Buckinghamshire holdings and here Manno and his successors concentrated their interests.

There was in any case much work to be done in Buckinghamshire. In the immediate aftermath of the battle at Hastings, William and his army moved north to London, but failing to gain a crossing there moved westward to Wallingford where they were able to ford the river. From here the army followed the course of the Icknield Way where there was a lot of harrying and laying waste of the countryside. Some of Manno's future manors lay directly in this path. The Domesday records record the impact of this devastation in the assessed land values.

- Ellesborough: Total value £6; when acquired £4; before 1066 £10.
- Chalfont: Total value £6 10s; when acquired 100s; before 1066 £6 10s.
- Aston: in total, value 100s; when acquired £4; before 1066, 100s.
- Helsthorpe: Value 40s; when acquired 20s; before 1066 £4.
- Drayton: In total, the value is and was £4; before 1066, 100s.

Ellesborough, Drayton, Aston and Helsthorpe were directly in the path of William's army, which eventually came to terms with the English at Berkhamstead, but all of these manors suffered some fall in value by the time of Manno's acquisition, suggesting that there were insufficient people to work the land in the aftermath of the Conquest. The dramatic drop in the value of Helsthorpe and its partial recovery 20 years later, may indicate that not much was done to restore the manor in the ensuing years. The rest of the manors had recovered their value after 20 years, although Ellesborough was apparently struggling to get back to its pre-Conquest valuation.

By comparison the North Buckinghamshire manors either retain or quickly bounce back to their pre-Conquest valuations.

- Lamport: In total, value 30s; when acquired 16s; before 1066, 30s.
- Padbury: Total value £12; when acquired £7; before 1066, £12.
- Stoke: The value is and always was £10.
- Loughton: the total value is and was £3; before 1066 £4.

42

The Barons of Wolverton

- Wolverton: Total value £20; when acquired £15; before 1066 £20.

The 1086 survey shows us how Manno managed his dispersed holdings. Some were given over to his knights in a practice later termed subinfeudation. In such cases a manor was given to a knight who would enjoy the revenue in return for military service. In this way Manno was able to fulfil his own obligation to the king. In Chalfont, which must have been largely wooded at the time, he installed two knights, one in the area known as the Vache and another at Isenhampstead, later known as Chenies. The Red Book of the Exchequer of 1186 records the names of those knights in the assessment of Hamon's 15 knight's fees. Among them, presumably descendants of Manno's knights, are Alexander de Ysenhamstede and Warnerus de Vacca. The Vache, which may have acquired its name as a cow pasture, was adopted as a surname by this family and the de la Vache prospered for a few hundred years. Isenhampstead is not mentioned in Domesday, but we can infer from the knight's fee of 1166 that it was part of the Chalfont Manor. By 1232 the family name was Cheyne, probably through marriage, and this family prospered there for centuries, giving their name to the manor and the parish as Chenies. There were a number of connections between the Chalfont manors and the Wolverton family over the centuries, suggesting a closer relationship than with the other manors of the barony. It has occurred to me (although it is pure fancy on my part) that the apparent importance of the Chalfont manors might be due to Manno granting them to close relatives, possibly even to younger sons who could not inherit the barony. There is no documentary evidence for this; it is only a hunch based on a plausible explanation. The South Buckinghamshire manors were 60 miles from Wolverton and Manno would need knights on those manors whom he could trust. Family ties were the best guarantee of loyalty and there is no reason to suppose that Manno was not conventional in granting key positions to his sons and close relatives or to his sons-in-law. We have no record of Manno's sons and daughters but it is reasonable to speculate that there may have been more children than a single son and that these children would have to be accommodated somehow. It is just possible that the de Wolverton and Chenies families were cousins.

Manno's Manor

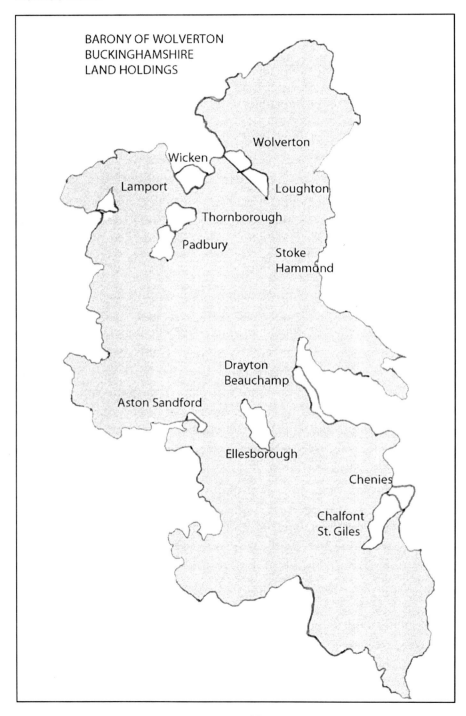

The Barons of Wolverton

Manno had granted the Drayton and Helsthorpe manors to Helgot and there may have been the expectation of more than one knight coming out of this arrangement. The 1186 list records Peverel de Bello Campo for two knights and Stephanus de Bello Campo for one knight. They may have been descendants of Helgot and had adopted the name Bello Campo – Beauchamp, which later attached itself to the manor and parish of Drayton.

The now non-existent Lamport, near Stowe, was also subinfeudated to Gerard and another follower, Berner, was given the quite large manor of Thornborough as well as Maidwell in Northamptonshire[2]. Two men at arms were given Loughton which may be the origin of two manors within the whole of Loughton. The de Loughton family emerges from one of these.

Mannou's knightly obligations could thus be met by two from Chalfont, two from Drayton, one from Helesthorpe, one from Lamport, two from Loughton, two from Thornborough, which possibly included Maidwell with the rest made up from Stoke, Wicken, Thenford, the Leicestershire holdings and Wolverton itself.

Knights were expensive. The armour might cost £10 and a good war horse might cost up to £40. On top of this the knight would need to support himself and his family in suitable style so it would require the labour of a large number of peasants to support a single knight, let alone esquires, who were in a sense apprentice knights. Knighthood did not have the high social standing that it acquired in the later middle ages, during the age of chivalry. There could be quite a range in wealth and social standing between a knight who enjoyed the proceeds of a whole manor and household knights who directly served Manno and lived off a small part of the Wolverton Manor.

All of this cost and the responsibility for delivery was borne by the feudal tenant, so the land grants had to be of a size to make the bargain feasible for both parties. The tenants-in-chief then made similar arrangements down the chain in the practice known as subinfeudation, described earlier, whereby the tenant-in-chief would hand over a manor to a knight in return for his required service. This, for instance, is exactly what happened in Manno's Manor of Aston, valued, as we have seen, at 4 ½ hides worth £5. In 1086 Odo held it from Manno in lieu of service and it

Manno's Manor

appears that his descendants adopted the name of Sandford. In time, as these feudal practices changed, first by excusing themselves from military service by a fine and by the 14th century seeking and expecting payment for military service, these small manors became customary holdings for the men whose ancestors once held them in lieu of service.

The vast territories awarded to William's followers, which would generate enormous wealth today, illustrated two realities: William's policy of securing his throne through an army that could be raised by a small number of barons that he could depend upon, and the low population (estimated at 1.5 million) and economic yield of the land.

The records of the reign of Henry II are slightly more informative and 100 years after the Conquest we have a snapshot of Hamon's feudal commitments.

In 1165 Hamon's knights and military commitments are spelled out in detail:[3]

> Bertram de Verdone 2 knights
> Peverel de Bello Campo 2 knights
> William son of Galfridi 2 knights
> Stephanus de Bello Campo 1 knight
> Alexander de Isenhamstede 1 knight
> Warnerus de Vacca 1 knight
> William son of Alan 1 knight
> Bartholemew de Loughton 1 knight
> Hamo Niger ½ knight
> Radulfus Macer 1/5 knight
> Owen de Stokes ¼ knight
> Roger Vis de Lou 1/5 knight
> Henry de Freine ½ knight
> Bernerus son of Azur 1/5 knight
> Azur Rufus 1/10 knight
> Simon son of Berner 1/10 knight

The list was drawn up as part of a new assessment and here amounts to 13 knights and "three parts of 1 knight", an attempt by Henry II to formalize a system which had become open to dispute after a century of use. At this distance 100 years does not seem like a lot but we need to remind ourselves that this was three generations and England was under the reign of its fifth king since the Conquest. Societies are always more complex than they appear on the surface and plainly, from this evidence, a system which started with a straightforward agreement of the exchange of land for military service had become subject to variation. Some idea of the varying arrangements can be divined from this list. Alexander de Isenhamstede and Warnerus de Vacca and Bartholemew de Loughton are each assessed for one knight on the basis of a manor, each one in the region of 5 hides, in other words little different from the Anglo Saxon relationship of a 5 hide manor to a thane. Henry de Fresne, who held the larger manor of Thornborough apparently has an arrangement whereby his military service (owed to the castle of Northampton) is assessed at only ¼ but we learn from a record of 1254 about a payment of 15s 10d per annum for the manor. Thus the baron was able to meet some of his own military obligations from Henry dee Fresne and secure some income from the manor. On the other hand Owen de Stoke, we learn from other sources, has only one hide on the manor itself, which is appropriately assessed at ¼ fee. There are other records in this reign where scutage, a payment in lieu of service, was assessed on two occasions against Hamon, one for £10 and another for £20. The customary provision of knights for military service had much changed over the century. Unlike their Saxon counterparts, who were mostly lightly armed foot soldiers, the 12th and 13th century knight needed an expensive war horse and costly weaponry. The customary recruitment was often difficult to arrange and over time fell into disuse as payment became normal.

Life on the Manor

When Manno le Breton settled his barony on Wolverton he brought a fundamental change in status to the manor. Peasants perhaps accustomed to direct dealing with a local lord, now had a baron with much wider interests who now employed a steward to administer the manor. And, as I suggest later, having a resident lord of some importance may have had an impact on the prosperity of the manor.

So far we have described what we know about the top end of this post-Conquest society, and even there with difficulty because the records

Manno's Manor

are sparse. It does appear, that apart from making the change at the top most of the rights and customs of the native inhabitants were initially respected. Manno most likely employed a steward, who might have been one of his household knights, to manage the Wolverton Manor, but most of the customary uses of the land continued as before.

Inevitably the picture is more complicated even in a small peasant society. Wool was spun into thread, cloth woven and fulled, leather was tanned, iron implements forged, trees felled and sawn, masonry chiselled. Were these specialist and skilled tasks undertaken full time by people who were paid for their work or, more likely perhaps, accomplished by specialists working part time in a forge, say, and part time on the land, possibly tilling a smaller acreage.

The most significant change over these two centuries was the gradual loss of status of the peasant, who was more-or-less free before 1066 and almost completely tied to the land by 1266. The Normans brought with them a more Roman conception of land management, where a central authority tied the peasants to land and service. They were not slaves in the Roman sense but at the end of this period they were more serf-like than they had been under English rule. There is an irony here. The Roman villa system of farming, from which this model was taken, had been abandoned after the Romans left in 400AD. The Celtic and Germanic model, while it may not have been as efficient, at least offered a peasant some notional freedom. Most, obviously, would stay with their customary plots, but it was possible for a young man to start out in another village, if the land were available. Under Norman rule this right was taken away and peasants were only allowed to move on the payment of a heavy penalty. At the end of the 14th century this oppressive arrangement broke down after the plague years.

But this social change was 300 years in the future. The revolution that was taking place in the first twenty years after the Conquest was to create a more centralised society. We have a record of the situation in 1066 and another in 1086. How these intervening years unfolded is not known in any detail that we could ascribe to Wolverton. It does appear that William initially left most landholders in place. He was able to appropriate King Edward's estates without objection and church lands likely stayed untouched, other than a change of bishop. The estates of Harold

The Barons of Wolverton

Godwinson were obviously forfeit and this may have extended to men of Harold, such as Godwin on the Wolverton manor. William began to change his mind after rebellions against his rule. There were smaller uprisings in 1067 and once these were put down the lands of the unlucky losers were appropriated. Marriages to daughters of some of the Saxon nobility also secured land for the invaders, but it was not until after the rebellion of 1069, involving the powerful Earl Waltheof and Danish invaders in the name of Edward the Atheling who had a more legitimate claim to the throne than William, that the new king changed his policy. He could only secure the realm by ensuring that his own followers held the land in service to the king. The only North Buckinghamshire Saxons to survive with their landholdings intact after 1086, were Leofwin of Nuneham, who held large estates in Oxfordshire and Buckinghamshire, Leofwin Oara who held small parcels of land in Simpson and Wavendon, and in Lavendon, on the edge of the forest, a man called Ketil held ½ hide from the King and appears to have been left alone twenty years later.

We shall never know what did happen to the local thanes, Godwin, Thori and Aelfric. Even if they had not lost their lives fighting against the invasions of 1066 their military allegiances probably made them easy to displace. They must have had families and brothers and sisters and cousins and one can only conclude that they were absorbed into the great mass of peasantry. It is probably not too far fetched to speculate that their genes survive in the Wolverton area today.

There is a timeless quality to the agricultural life. The seasons rotate, seed is planted and harvested. Food is stored for the winter and the cycle repeats itself. A new generation replaces the previous one and life and work continues much as before. Along the way small improvements are made - a new plough board perhaps, more refined milling of grain, grain is stored in houses that are raised off the ground to keep out rats. But these technological improvements are spaced over centuries and appear to the historian as slow-developing and unexciting. In the meantime human affairs are more volatile and change in this area can be rapid, sometimes for the good, and often for the worse.

Sir Frank Stenton has observed that apart from the imposition of forestry laws and the restriction on transferring their allegiance to another

Manno's Manor

lord there was remarkable continuity between Anglo Saxon England and Norman England in all other laws and customs.

> In these ancient institutions the Anglo-Saxon tradition was never broken. The virtue of the Old English state had lain in the local courts. Their strength had been due to the association of thegns and peasants in the work of justice, administration, and finance, under the direction of officers responsible to the king. The memory of this association survived all the changes of the Conqueror's reign. To all appearance, his barons and their men had accepted as a consequence of their position the share in local business which had fallen to their predecessors.[4]

One of the great "what if" questions of English history relates to the Norman Conquest of 1066. The outcome of Harold's engagement with William hung by little more than a Bayeux tapestry thread and could have gone either way. In the end William was the lucky one and with Harold dead the English lacked the leadership to withstand William's eventual triumph. Would English history have turned out differently? I suspect it would and this is apparent in the microcosm of the Wolverton Manor.

Anglo Saxon England was in many ways a more equal society. I don't want to use the word democratic because it does not apply in any modern sense, but people then did have more of a voice in community affairs. The chief reason for this was that it was a smaller, more manageable society. 98% of all people's affairs could be managed locally. Larger issues, usually those affecting the lords were addressed by the hundred court, which in Wolverton's case was held at Seckloe Hill. The king's justice was required only in a few cases and the usually in disputes between the magnates and the church. The council, (witan), was a feature at all levels of society, and, as can be seen in this Wolverton example, the presence of three thanes within the manor meant that neither one of them could become too powerful. The Norman centralisation of power was the significant revolution of 1066 and has had its long-term impact to this day. Even if there was intermarriage the Normans held themselves a class apart from the natives they had subjugated, even maintaining linguistic differences for 300 years.

The Barons of Wolverton

The Succession

The rule of Manno, Baron of Wolverton, must have been a long one and the indications are that he lived to an advanced age. He came to England in 1066 as a leader of men and a successful warrior and he had enough status to be rewarded by William with a barony. His birth can be estimated at any time between 1040 and 1045 and if he lived to 1114[5] he must have been at least 70 years old. His successor was Meinfelin. Meinfelin himself lived to about 1154 or 1155, so his three-score and ten years (if he achieved them) would place his birth in the region of 1085, when Manno was at least 40. The record of Manno's immediate family does not exist. We do not know the name of his wife nor how many sons and daughters he had. We know only the name of his heir, Meinfelin, possibly, but not necessarily his son. Meinfelin appears on record in 1125 as Sheriff of Bedfordshire and Buckinghamshire and we know that he died in or around 1155.[6] There are three key dates only: 1086, when we know of Manno and his land holdings, 1125 when Meinfelin was Sheriff of Bedfordshire and Buckinghamshire and 1155, when the Pipe Rolls of Henry II make reference to Hamon, son of Meinfelin. We therefore have clear evidence that Hamon is Meinfelin's son and heir. The rest is guesswork.[7]

If, as I remarked earlier, we can reasonably infer a birth date of no earlier than 1040, there is a span of almost 115 years between the estimated birth of Manno and the death of Meinfelin. It is possible that Meinfelin was Manno's son, either by being the youngest, or by being a son of a second marriage, but we should also entertain the possibility that he was a grandson and that he may have inherited the barony as his own father died before Manno passed on. There is a 13th century document which appears to confirm the succession but does not establish a father-son link between Manno and Meinfelin. It records a grant of land for the chaplain (presumably at the new chapel at Stony Stratford) from the Lord William, and one of the conditions is that prayers are spoken on three days a week

> for himself, his wife Helwisia, Mayny, Maynfeling, Beatricia, Hamon son of Meynfeling and Annable Mauduit and Hamo son of Hamo and the spirits of the faithful departed.[8]

Manno's Manor

Pointedly, it does not identify Maynfelyng as the son of Mayny.

As with eveything about Manno, there are no satisfying conclusions one can reach from scarce facts. Meinfelin was born almost 20 years after the Conquest and it would be surprising indeed if there were not older siblings born between 1066 and 1085. How then did he succeed to the Barony? One explanation may be that older brothers (if indeed they existed) died before their father without issue. Another, which sounds more plausible to me, is that Meinfelin was the eldest son of the eldest son, and this man died before Manno, leaving Meinfelin as the heir.

The second baron, Meinfelin, was appointed to the important position of Sheriff of Bedfordshire and Buckinghamshire between 1125 and 1129. We can therefore assume that he was a significant and powerful figure in the region and that his position enabled him to augment and consolidate the wealth of the Barony. We can also learn from a later document that Meinfelin married into the de Warenne family. William de Warenne, who held some land in Buckinghamshire, became Earl of Surrey and as one of William the Conqueror's closest companions, was a very powerful figure. The deed cited above, in the briefest of references, does give her a name - Beatrice. The union would indicate that Meinfelin was of sufficient status to enter into the marriage.

Apart from these fleeting references our information about Meinfelin is also scant. His appointment to the lucrative office of Sheriff tells us that the family was by this time well enough established and powerful enough to be respected in this role. King Henry I obviously felt that Meinfelin could be trusted. The Sheriff was responsible for the administration of justice in the county – the shire reeve - and before the emergence of a specialised judiciary, the sheriff would preside over courts in the county where the king's interest was at stake. Local justice was administered by the local Lord or the Church. More serious cases were the province of the king's justice. The Sheriff was often charged with the collection of taxes when they were levied. In both functions the sheriff would take some part of the money collected as his fee for the service, so the position of Sheriff was beneficial to the holder, and tolerated as long as one was not too greedy, which could bring its own penalties.

The Barons of Wolverton

The Barons of Wolverton

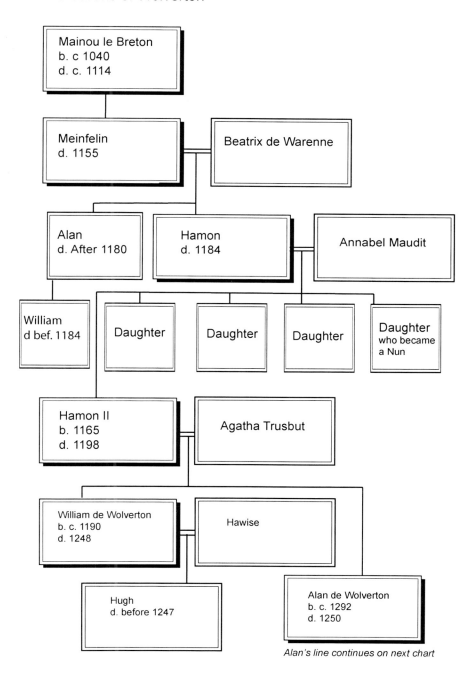

Alan's line continues on next chart

Manno's Manor

Since there is no record of any complaint against Meinfelin and neither is there evidence of any great wealth, it might be fair to assume that he conducted himself in his role without a great deal of excessive peculation. He certainly had sufficient surplus wealth at his death to endow the Priory of Bradwell in his will, a foundation that was to last for four hundred years, although it never became a rich priory. The first two barons, whatever their precise relationship, lived long lives, and the third baron, Hamon, comes into the inheritance some time before 1155.

The Third Baron

The third baron, Hamon (d 1184) also left his mark by making a bequest of part of the manor of Thornborough to the Priory at Luffield. Luffield had been founded by Robert de Bossu, earl of Leicester, earlier than 1133 and was the first priory in the county. As such it took a senior role in the affairs of the Bradwell Priory. This Hamon also gave his name to Wicken (Wick Hamon) and Stoke Hammond. He was the younger of two sons that we know of, the elder being Alan, who pre-deceased him.

We know a little more about him than his father or grandfather because the records of the reign of Henry II are more carefully recorded. He appears in fines for scutage ("shield money" paid to the king in lieu of actual military service)[9] In 1161 he is assessed £50 against his 15 knights-not a small sum of money it has to be said - and again for the same amount in 1162. In 1166 he is listed with the names of the fifteen knights for which he he is responsible.

In 1176 he appears again in the rolls to pay a fine of £100 for the very serious crime of hunting in the king's forest. This was a common enough transgression and the issue of hunting was a bone of contention between the king and his nobility. The king had reserved most of the forest, that is land for hunting, for himself and set heavy penalties against those who hunted on his forest. Sometimes these forests swallowed up huge territory. Almost half of Hampshire, for example, was covered by the New and Bere Forests. In North Buckinghamshire and South Northamptonshire the Whittlewood and Salcey Forests took over many acres. The barons remained resentful that their hunting activities were restricted. In addition the land was economically unproductive.

The Barons of Wolverton

It was easy to stray. Hamon's land at Wicken bordered Whittlewood forest which was a royal reserve so it was almost a casual crime, wittingly or unwittingly, to move on to the king's territory.

Hamon died in 1184 or thereabouts for the barony fell into the hands of the king, as was the practice when the heir was in a minority. The rotuli for Michelmas 1185 records Hamon as recently dead "obiit die Veneris ante Acsensionum" or May 23rd. 1185 and leaving a widow and a son aged 20. The King's exchequer accounts for £10 18s. 1d. from the issues of Hamon's landholdings and a further £2 for Wyke Hamon, now known as Wicken. These are probably the earnings for part of the year. Since there is no further mention we may assume that Hamon's son, also named Hamon, came into his inheritance shortly after on payment of an entry fine to the king – again customary practice. Often these relief fines were paid in instalments but it appears that in 1190 he still owed £62 6s. 8d. to the crown. This same brief record also tells us that Hamon had four sisters, one of whom was a nun. This is a rare instance in those early centuries of recording the existence of siblings who could not inherit the main estate.

We also learn from the same document that Hamon had married Matilda,[10] a daughter of the powerful William Mauduit, sometime chancellor. She had brought the manor of Fyfield in North West Hampshire into Hamon's hands as her marriage portion. It remained with the de Wolvertons until 1280 when it fell into the king's hands, possibly for payment of a fine. Maud was given the manor of Stoke for dower as a widow and it is possibly at this time that the suffix Hamon (later Hammond) became attached to it. This record shows us that Meinfelin had entered the orbit of Earl Warenne. Hamon, son of Hamon, son of Meinfelin was very well connected. Somehow, little of this rubbed off on the Barons of Wolverton.

This information does enable us to arrive at an actual year of birth for Hamon fitzHamon, 1164. And so at the age of 21, at the king's command, he married Agatha Trusbut, daughter of Sir William Trusbut. William Trusbut, according to Orderic Vitalis, came from very humble parentage but clearly had talent as he was raised to an Honour of 10 knight's fees by Henry I, putting him more-or-less on a footing with Hamon son of Meinfelin. Not one of William Trusbut's four sons had issue and the

Manno's Manor

estate was divided between two daughters, Agatha and Rohese. In 1995 Hamon paid a fine of 300 marks to the treasury for his share in the inheritance. What these lands were is unclear as there is no further mention of them.

It is possible that the de Wolvertons did not gain in the long term from this inheritance, because Agatha, who must have been widowed by 1198, was scooped up in marriage to William de Albini from Clifton Reynes. William was about 30 at the time and Agatha, who was by now 38, was his second wife. That the inheritance went with her is shown through William's payment of a fine of 600 marks to the King upon his marriage to Agatha and his absorption of her inheritance. She probably had a more exciting life with William who was part of the baron's uprising against King John in 1201 and who, in 1217, held the command of Rochester Castle against the siege of the king. For his rebellion he forfeited his estates to the Crown but regained them from John's son, King Henry III.

During her 13 year marriage to Hamon, Agatha bore at least two sons, William and Alan. Both succeeded in turn to the barony, as William had no heirs. William makes his appearance in the Red Book of the Exchequer in 1211, when he is required to pay scutage, which would indicate that he was of age to do military service, but chose to pay the fine instead. Thus his birth year can be estimated as 1190 or earlier.

The last reference to Hamon son of Hamon paying scutage is in 1198, which might help to confirm his early death in that year at the age of 34. The cause is unknown.

It is very difficult from fragmentary facts to gather some concept of personality but we do appear to be entering a period with William, of gradual erosion of the family's prestige. Sir Frank Markham considers them "a feeble lot" and this is a fair judgement. While contemporary families were aggressively pursuing greater power and land ownership, the de Wolvertons, as they were now beginning to style themselves, were content with what they had. Compared with some of the thrusting barons of the 13th and 14th centuries, even nearby families like the de Greys or the d' Albinis, the de Wolvertons seemed content with their status and kept a low profile. And who is to say that it was a bad policy? Many ambitious barons paid for their elevation with their lives; some even lost both their lives and

The Barons of Wolverton

their estates for their posterity. The de Wolvertons, by not venturing for risky acquisitions, at least held on to what they had. In consequence the people of Wolverton enjoyed a comparatively placid existence. They were, like everyone, subject to famine and disease, but at least they were not the victims, from the time of the Conquest onwards, of rapine and devastation.

The fines for failure to meet their military obligations demonstrate William's lack of interest in advancement. In the 13th century, the only way to improve family fortunes was to perform some useful service for the king and look for reward. William showed no interest in this. He makes the record in the rolls during the reign of King John in 1215 when he had to pay 50 marks to recover his lands after losing his rights for failure to provide military service. The same thing happened again in 1223, during the reign of Henry III.

A similar lack of ambition centres around the status of Bradwell Priory, founded by his great grandfather, Meinfelin. Little effort was made to advance the interest of this Priory and it was during this period it became a cell of Luffield Priory with corresponding secondary status.

Many deeds from the time of William's tenure survive; they all relate to land transactions on the manor. The early ones are undated and many of these deeds are difficult to place in context. However, for the first time since Domesday, we have documents which can afford us a little insight into the workings of the manor. The deeds were kept because of their legal importance and were passed on from generation to generation through the Longuevilles and finally to the Radcliffe Trust. This chest of documents was deposited in the Bodleian library in 1923. Each transaction of land or property is carefully written as a deed and witnessed on the appropriate occasion by various important retainers.

William married a woman called Hawise. Nothing is known about her origin. There were no surviving sons although there is a reference in one of the deeds to Hugh of Wolverton *dominus* and I would take him to be a son of William. Hugh must have died before 1247. Certainly when William died in 1248 he had no surviving male issue and he was succeeded by his younger brother Alan.

The Barons of Wolverton - continued

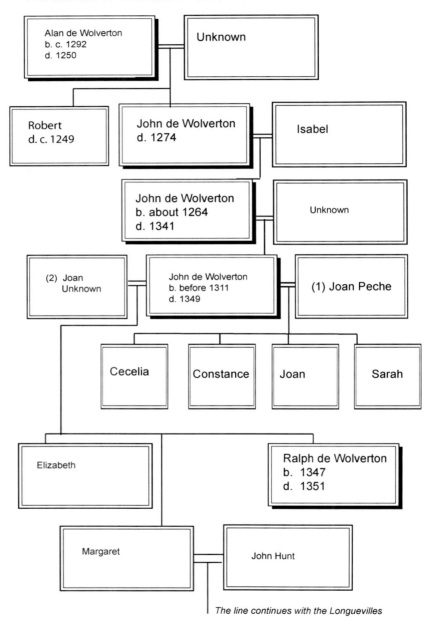

The line continues with the Longuevilles

The Barons of Wolverton

Alan outlived his brother by no more than two years, not long enough to leave his mark on the barony. Alan was the first to style himself de Wolverton and he was the only one with a male heir, John, who lived to 1274.

In 1274, John's son, Sir John de Wolverton, succeeded to the title as a minor. He appears to have been an uncooperative character, at least as far as the crown was concerned, and from the standpoint of history his accession continues the slow decline in the de Wolverton fortunes.

In 1284, as he was a minor and a ward of the crown, Queen Eleanor chose a bride for the young Sir John. He refused to marry her. In 1297 he was required to undertake military service overseas. He declined and paid a fine. In 1328 he argued for exemption from the Assize and in 1342 it was suggested that he had not been fulfilling his service duties at Northampton Castle. He was the last of the de Wolvertons to be summoned to Parliament and it seems that the Barony died with him. He died in 1342 and his son John succeeded to the remaining estates but not the dignity of Baron.

This John had four daughters by his first marriage and two daughters and a son, Ralph, by his second marriage. When John died in 1349 (the date would suggest death from the Bubonic Plague) Ralph was only two years old.

Ralph did not last long and died in 1351 leaving a complicated succession.

The End of the de Wolverton Line

During these turbulent 14th century years the male succession to the barony was lost. The Chalfont St Giles Manor of the Barony was divided between the daughters of the first marriage to Joan Pecche. She died before 1331 and four daughters survived her, Joan, who married Hugh Wake, Sarah who had a son called Adam Basing, Cecilia, whose son Theobald Grossett was also an inheritor and Constance the youngest daughter. From 1349 onward this manor is no longer connected to Wolverton and there do not appear to have been any claims against the major estate. John's second wife was also called Joan and she bore two daughters, Margery and Elizabeth and a son Ralph who died young in 1351. Margery was at that

Manno's Manor

time betrothed to John Hunt of Fenny Stratford and she married him in 1352.

Elizabeth in the meantime married William Cogenhoe of Cogenhoe Manor in Northamptonshire, and they signed a deed in 1378 to the effect that if they had no heirs, their portion of the Wolverton estates would be granted to Sir John Cheyne of Isenhampstead Chenies. The reasons for this are not obvious but I have hinted before they may have been cousins. The Isenhampstead family, who later adopted the name Cheyne, were certainly prominent in Buckinghamshire and even at this date were still a rising family. William and Elizabeth de Cogenhoe did have two children, William and Agnes. The elder child, William died in 1389 and his son died in 1399, still a minor. The heir to the estate was Agnes, who John Cheyne promptly married in 1400 to cement his interest in the Cogenhoe manor and the portion of the Wolverton estate.

In the meantime Margery produced one heir, Joan Hunt who married John Longueville of Billing and it is here that the Longuevilles enter the Wolverton story. Even though John Hunt died before 1365, Margery remarried and outlived two further husbands, dying herself in 1383.

At this stage what was left of the Wolverton barony was divided between Joan the wife of John Longueville and John Cheyne and his wife Agnes. She died in 1421, but they had one son, Alexander. He had no issue, and at the death of John Cheyne in 1445 their portion of the Wolverton manor was restored to the other half of the family, by now in the person of George Longueville.

For just over a century the Wolverton Manor had been a divided inheritance. It is hard to see at this distance in time whether or not it made any difference. Presumably it made none to the ordinary peasant but it must have had an impact on the income of the lord of the manor. Perhaps it is not a coincidence that the building of a tower at St Mary Magdalen begins soon after this date when the manor was finally re-unified.

William Vis de Lou and the Knights

An undated deed from the early 13th century has a perfectly preserved wax seal suspended from it by a ribbon. It bears, in relief, the likeness of a

The Barons of Wolverton

wolf's head and the inscription around it to tell us that it is the seal of William Vis de Lou. It is an extraordinary connection to a man and a family that lived and prospered in Wolverton 800 years ago. The name Vis de Lou (Vis de Loup) probably started as a nickname and means "wolf face" or "face like a wolf" and it is probable that William's ancestor, a man who accompanied Manno during the invasion of 1066 had facial features that could be likened to a wolf. Nicknames were common in the 10th and 11th century, and if a man did not bear the name of his place of origin (for example, Longueville) he often bore a nickname which was carried through the generations. Miles Crispin, for example, had a forebear with stiff, wiry hair. Walter Giffard's ancestor was probably on the chubby side. In the case of Manno the Breton of Wolverton and Winemar the Fleming of Hanslope the general area of their origin was enough to define them but the Normans who did not have a nickname tended to be more precise in naming the village of origin - William of Warrene, Roger of Ivry.

The seal of William Vis de Lou, attached to a 13th century deed.

Manno's Manor

It is quite possible that William was a descendant of Humphrey Vis de Lou who was given a manor in Berkshire. Over time they expanded their interest into North Bucks and Northamptonshire and it is possible that one of the family (perhaps a younger son) found a position with the Baron of Wolverton.

We first hear of a Wolverton Vis de Lou in 1166 when Roger Vis de Lou is named as one of the Wolverton barony knights in the inventory of Henry II. Roger accounts for 1/5th of a knight's fee and while we are not told which part of the barony he is from it is a fair assumption that for this amount he held some land on the Wolverton estate itself. The fact that he represented a fractional amount suggests that the grant of land was for payment and that no actual military service was undertaken. It does appear from other records of the period that a full knight's assessment might approximately translate to 4 or 5 hides of land. A quarter knight's fee, as in the case of Owen of Stoke Hammond was 1 hide. We might deduce, although not with certainty, that Roger Vis de Lou's 1/5 could be 3 virgates - about 90 acres. If he had this land on the Watling Street he was probably in position to generate a good income and his descendant William was probably well placed to make bequests to priories.

William, who may have been Roger's son, was in the early 13th century able to make bequests to religious foundations in the interests of his immortal soul. In one deed he made a bequest to the Priory at Snellshall and in others he granted some land to Bradwell Priory. If we assume that William was able to look after his own family (and there is a Geoffrey Vis de Lou in later documents) then he and his family were surely in a position, some 150 years after the conquest to give away some of their accumulated wealth. For the most part these parcels of land abut Watling Street.

These early 13th century deeds, even taken as a whole, give us only fragmentary information, very much like a shard of pottery found in an archaeological dig: there is evidence of human activity (in this case land transactions), but very little to go on in constructing a coherent narrative. The parcels of land are described in ways which made perfect sense to the men of the time but are impossible to locate today. For example:

One ½ virgate of land which Hugh, father of Robert held.[11]

The Barons of Wolverton

Or more specifically:

2 acres above Severungfurlong[12] of which one is between the land of Simon of Eltesdun on one side and of Thomas Vivian on the other.[13]

Everybody at the time knew what the boundaries were. They were physically defined on the ground. Each cottager knew the boundaries of his yard and every villein knew the limits of his furlong strip. What may now appear to us as a vague description was precise to contemporaries. Encroachments then, as today, were zealously resisted.

When Manno established himself at Wolverton he had to look after his own followers. The major figures were given manors of their own in various parts of the barony, but in the second rank men like Vis de Lou had to settle for smaller acreages - enough certainly to maintain themselves in the status of a knight and to be on hand to provide immediate services for Manno. It is quite probable that this condition did not last long. Already by the reign of Henry II barons were paying scutage (*shield money*) which was a fine to excuse themselves military service. A man like Roger Vis de Lou, for example, representing 1/5 part of a knight would probably willingly pay the required fee to his lord, who would then pass it on to the king and be excused the expense and uncertainty of military service. It is more likely that men like the Vis de Lous prospered in Wolverton and Stony Stratford during these years.

We are offered other glimpses into the names of others at this time, some being families from nearby estates, like the de Fresnes or Fraxinos from Thornborough, or the de Luctons from Loughton, the Barrés from Stanton Barré. These meetings to discuss and witness land transactions were probably held twice a year, at Lady Day in the Spring and Michelmas in September. They were probably occasions for merrymaking and for the baron to find out what was going on in other parts of his domain. Apart from the local names there are Bello Campos (Beauchamps) who may have come from the Drayton Manor. And too there are other men, possibly local, who have sufficient status in the community to witness these deeds. We find a Hugh de Stratford, John Hasteng (Hastings), Robert Race. These last two names indicating that Saxon names did not completely die out. Some of these men must have been descendants of Manno's household knights. There is a Richard le Frankelein de Calveruntun. A Franklin was a

Manno's Manor

freeholder who held land that was not tied to service. In other words he owned it outright.

Thus a significant, if small middle class was growing up around Wolverton with sufficient land and prestige to raise them above the common herd. Adam le Coc, for example, may have owned the strip of land on which the Cock Inn was built and may have been quite well to do.

For a period of years William Vis de Lou appears as a witness to every surviving deed. Sir Frank Markham infers from this (at least I can find no other evidence) that he was Baron William's steward. He may have been.

The Vis de Lou name becomes less active in the next generation and might be thought to have died out but we find some documents in the early 15th century which suggest that the inheritors of the name carried with some pride in the 13th century were uncomfortable with it. In 1421 a sale of some acres in Stony Stratford was made to John Oxe, alias John Vydeloue[14] . Some 45 years later, in 1466, the former name is still being recorded[15]. "John Videloue of Wolverton alias Oxe Senior grants etc." An interesting side note on this transaction is that even at this late date the land grant is made "saving service to chief lords of fee" telling us that the original grant from the baron of Wolverton to the original Vis de Lou was for knightly service. Four centuries later life was very different; although technically the land came with the expectation of military service to the lord, and hence to the crown, in practice this obligation would be dealt with by a cash payment and of military service was required mercenaries would be hired to do the job.

The eventual decline of the barony coincides with the decline of the knight. The military men who had accompanied Manno and settled with him on the Wolverton Manor had receded into history and their descendants had become sheep farmers and innkeepers and men of property. By the middle of the 14th century the knight was usually a man of high status, usually from a high-born family. Chaucer's "verray parfit gentil knight", described in his Canterbury Tales, and thought to have been modelled upon Henry Grosmont, Duke of Lancaster, was a very far remove from some of the rough and ready bruisers who were the ancestors of some of the Wolverton families. There is more than a hint in Chaucer's verse that the knight was becoming an anachronism. Wars were by that time

The Barons of Wolverton

fought by mercenaries led by the like of Sir John Hawkwood, the famous (some might say infamous) leader of mercenary bands in Italy in the 14th century.. The amateur knight who tended to his estates and answered the call of duty when it came were a vanishing breed. More typical were men like Sir John Longueville, about to come into the Wolverton inheritance, who held the status but not the old fashioned obligations.

The story of the barony of Wolverton charts a period of 300 years. The barony was a loose agglomeration of manors under the tenancy of one man who owed his allegiance to the king. He in turn, parcelled out a good part of these extensive territories to his own followers. The first three, possibly four barons held some status with a high point in the 12th century. Thereafter, because the titular barons were not ambitious, the barony declined and more-or-less disappeared under the relaxed watch of the de Wolverton family.

Part of the reason for this was that the term baron itself had no precise definition in the Norman and Plantagenet periods. Earls, and later Dukes, had specific status, as did Bishops, but the status of Barons was elastic. Some of William's followers were granted huge estates (in some cases on both sides of the channel) and their wealth, compared to Manno, was disproportionately high. Walter Giffard, for example, Manno's Buckinghamshire neighbour, had vast estates and correspondingly more influence. In this period baron was more of a description than a title - a general collective term applied to William's senior followers.

The Barony of Wolverton was certainly an historic entity and came later to be known as an "honour" which could expect certain rights and dues. It did not carry with it the status and dignity of an earldom.

As the successors to the honour of Wolverton lapsed into an unambitious torpor the barony seeped away in the 13th century and by the time the de Longuevilles came to Wolverton at the end of the 14th century is is doubtful that the word baron had any meaning at all in the Wolverton context.

Manno's Manor

1 Sir Frank Stenton. Anglo Saxon England. OUP 1970.

2 There may have been two men named Berner.

3 Red Book of the Exchequer. (Rolls Series) p. 314-5.

4 Stenton. op.cit. p. 684

5 A date suggested by Frank Markham.

6 Great Roll of the Pipe. 2-4 Henry II, 22. (Rec. Com.)

7 Hyde puts the death of Manno at 1110 on the basis of "some evidence". Markham offers 1114 with no evidence. VCH Bucks. refers to VCH Northants i. p 368, 374, 385.

8 Bodleian, dd. Radcl. Deed 49, undated but before 1246.

9 This was beginning to be a good arrangement for both sides - the baron could be excused military service and attend to his other affairs and the king could use the money to hire mercenaries, who in many ways were more dependable.

10 She is named as Matilda or Maud here but the Wolverton deed, cited earlier, calls her Annabel. Both names must refer to the same woman.

11 Bodleian. MSS. dd. Radcl.. Deed 50

12 There is a piece of land of 8 acres in a 1710 document described as Severins Close, which may be a variant on Severungfurlong or the Severidge.

13 Bodleian. MSS. dd. Radcl.. Deed 474

14 Bodleian. MSS. dd. Radcl. Deed 8

15 Bodleian. MSS. dd. Radcl.. Deed 502

FOUR

TOWN AND COUNTRY

There was a long period, up to the middle of the 19th century, when Stony Stratford was more populous than Wolverton and had by far the stronger economy. Eighteenth century travellers would know about Stony Stratford but could remain ignorant of Wolverton. By the mid-nineteenth century the reverse may have been true. The coaching trade went into steep decline and Stony Stratford returned once more to being a smaller part of Wolverton's economic strength. Before the 12th century the roadside settlement had no separate identity from its parent manors, Calverton and Wolverton, but by 1200 it was able to assert a distinct identity even though it was still tied economically to the two bordering manors. By the late middle ages Stony Stratford had become a separate entity, with some independence from the two manors that had once controlled both sides of the Watling Street, but since much of the Wolverton side was still owned by the Lord of the Manor this part of Stony Stratford could still be reckoned as a substantial part of the Wolverton economy. Any history of the manor must consider the emergence of Stony Stratford as a notable part of the story.

The story of Stony Stratford starts fairly late. Although there have been some claims for Stony Stratford as a Roman settlement there is as yet little archaeological evidence to support this idea other than the discovery of some Roman coins and pottery fragments. There were garrison settlements along the road at Fenny Stratford (Magiovinto) and Towcester (Lactodoro) but evidence of even a posting station at either Stony Stratford or Old Stratford is skimpy at best. White Kennett, writing in the 17th century, blithely refers to Stony Stratford as "old Lactodorum"[1] and earlier William Camden (1594) makes the same assertion. Even as late as 1760 the map maker Thomas Jeffreys was able to mark Lactodorum in Old English script beside Stony Stratford. By the 19th century this placement was questioned and present day opinion and evidence places the site of Lactodoro at Towcester and although this does not exclude the possibility of a settlement at Stratford in Roman times, it does pour a certain amount of cold water on the idea that it was a significant Roman station. If we were

Manno's Manor

to make an argument against the idea of a Roman station at Stony Stratford we could note that the 16 miles between Magiovinto and Lactodorum could be accomplished in a day's march. A case can certainly be made for a station every ten miles or so. From London the known stations are 13 miles to Sulloniacis (Brockley Hill), 9 miles to Verulamo (St Albans), 13 miles to Durocobrivis (Dunstable), 12 miles to Magiovinto (near Little Brickhill) 16 miles to Lactodoro (Towcester), 12 miles to Bannaventa (Whilton Lodge), 19 miles to Venonis (High Cross), 11 miles to Manduesedo (Mancetter), 16 miles to Letoceto (Wall), 12 miles to Pennocrucio (Water Eaton), 11 miles to Uxacona (Redhill) and 11 miles to Urioconio (Wroxeter). Interpolation from this evidence should reasonably predict a station either side of the river at this crossing and reasonable grounds to plan an excavation. There is no surviving name for this camp. If it existed, and the case is yet unproven.

If we try to take a Roman view of the matter, military units leaving either Lactodoro or Magiovinto could reasonably expect to reach the Ouse crossing by the middle of the day, even if encumbered by baggage, which would mean that the river could be negotiated within an hour before moving on to the next station in the afternoon. So, far from being a natural stopover point the Stratford crossing may have been one that the soldiers preferred to manage when the sun was high.

Professor Hyde points out that the river crossing was never one of the better crossings and was always liable to flooding. An easier crossing could be found at Passenham and at Wolverton Mill and indeed there remained ancient roads or pathways at these points until recent times. By either route it was possible to negotiate the river more easily and continue the northward or southward journey. However, the Romans had a preference for building straight roads and coping with whatever engineering problem came their way. In this case it meant building a stone causeway to negotiate the marsh and laying stones and gravel on the river bed to ford the river. This is commonly believed to be the basis for the name of the place, although Hyde advances the view that it is more likely to derive from Stane Street: thus Stane Street Ford, rather than a stone bed at the river crossing. He notes that in many surviving medieval documents the place name is written as Stani Stratford. That having been noted, later reports up to and including the 16th century of difficult river crossings here may have been

Town and Country

more attributable to the general neglect of roads once the Romans had departed rather than the impassability of the river itself.. The Romans had a military imperative in maintaining good roads so that they could move troops quickly and effectively across country. Once the imperium had gone and the country broke up into smaller tribal kingdoms there was no longer any incentive to maintain roads even if the successors to the Romans had the engineering knowhow.

One fact we do have is the existence of the road itself and it would be unusual indeed if the river crossing did not attract residents who could enhance their livelihood by providing services to the itinerants. It is not until the compilation of the Domesday Book in 1086 that we encounter any documentary detail, and even there no mention of Stony Stratford is made. In his *History of Stony Stratford*, Hyde is of the view that there was a settlement there in Domesday times. He infers this from the rather high assessment of Wolverton at £20 compared to much lower assessments for equally fertile land along the Ouse valley - Beachampton at £7, Thornton, Haversham and Stanton at £6. Calverton, even though heavily wooded in the Weald part of the manor is valued at £12. Hyde's conclusion is that this relatively high valuation must include the economic life of inns and commerce along the old Roman road.

The other question that ought to be posed is why the settlement was built on the south and not the north side of the river. The bank is higher on the north side, less prone to flooding and closer to the river itself. It was also at the crossroads for the high road to Buckingham and the road to Northampton. Any garrison, if indeed there was one there, would find this a much more commanding position for the river crossing. So in many obvious respects the "Old Stratford" site was a better location and we should at least consider the theory that a Roman station was located on the north side of the river and that in the more secure Middle Ages the inns relocated south of the river. With the passage of a few hundred years, the settlement (if it existed) was forgotten. Theory is all we have because when it comes to evidence there is little to be found. Despite its name, Old Stratford as a recognised settlement was never older than Stony Stratford and throughout known history never amounted to much. The community, even in more recent centuries, never had a church or a school, and any

Manno's Manor

development that is there is more recent than Stony Stratford. It remains a puzzle.

There may not be a ready answer as to why a settlement grows on one side of the river and not the other. The name "Old" Stratford did not make an appearance until the 15th century when Stony Stratford was well established. Earlier references call the place *West Stratford* or *Far Stratford*. The name "Old" Stratford does suggest that there was some belief, possibly based on oral tradition, that the settlement was older. Stony Stratford was a focal point for the several crossings over the River Ouse and this may be one reason for the settlement on the site.

> A glance at the map will be sufficient to show the relative importance of Stony Stratford's position in this road system. The town stood at the very focal   point of a number of fords across the river, and thus was the junction for traffic coming in from many parts of the country. From early times its   streets saw the passage of soldier, trader, and pilgrim; and their needs, military, commercial, or religious, led to the multiplication of trading facilities, which in turn reacted on the economic nature of the town's development.[2]

The choice of Stony Stratford as a settlement may also be as simple a matter as access to water; wells were easier to dig on the lower land.

What gave Stratford its later importance was the intersection with the Watling Street of the cross country trackways. There appear to have been two, both ridgeways in that they followed the high ground above the river. The northern side was crossed at Old Stratford and followed a line through Cosgrove and Castlethorpe to Haversham. The southern route came through Calverton and crossed at Gib Lane along the line of the road now known as Ridgeway), taking the route eastwards across to Stantonbury and Linford. The core of the eventual settlement is at a mid-point between these two cross country roads. As commerce developed in the early middle ages the crossing of these two roads and the ancient road from London to the North West gained more significance and businesses to serve travellers grew up here. Later another cross country road, from Horse Fair Green to the old medieval village of Wolverton and continuing towards Newport Pagnell became the more used cross country road.

Town and Country

There was probably no compelling reason to travel on cross country roads until 1061 when Walsingham acquired fame as a shrine. The Middle Ages were dominated by Christianity and the fervent desire of all to achieve salvation. The rich could achieve this through good works, such as building churches or priories and going on expensive pilgrimages to Jerusalem or Santiago de Compostela. The merchant classes, could make smaller bequests or travel on pilgrimages closer to home. These opportunities expanded in the later Middle Ages and one such related to a woman who became known as The Lady of Walsingham. She was the Lady of the Manor of Walsingham Parva in Norfolk. Her name was Richeldis. In 1061 her devoted life of prayer and good works brought her a vision, in which she was taken by Mary and shown the house in Nazareth where the angel Gabriel had announced the birth of Jesus. Mary then urged Richeldis to build a replica of this house at Walsingham. Accordingly the house was built and Walsingham acquired a reputation as England's Nazareth.

As the news spread across the country Walsingham became a magnet for pilgrimage and travellers from the west tended to take a route that would bring them close to Stony Stratford.

The other significant event was the breakaway of Oxford scholars and their foundation of a new university at Cambridge in 1202. Any journey between the two centres of learning would take them close to Stony Stratford.

One further thought (and this is simply a theory) is that the growth of a town in medieval times may have been due to the central presence of a powerful baron in Wolverton. Even when not in residence on the manor he would always have retained an armed contingent of sorts, however small, and this alone may have proved a deterrent to footpads and brigands who were wont to operate on the highway. This security may have allowed trade to develop along the Watling Street at Stony Stratford, while other potential sites remained risky. The siting of new development on that part of Watling Street would place it within view of the castle and could be quickly reached by the castle guard if necessary, whereas any possible settlement at the Gib Lane crossing would have placed it beyond view.

From surviving 13th century records we tend to see more early development on the eastern side of the Watling Street and we can deduce from some of the recurrent names that the early barons accommodated

Manno's Manor

some of their knights through grants of land. Before too long the income possibilities through serving travellers must have quickly come apparent and this led to a cluster of houses and inns.

And who knows? Perhaps there was once an inn at the corner of Gib Lane but after the baron and his knights began to develop Wolverton the centre of gravity moved northwards. For, if as I suggest above, the new development closer to Manno's castle offered greater security, then the extra detour for east-west travellers would not have seemed onerous.

The idea of early settlement at Stony Stratford is highly speculative and to this date, as the previous discussion has perhaps shown, no real evidence can be brought forward to support that idea. Historians from the 16th century onwards have tended to work backwards from the fact of Stony Stratford. As there was an historical settlement there the likelihood of an earlier settlement was assumed without rigorous questioning; however, as I have tried to show, its location at a river crossing and at a medieval crossroad cannot be defended as a plain fact. If it were to grow organically at a cross road then why not at Gib Lane or at Old Stratford? If at a river crossing, why on the south side and not the north? There are answers to these questions but they do enter the realm of speculation.

My own view now is that the placement of the buildings that evolved into the town of Stony Stratford had much to do with the way it was colonised after the Conquest. Later evidence shows that Manno granted land to his retainers in the lower valley close to the Watling Street. Most of this was good pasture land which held a higher value than arable land in that period. It may have been the case that earlier inns (if they ever existed) might have been found at the Gib Lane crossing in the Fuller's Slade area prior to 1066 and moved northwards after that date because of the greater security of the new settlement. As we have already seen on the manor of Wolverton settlements did become obsolete as newer economic forces came into play. There is no reason to assume that this may not have happened along the Watling Street.

The Birth of the Town

The first official record of Stony Stratford comes as late as 1194. when it was given a charter (confirmed in 1199) to hold a market. This indicates that Stony Stratford had by this time reached a size of some

Town and Country

importance, even though the traders on either side of the Watling Street were under the separate jurisdictions of the manors of Calverton and Wolverton. It was during his reign that Stony Stratford came of age. Up till then it must have been a growing collection of inns and dwellings on both the Wolverton side and the Calverton side to service travellers, but (and I am increasingly coming to this view) may have only started a few years before with Baron Hamon's allocation of a few one acre plots along the street. However in 1194, under King Richard's seal, Stony Stratford was given the right to hold a market - a much-prized licence in those days as it allowed a community to grow economically, often at the expense of nearby communities It may appear curious to us now that a small market was a matter for royal dispensation, but as with many of these things it comes down to money. A commercial market was a opportunity to make money and the regulation of such markets was an opportunity for the king to increase his revenue by charging a fee. Richard was an expensive king who led a large crusade, was captured on his return and the country had to pay a huge ransom to redeem him, and for the last five years of his life was engaged in war with the King of France to recover lost territory. The king's agents would be looking for any opportunity to fill the king's coffers and the application by Stony Stratford burgesses could only be favourably considered in these circumstances.

The first charter was issued to Gilbert Basset and his wife Egelina on 30 April 1194 and this charter was confirmed with the king's seal on 20 January 1199 for a Sunday market at their manor of Stratford. Egelina, a daughter of Reginald de Courtney, had previously been married to Walter de Bolbec, who held the Calverton manor as part of his barony and Britnell suggests that Egelina may have received this land in dower after the death of her first husband in 1190.[3] This part of the manor, possibly centred on the present Market Square, may have extended north to the river. On it's own it was not especially productive for agricultural purposes, but the commercial potential was great, which was why Gilbert and Egelina were anxious to secure a charter twice during Richard's brief visits to this country and a third time under John in 1200.

On the Wolverton side there are some extant deeds which show that small parts of the manor on the Watling Street had been granted to others. There are not very many - only three - dating from the 12th century,

Manno's Manor

but these, together with inferences which we can draw from the 13th century deeds in the Radcliffe Trust deposit, are probably enough to conclude that there was already sufficient commercial activity on the road to make grants of land as small as one acre worthwhile.[4] Gilbert and Egelina could see clearly enough what was happening on the other side of the street and were anxious to garner a piece of the trade.

There is other evidence that small portions of the Wolverton Manor had been sold and even though these were small acreages compared to the main manor they were referenced in other deeds as *manors*. One example of this is land owned by the Priory of Chicksand which makes reference to their land on the east side as their *manor at Wolverton*. In another grant Simon Barré makes a gift of some land he holds on the Watling Street to the Priory at Bradwell. There are several other examples that show us how lands that had once been granted for service three generations earlier were now being transferred for its monetary value. Simon Barré's piece, for example, was worth 9 shillings a year for its intended recipient - not a small sum in those days. At any rate this appears to be the beginning of Stony Stratford as an entity. The grant was confirmed by King John on 21 Mar 1200.

This period is also important as it marks the beginning of a transition of Wolverton from as purely rural to a mixed agricultural and mercantile economy. Overall, agriculture was still dominant, and was to remain so for hundreds of years, but now Woverton had an economy which included a commercial centres - subsequently known as towns or market towns. Stony Stratford therefore had a transforming effect on both Wolverton and Calverton. King John in particular encouraged the growth of new market towns, largely because he was able to see the tax-gathering potential in such a policy. Liverpool, for example, was his own personal creation on his own land. There were great attractions to these new towns for those who wished to free themselves of the bondage of being tied to the land. From this point Stony Stratford begins to grow as a commercial entity and the population starts to outstrip both Calverton and Wolverton.

During the reign of King John specific documents make their appearance with references to Stony Stratford, the first surviving one being in 1202 when a grant of land is made to Richard the Clerk from John de Calverton. Other references to property grants occur in the reign of Henry

Town and Country

III and by the mid century there are several surviving grants in the papers of the de Wolverton family. From this time forth Stony Stratford has its own identity, although the lords of Calverton and Wolverton continued to maintain a strong and active interest in the affairs of the town.

The development of a town on the borders of Wolverton and Calverton was a genuine innovation. Urban living had been unknown in England since the Roman departure in 400AD. The native population and the Anglo-Saxon incomers preferred to live and work in a rural economy. Specialist workers were rare and virtually the whole community, with the exception of the lord and his family were directly employed in agricultural production. With the development of money it became possible for a miller or a blacksmith to earn a living from their trade without tilling the soil. But most rural economies remained rooted, so to speak, in their agricultural production. Production surpluses and other goods from Wolverton could be satisfied through seasonal fairs held at Buckingham or Newport.

The emergence of towns in the Middle Ages brought out a new class of people into being - the merchants, who could, by buying and selling products and commodities, earn their living and generate wealth. These new men of the merchant class could acquire capital and deal with the lords to acquire land for themselves. This process is illustrated in the surviving deeds of the 13th century and 14th centuries. By the 15th century men of the merchant class, such as John Edy, were prosperous enough to make public benefactions on the scale that had once been the preserve of the earlier lords of the manor. What this must have meant to the residents of Wolverton and Calverton was that there were employment alternatives without leaving the manor or the parish - something that was generally difficult to do until modern times Stony Stratford therefore became important to the economic life of both manors. It is instructive to contrast the impact of Stony Stratford on the two manors with with the neighbouring Loughton and Shenley manors, also divided by the Watling Street, which remained completely rural until late in the 20th century because it never developed a town alongside the road. A similar observation could be made about Passenham and Furtho to the north.

Manno's Manor

A Child of Two Manors

While this book is about the manor of Wolverton, it is impossible to account for Stony Stratford as the child of one manor. Calverton of course was the other parent. In 1066 the Calverton Manor was held by Bisi, a thegn, with a smaller part, assessed at two hides, held by a "man of Queen Edith". After the conquest the manor was given to Hugh of Bolbec who may have been a relative of the Giffard family. The manor was not as wealthy as the Wolverton manor which had a lot more cleared land, but it was not insignificant. After almost two centuries the male line died out and the estate came into the hands of the de Vere family through marriage to Isabella de Bolbec. Robert de Vere, who came into the manor in 1244, was then Earl of Oxford and quite powerful. In fact the rise of the de Veres seems to correspond to the decline of the de Wolvertons and this provides a counterbalance, encouraging more development on the Calverton side. The competition between the two lords must have generated a creative tension which might have been smothered if the town had come under the control of a single lord. Hugh, the son of Robert and Isabella, began to apply some energy to the development of Calverton, and thereby Stony Stratford. In 1257 he established a separate manor on the west side, which may in part have been the historical manor belonging the the man of Queen Edith but it would probably correspond to that neck of land between the river and Watling Street. The manor once owned by Gilbert and Egelina Bassett was now formally its own place. In 1257 he acquired fair rights for a three day event "on the vigil, the feast and morrow of St Giles." In 1290 his son Robert was able to get a further grant for an annual fair on the vigil and feast of St Mary Magdalen. It appears also that the de Veres were able to buy land from Sir John de Wolverton, some 40 acres, probably the meadow land bordering the river. This gave the de Veres control of the river crossing tolls.

Sir John may not have been immediately conscious of the significance of the sale. From his point of view the land was mostly liable to flooding and unproductive. He was thinking in old economic terms. The de Veres were very much awake to the opportunities coming from the new economy and that unproductive land in the right location could yield far greater revenues than traditional farming. Sir John, later, realizing his blunder he

Town and Country

tried to redress the balance by acquiring land on the west side. Through one of his kinsmen he obtained "two closes there containing two acres of land" from "Watlynge Street to Mill Lane". It was not a large amount of land but this strip gave him some control of the river crossings and the revenue therefrom.

Markets or Fairs were a lucrative business and represented an opportunity for people to sell their products. In that economy everything was made by hand and tools were limited in their application so it took a long time to make, say, a pot or a pan or weave a cloth or make a bracelet. The fair was an opportunity to sell the product of several months work. There were no shops as we later came to know them nor was there a retail distribution network as we might understand it. Most villages or manors were self-sufficient but if your production exceeded local demand then the fair was the opportunity to sell the surplus. Valuable goods were often transported over long distances but everyday items were likely to have been made locally within reach of the market. He who held the rights to the fair collected the tolls and dues and probably administered the law in the case of disputes - again a source of revenue.

So the opportunism of the de Veres was probably the spur to the growth of Stony Stratford. The 13th century saw the two sides of the street begin to coalesce into a town - still not a borough, nor entirely independent of manorial control, but emerging as the place we can recognise as Stony Stratford.

And due to the de Vere initiative the town development on the west side of the High Street was around a square. Naturally enough the prime space was on the high street itself and this ribbon development was the pattern on the Wolverton side until the 19th century. The Calverton side experienced the development of a Market Square, Horsefair and Cowfair and some associated back lanes. Almost all the properties on the Wolverton side of Stony Stratford stretched back to what is now Russell Street and Vicarage Road, both built in the last quarter of the 19th century. Previously this was known as the Back Way. It probable that these plots stretched further east at one time and enveloped one acre of land. Each plot served as a garden and pasture for the house or inn and are generally known as burgage plots. Their extent can be seen on the map on page 84. Possibly as much as two thirds of these plots on the Wolverton side were in private

Manno's Manor

hands by the 13th or 14th centuries, which is the period when we have surviving deeds relating to manorial property and it must be assumed that some at least had been sold or granted before the early 13th century when we have surviving deeds to work with. *The Cock Inn*, for example, never once features in any deed, and by the late 17th century, when lease documents survive, some of the inns, like *The Bull* or *The Three Swans* are detailed, whereas *The Cock* is conspicuously absent.

Economic Development in the 13th and 14th Centuries

Stony Stratford's divided lordships led to the eventual foundation of two churches on either side of the Watling Street. The church on the Wolverton side was dedicated to St Mary Magdalene; on the Calverton side to Saint Giles. Their dates of origin are obscure but we can begin to find references to chaplains and buildings from the first half of the 13th century. So we might infer that chapels of ease were established in the early decades of the 13th century for travellers and some of the local inhabitants. An undated deed in the time of William, baron of Wolverton (d 1246) records the grant of a ½ virgate of land to William, chaplain, land once held by Hugh Capellanus. So even if this were dated at, say, 1240, William the Chaplain at least had a predecessor.[5]

Hyde[6] interprets church activity as underlying a unity in Stony Stratford. Possibly so but administrative differences persisted until almost the 20th century. The Watling Street became a de facto parish boundary and 19th century censuses record two distinct parishes. There must have been differences, such as more favourable land arrangements, which caused the largest inns, such as *The Cock, The Bull, The Three Swans, The Red Lyon* and *The Horseshoe* to establish themselves on the east side. There were also disputes arising from men of Calverton using their property holdings on the east side to entitle them to use of Wolverton's common lands, and vice versa. Bradwell priory, founded in the 12th century had been endowed with the Wolverton Church and later received gifts of land in the Calverton manor, so it did have interests on either side. This does not necessarily speak to the unity of the two parishes. The Wolverton Church and the Calverton Church would both interpret their missions as administering to their own parish and the parishioners would likewise attach their allegiances to their respective churches.

Town and Country

The Church of St Giles may be the earliest foundation, although perhaps by not many years. The documents mentioned earlier, surviving from 1202-3, relate to a grant of about 3 acres from John de Calverton to Richard Clericus who put some buildings on it. Subsequent documents mention Peter the Clerk, Roger the Clerk and William the Priest and while it is clear that a transaction has taken place the succession is not. However we can say with some assurance that a chapel or some such structure dates from this period and that was likely on the site of the present church.

The church of St Mary Magdalen appears to have its origins in a similar set up, as a chapel of ease for travellers under the jurisdiction of the parent church at Wolverton. In 1238 we learn of Hamo the clerk living in the house which formerly belonged to Richard the Weaver. The house was attached to a chapel on the Wolverton side. So we do get a sense of parallel development on both sides of the street, even allowing for manorial variations.

By 1290 when Queen Eleanor's body was carried through Stony Stratford it is thought that overnight it rested in the church of St Mary Magdalene, so a building must have been established at this time - although the towers came much later.

This is evidence enough that Stony Stratford was a settlement of some size. The funeral cortege of Queen Eleanor was a large royal party that could only be accommodated in a town with well-developed provisions for hospitality. She was the much-loved consort of Edward I and the mother of 16 of his children, the last one, Blanche, born only a year previously. Eleanor, born into the royal family of Castille was between 45 and 49 years old at her death at Harby in Nottinghamshire.

It has to be said that she was not a popular queen. She was acquisitive and often took advantage of distressed sales to take over manors and then to run them in a manner that might be considered exploitative. She also avoided, or showed no interest in such acts that might have won her some favour such as distributing alms to the poor. In addition she was Spanish and had throughout her life demonstrated little empathy for the English. Edward however was devastated. She had been his constant companion as he had travelled the realm, pausing only to give birth on at least sixteen occasions. And so he set about extravagant preparations for her burial and for her memory. Her body was first taken to Lincoln where it was prepared

Manno's Manor

in medieval fashion for eventual interment. From here, the cortege started its two-week procession to its final stopping place at Charing between London and Westminster. The royal party probably reached Stony Stratford at the beginning of December and those who could be accommodated in the inns must have welcomed the warm fires.

After the funeral at Westminster Abbey the King commissioned a series of memorial crosses to be erected at each stopping place on the way to London. One of them was Stony Stratford. The monuments were known as "Eleanor Crosses". Only three have survived the passage of 700 years, at Geddington in Northamptonshire and Hardingstone, just outside Northampton, and at Waltham in Hertfordshire. Each of these survivors gives us some idea of the appearance of these memorials although it appears that some were much more elaborate and expensive than others.

The Stony Stratford Cross did not survive the 17th century Civil War, when it was deliberately destroyed by Parliamentary soldiers during the occupation of Wolverton, and Browne Willis, making notes in 1755, records a conversation with an 80 year-old who remembered the base still standing. Most agree that the cross was erected at the north end of the town, probably opposite the old *Horseshoe Inn*, which would have provided accommodation for some of the travelling escort. The High Street widens at this point suggesting that houses were built around the cross which may have been placed at the side of the road.

The monument itself may not have been one of the more expensive crosses. Camden (16th C) describes it as "none of the fairest". The mason, John of Battle, was paid £63 13s 4d. for making the cross, not a small sum in those days but relatively paltry when compared with some of the others. The marble decorative elements were provided by Ralph of Chichester.

The medieval royal court travelled constantly and this was not only the king and his entourage but the entire administration of government. Judgements were made, justice dispensed, fees paid on the hoof as it were. This was not merely the king and a few retainers but every court functionary. There were two consequences to this: travel was slow and a large party had to be accommodated. From Northampton, the party managed the 14 miles to Stony Stratford and the next stop was off the highway at Woburn Abbey, there being no accommodation large enough before Dunstable to accommodate the royal party. What this should tell us

Town and Country

is that by 1290 Stony Stratford was sufficiently organised to provide food and accommodation for the English government.

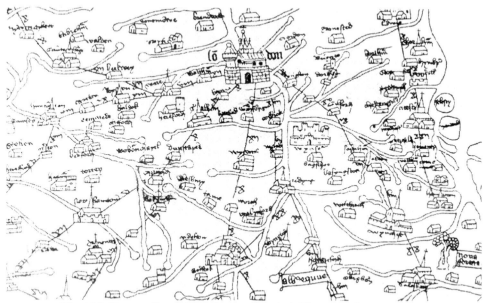

The 14th Century Gough Map showing Stratford. The top of the map is East.

By then, almost 100 years had passed since Stony Stratford first got its market charter and it was clearly a significant stopping place by this time. King John, constantly on the move, during his reign stopped over for a few days in 1215[7] After staying at his royal manor of Brill, so there must have been sufficient accommodation even at that time. What exactly there was we do not know but there must have been adequate provision for the accommodation of people and stabling of horses, together with the victualling of both horse and man. In 1314 we have another deed which relates to building "in le cheapingstede de stonistratford"[8] - one of these curious medieval documents where Latin, French and English are freely mixed . A *cheapingstede* is a place for buying and selling. It is found in some place names such as Chipping Norton, which is as good evidence as any that not only was a market established but that building was going on around the marketplace. And finally, as proof of Stony Stratford's quick rise to prominence, there is the early 14th century Gough map, which clearly marks Stony Stratford as a place of significance north west of St. Albans and Dunstable, with branch roads to Northampton and Buckingham.

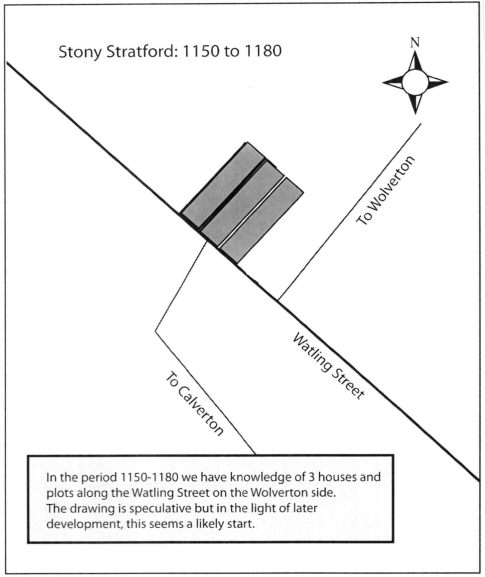

The Beginnings of Stony Stratford

Professor Hyde's study of the economic development of Stony Stratford in these years provides us with some data whereby we can assess the growth of Stony Stratford. He has estimated that during the period 1150-1185 there were three houses in Stony Stratford. In the period 1200-1230 he counts 19, 16 in the period 1250-1280 and 29 in the period

Town and Country

1290-1310. Thereafter the figure appears to stablilize until his assessment end in 1500. The figures are not presented as an accurate census but as an indicator of the growth of the town. Each of these houses or cottages would have some land attached.

These data accord with what we already know and we can fairly conclude that, while there was some settlement on the Watling Street prior to 1200, it is only in the 13th century that the new economic model for Stony Stratford starts to take off. The produce of the land was available for sale at markets as was that of manufactured goods. Stony Stratford became a centre for exchange. Its position on the road also made it a stopping off place for travellers and inns, together with associated services for the travelling public, and it grew in prosperity. The gradual freeing of the bonds of service on the neighbouring manors meant also that new people could come into the town to establish themselves with some craft or trade.

One deed, which, although undated, can be given an inferred date of 1248, right in the middle of the century, illustrates how a man could accumulate scattered plots of land. Included are a Messuage with houses and an orchard, 4 acres in the west field six separate ½ acre strips which are in various parts between Fuller's Slade and the river meadow. In addition he also bought the mill in the west of Wolverton from Lord William together with a virgate of land attached to it. The sale is from Richard, son of John, Clerk of Wolverton. It is not clear whether Richard is also a cleric but the mill and the scattered acres may suggest that he was not himself tilling the soil but renting out this land for income. There is not enough information to tell us if he was the practising chaplain at St Mary Magdalen and living off the rents but it does illustrate how relatively complex society had become almost 200 years after the conquest.[9]

The houses that do develop during the period were developed around a courtyard or "place" as it is termed in the deed. This was probably a forerunner of the inn courtyard which still survives today in the town. We can also infer that these smaller plots were mostly drawing their income from commercial activity. That a considerable income could be drawn from a relatively small amount of land might be deduced from the information we have about Nicholas de Arderne. The man who was probably his father, Ralph, married Isabella, the widow of John de Wolverton. It was unlikely that she would marry someone without resources. Isabella herself had the

Manno's Manor

manor of Wick Hamon (Wicken) in dower. In Stony Stratford Nicholas possessed 2 messuages, 1 croft and 45 acres. This would not have been very much if he had owned it in 1086, but 250 years later this alone would put him amongst the more well-to-do citizens on the manor.

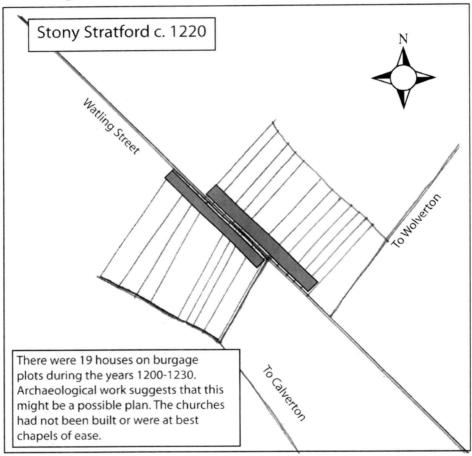

Stony Stratford in the early 13th Century

So we can summarise the development of Stony Stratford. At some time between 1150 and 1185 three small plots were granted along the Watling Street on the Wolverton side. The maximum size was one acre. These we now describe as burgage plots and they determined the development of the town, at least along the Watling Street. Possibly the starting point was the present location of the Cock and they grew outward, at first toward the river and then towards the south. That this was the

Town and Country

sequence can be inferred from the location of the Church of St Mary Magdalen, which was established somewhat later than the first burgage plots.

The beginnings, at least on the Wolverton side, can be traced to a bequest by Hamo, Son of Meinfelin, which makes reference to three plots abutting the Watling Street. At least thirteen of these plots can be determined on the Wolverton side varying in length from 115 to 125 metres, and mostly with a width of 15 metres. These approximate to about half an acre and it can be inferred that they once extended further beyond the back way.

North of St Mary Magdalen the burgage plots are smaller and it is suggested that these were later than the early medieval development. In any case, these plots were likely developed after the building of the church.

The Calverton side developed along the same model and lines of the old burgage plots can be traced north of church Street. One difference is the planned development in the late 13th century of a Market Square off the High Street. This may have been determined by available land behind the church. The earl of Oxford was probably the instigator of this development. The west side does have a different character. Whereas the Wolverton markets and fairs spread up and down the street, the Calverton side markets and fairs had their own sections off the min road. This was replicated in the later developments of Horse Fair and Cow Fair.

The three maps presented here are speculative, but do draw on some actual evidence. Records gleaned by Professor Hyde in his articles[10] do show a trend in growth from our first awareness of a settlement. One shows the possible start of the development at some date in the period 1150 - 1180 on page 82, another at 1220 when the town became recognisable and illustrates the quite rapid development in those years on page 84, and a third at 1300 when the churches were established (page 86). It is fair to say that there are a lot of assumptions behind these maps, although they are informed by the available documentary and archaeological evidence.

Across the road, a similar development took place on the Calverton side, moving northwards from what is now Church Street. Most of these plots were 1 acre or half an acre, although some may have been smaller. One deed describes one piece on the Watling Street as 10 1/2 perches long by 3 perches and 5 feet.

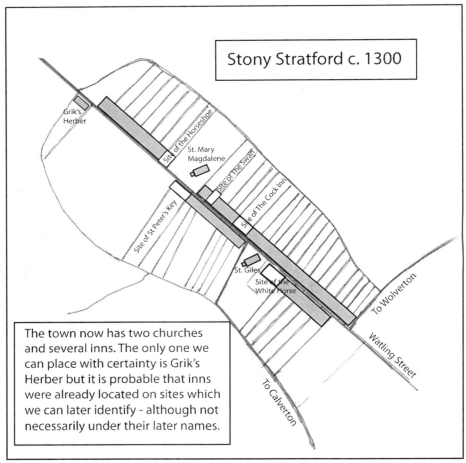

Stony Stratford in the 14th Century

Barbara Tuchman draws parallels with the events of the 20th century and the turbulence of the 14th century in her famous book *A Distant Mirror,*. She has a point. Just as 20th century europe was racked by war and social upheaval so indeed was the 14th and we can see a very great difference between life at the outset of the reign of Edward II and the abrupt end of Richard II's reign in 1399. There had been war certainly and even in 1399 France and England were still locked in the struggle that would come to be known as the Hundred Years war. But there are always wars. The really dramatic change in the 14th century was brought about by the great plague in the middle of the century known as the Black Death, which reduced the

Town and Country

population by a full 40%. The steady growth since the conquest was severely cut back in a matter of months.

The immediate impact was an extreme labour shortage. The longer term impact was a shift towards a wage economy. The feudal model relied upon a system of tied service, but after the plague years this model was no longer sustainable. Villeins who had been perennially tied to a plot of land on one manor could now, if they wanted to better their circumstances, move to another manor where the lord was willing to offer better terms of tenure. Or, even better perhaps, they could demand wage payments for service they had customarily given free to their lord.

In these years there was a general improvement in prosperity among the lower orders. Merchants became richer; tradesmen were able to make a good living. The ruling classes were so alarmed at one point because members of the lower orders were now dressing in fine clothes that the upper echelon saw as their traditional and exclusive preserve, that they even passed a law trying to restrict dress. It failed.

Further unrest developed in 1381 with the so called Peasant's revolt. It was quashed and achieved nothing, but it was symptomatic of the kind of eruption that can occur when the old order is under stress.

Wolverton was almost certainly affected by the Black Death. The death of Sir John de Wolverton in 1349 and Ralph his heir two years later were in all likelihood plague deaths. Bradwell Priory lost a number of monks during this period and was scarcely able to function. Nothing else is documented but we can reasonably say that Wolverton was no less affected than anywhere else.

What we begin to notice in the Wolverton deeds is that the names of prominent citizens change. The names of those who were prominent in the 13th and 14th centuries are gone and a newer range of prominent names make their appearance. The Anketyls, Tourams, the de Hyntes, for example, families which may have been there from the Conquest, now fade from the histories of Stony Stratford and Wolverton. Possibly some of their descendants survived but not obviously through the male line. Instead we discover a new cast of characters. Late 14th century deeds begin to furnish names which we might regard as typically English - King, Stead, Ward, Sawyer, Brende, Cole, Bruton. Tradesman's names, invented as it were earlier in the century, come to some prominence, which means that some

Manno's Manor

of them, within a generation were starting to rise in prosperity. The name of Hastings still persists in the late 14th century, indicating that not all were wiped out, but the name declines in importance, suggesting other factors. The name Edy first makes its appearance in the later part of this century. It is a name which will take on more importance in the next century.

Looking at names in documents can only provide us with the roughest guide. There are no genealogies to guide us. In the normal course of events, in a monogamous society, male names do eventually die out leaving the genes to be passed on through the female, so this is not unusual. The unique feature of the 14th century was the extreme impact of the bubonic plague which, as we can see even in Wolverton, did cause great social upheaval.

Take for example William Sawyer, who was conducting land and property transactions in the 1370s. Sawyer as a surname could not be earlier than the reign of Edward II so clearly the Sawyers have risen from anonymity to some prosperity within two generations. The transactions include a croft in Stony Stratford, a tenement in Wolverton and some small land transfers, none more than 5 acres, but the deeds do indicate that the Sawyers had in some small way "arrived". We learn too that William and his wife Margaret had a plentiful supply of sons - John, Richard and Stephen. This is probably as good an illustration as any of how dynamic any society can be at any period in history. Too often we are tempted to imagine the past as a neat model where everyone dutifully conformed to their allotted role.

Stony Stratford came of age in the 14th century. Poor harvests and famine in the first decades, plague and war with France in the middle of the century and disruption to the social order in the last quarter may, perversely, have enhanced the importance of Stony Stratford. The town, with its ability to create specialised trades and new wealth may have been the bulwark that Wolverton needed during a period when the old agricultural economy was suffering.

Town and Country

1 White Kennett, Parochial Antiquities attempted in the history of Ambrosden, Burcester Vol 1, p 24. 1695.

2 F.E. Hyde. Stony Stratford from the Earliest Times to the end of the Seventeenth Century. p.7

3 R H Britnell. The Origins of Stony Stratford. Records of Bucks. Vol XX Part 3, 1977.

4 Britnell. op.cit. p. 452-3. discusses three small plots granted in the time of Hamo, son of Meinfelin, details in the *Luffield Priory Charters* and the *Records of the Templars*.

5 Bodleian. MSS. dd. Radcl. Deed 49. Since the vicar of Holy Trinity was under the appointment of the Prior of Bradwell at the time, I think I am right in reading this chaplaincy as separate, and new

6 ibid

7 22 Feb to Mar 5th 1215

8 Bodleian. MSS. dd. Radcl. Deed 255

9 Bodleian. MSS. dd. Radcl. Deed 59

10 F.E. Hyde The Development of a Town: Part II.

FIVE

MEDIEVAL LIFE IN WOLVERTON

While change was taking place on Wolverton's western edge agriculture still remained the engine house of the economy. The new types of business at Stony Stratford may have been a welcome supplement to the manor's economy but manorial life on the largest part of the manor was probably unchanged from the 11th century.

The Development of The Manor

500 years elapsed from the Anglo Saxon settlers to the Norman establishment and we know extraordinary little about the period. Most of what we know can only be pieced together from archaeology and studies of land use form the period. There is very little documentary evidence which we can tie to Wolverton.

It requires a real effort of imagination to reconstruct life in those times. The local lord probably had the resources to construct a cruck-built hall, which could house his family and his principal followers. There was no privacy. People ate, talked, entertained, copulated and slept in a single room. It is possible that the kitchen was an outbuilding. The poorer peasants lived in small hovels of their own making, with low walls made of interleaved branches and filled with mud, together with roofs of thatched straw, unsupported by strong timbers and vulnerable to storms. Farming, as described earlier, was limited by the technology of the age, and probably only supported a handful of families.

Beyond the time of Wulfhere, who probably prevailed in the late 6th century we know little detail until the evidence of the Domesday Book. As the kingdoms developed Wolverton fell largely under the control of the King of Mercia where it became a frontier settlement on the edge of the Danelaw, where the Ouse became a border. It appears unlikely that Wulfhere founded a dynasty and at Domesday there is no single ruling family. It is almost certain that in the upheaval of these centuries no single family left its mark. Indeed, by the time of the Domesday record, there were three thanes on the Wolverton manor, neither one of them particularly powerful. Circumstances may have been fluid in each of these centuries.

Manno's Manor

The only stable pattern that one can detect in the trend to land ownership and the development of hierarchies. The frequently-used phrase in the Domesday Book is "he could sell" when referring to the saxon thanes who once had possession of land, indicating that they had independent rights of ownership.

The peasantry meanwhile continued to do what they always did, try to scratch a subsistence living from the soil. Lords came and went, but while they were there they exacted their demands. Death and taxes it seemed were life's only certainties. It would be wrong, however, to envision the peasantry as a homogeneous mass. Social mobility was possible then as in all societies at all times. And although all peasants were engaged in more-or-less the same activity, there were degrees of social and economic standing.

A treatise on estate management, known as the *Rectitudines Singularum Personarum* The Management of People), written in the early 11th century sets out three classes of peasant and probably fairly reflects the existing or emerging economy. The author describes three classes: the *genat*, the *gebur* and the *kotsetla*. There were of course slaves below these ranks. The *geneat*, at the head of the peasantry, while not free of service, was free from much of the routine drudgery and was expected to perform a range of general duties, often requiring some skill. He was entrusted with errands for his lord, some guard duties, maintaining the fences around the lord's house. The *gebur* was probably the forerunner of the Norman villein, a man who may have had up to 30 acres to tend and was committed to two days a week service on the lord's land and three days a week at harvest and seeding time. He was also assessed at various rents from his own land. The *kotsetla*, in the third tier, was the cottarius or bordarius of the Domesday Book, probably with 5 acres or so to till for his personal needs in return for work on the lord's desmesne every Monday and three days a week in August.

By the 7th century Western Europe was connected by trade to the Mediterranean world. The Caliphate of the Islamic world and the Byzantine Empire fostered a demand for extensive trade and even the outlying fringes of Europe were drawn into this highly developed web. Archaeological evidence provides us with artefacts from the Mediterranean, probably traded for metals such as tin and slaves to reinforce the labour force. During this period market centres, or emporia, began to emerge, or

Medieval Life in Wolverton

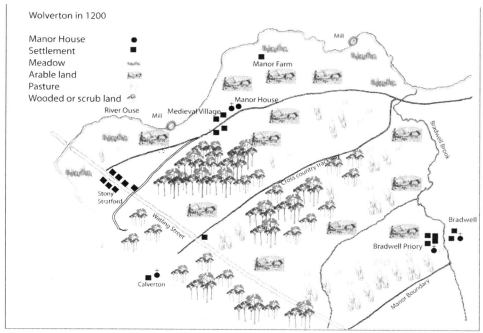

The Manor in 1200

re-emerge in some instances. The overall picture is incomplete. Sites at London (Lundenwic), Ipswich (wic) and Southampton (Hamwic) are known to have been quite important. Other settlements across the south and east have been identified although the overall picture is indistinct.

In our local context there may have been some sort of trading centre at Buckingham and at Newport. Based upon our assessment of the later evidence one can assert with some confidence that there was no such trading post in Wolverton. Any trading needs (and this was still a society without much currency) could probably be met through occasional fairs at other centres.

The 12 to 15 generations from the departure of the Roman colonisers in 400 AD to the eleventh century, is a period where we can witness the results of social change without being able to supply a narrative as to how and why that change occurred. Historians of the 19th and 20th centuries who nourished the idea of the "dark ages", a period of barbarity between Roman and Christian civilization. Even so, the archaeological evidence is accumulating from partial excavations and more advanced

Manno's Manor

techniques of analysing land deposits and consequently newer theories are emerging which cause reconsideration of traditional views.

One agricultural practice which did emerge in these years before the conquest was the open field system. Rather than the system which might have applied during the Celtic period where families farmed sections of land around their own households, a highly organised system emerged whereby large open fields were farmed in strips by individuals. Crop rotation was practiced, with one field being left fallow each year. Anglian society had reached a level of organisation that permitted the development of the sophisticated three field system which allowed two fields under cultivation and a third lying fallow to allow the soil to recover its nutrients. Some have theorized that this system developed from a two field system, but more recent scholarship takes the view that the two field system was localized to Wiltshire and the south west and that the Midlands had always practised a three field system of cultivation. This open field system was the means by which these Anglians practised agriculture. That is, the cultivatable area was divided into strips of land. Individuals or families cultivated these strips and acquired customary rights over time.

It is possible that this agricultural revolution was the cause of the relocation of the Wolverton village. The first Anglian settlers had established themselves on the unoccupied land at Wolverton Turn, as mentioned earlier, but at some time before the 9th century they appear to have relocated to the lower ground. There are no clear reasons why. It may have had something to do with the growth in numbers of the Anglian community or to developments in farming practices, or a combination of these and other factors. As they were able to claim and farm the better land it must have made more sense to relocate the core of the village closer to the great fields.

The higher ground may historically have been wooded or scrub land and was probably undeveloped at the time of the conquest. A lot can be learned from names. The weald at Calverton probably extended across the Watling Street for some way and names from this area can offer some insight into the gradual clearing. Fuller's Slade, for example, was a green clearing in a wooded area either cleared by a man named Full, or Fuller or Fowler, or held by someone of that name when it was first recorded.[1] Greenleys (sometimes Grindleys) suggest also that green meadows have

94

Medieval Life in Wolverton

been cleared from wooded land. The furzes and bush fields to the south east of the manor suggest rough land that was probably not cultivated early. The area now known as Warren farm was likely a wooded area used for hunting rabbits – the warren.

The Warren may still have been wooded at this time, and certainly the higher land adjacent to the Calverton Weald must have been covered with woods. Wood was a resource for building and for fuel and probably under the control of the lord. Peasants would be given permission to harvest broken twigs and deadwood on the ground but would not be allowed, on pain of severe punishment, to cut down trees without payment.

So you could draw a fairly convincing picture of a manor that by the late 11th century had only developed alongside Bradwell Brook and the Ouse. Gradually, and probably over these two centuries, more land was cleared for arable purposes and for pasture. The work was extremely hard. Each tree had to be cut down by hand and the stump dug out. In addition these assarts, as they were called, were undertaken in a man's spare time, on top of his hard work in his own fields and on the lord's domain.

One practice, which expanded the amount of available land, was the founding of priories or monasteries on poor land. The foundation of Bradwell Priory by Meinfelin was typical. Meinfelin could earn some credit in heaven at no great cost to himself and the monks in subsequent generations would do the work to clear the land and make it productive.

This land usage continued until the enclosures began in the 16th century, but even if it had provided for a growing population for a century or so it was never much more than subsistence agriculture. While everything looked promising when Edward I's youngest son succeeded to the throne in 1307, matters were infinitely worse eight years later with two successive harvest failure. The years 1315 to 1317 were subject to abnormally heavy rainfall and the yield was dire. In Wolverton we can picture most of the meadows close to the river being flooded and the higher clay lands becoming waterlogged. Prolonged rainfall inhibiting the ripening of crops and delayed the harvest. It was hard enough to preserve enough food for the winter months in normal years, but to encounter successive crop failures must have led to famine and the consequent death of both people and animals. Wolverton villagers would have cared more about this than Edward's disastrous defeat at Bannockburn in 1314,

Manno's Manor

although in their superstitious minds they may have connected the former as a presager of the famine.

There was no happy way out of a famine in medieval times. Food storage was limited and once supplies were used up there was no vehicle for providing aid. Valuable stock animals had to be slaughtered and inevitably people died of malnutrition or starvation.

Stock animals were expensive and not every peasant could afford them. Cattle and sheep were smaller animals than they are today and their yields of milk, wool, leather and meat were correspondingly diminished. The biggest challenge was to keep the animals away from the crops, in part the responsibility of the cow herd and shepherd, but just in case the village also employed a hayward (hay guard) to make sure that animals did not stray onto arable land. Some enclosures may have been built, either hedged or protected by earth bank or ditches to keep stock animals enclosed in winter.

Certain specialized jobs developed in this economy. The Reeve was a man employed by the lord of the manor as an administrator. He would ensure that services dues were met, that tithes were paid, and that disputes between the villagers were resolved.

The Hay Ward was often an assistant to the Reeve but his main function was to organise and control the cropping of hay. In all communities tis was a significant crop necessary for winter feed. All of the meadows in the north of the manor would be closely supervised by the hayward. He would determined when the grass could be mown and what portions were taken by the peasants and what portion reserved for the lord. He would determine the times when the meadows could be used for pasture and when they could not. At other times of the year he would be the enforcer if livestock on the commons got out of control and started to feed on the arable fields. He would give warnings to the owners of the cattle and possibly levy fines.

On the Watling street it was probably more of the same, except that here, innkeepers would have larger buildings and outhouses and a strip of land going back from the main street.

We could also present the argument that Wolverton grew as two villages. The manor village and the settlement at Stony Stratford. Their different purposes meant that they grew on different models. Whereas the

Medieval Life in Wolverton

Wolverton village developed irregularly, (and as it turned out impermanently) the west side of the Watling Street was defined by the road, and houses that were built there fronted the street with a back yard that may have extended to the footpath that once marked the eastern edge of Stony. And it is clear from later developments that these plots varied in size.

The Open Fields

Medieval Farming was based upon large open fields which were communally farmed. The lord controlled rights of access to the land, usually in return for payment of a portion of produce, or services, or money, or sometimes a combination of all three. From the labourers point of view these rights were customary and could be passed from father to son and so on. Typically 30 acres was held to be sufficient to support a family. The local picture was often more complicated than this, but as a general description this is how the manor worked. The large fields were divided into strips and crops were rotated each year. One field could be left fallow for one year in every three.

Professor Hyde's analysis of Wolverton's three great fields and the Lord's demesne was developed from the 18th century enclosure map on page 179. He uses the later names to describe the make-up of the three fields of Wolverton. One of the fields, he explains, extended from Stony Stratford to the mill drive and was bordered to the south by the Wolverton Road. Thus all the fields named Rylands - a good giveaway to the arable properties of the soil - were in this field.

The second field was to the south of the Wolverton Road, starting at the corner turn and encompassing Barr Piece and Barr Close, Marron Fields, Dean's Close, Roger's Holm and Lower Slade. This was the land mostly covered by the Railway Works, McCorquodale's and the 19th century town.

Barr (OE baere) means barley and plainly takes its name from what was grown there. It is likely that the name Atterbury, often found in Wolverton and area, can trace its origin from this or a similar named field in the area. When surnames originated in the 14th century people were quite as likely to take their name from the place where they lived. Thus John atte Barre (John at the Barley Field) became in time, Atterbury.

Manno's Manor

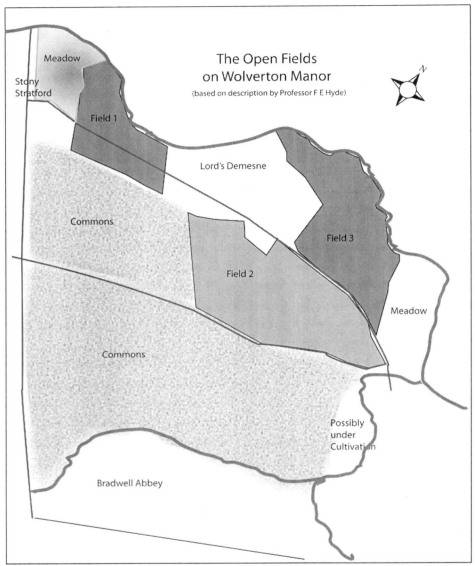

Possible arrangement of the three open fields

I am not certain of the origin of Marron, but it may possibly come from the Old English maere, meaning great

The third field included Colt's Holm, Linces, Upper Hey, Kent's Hook and Debb's Hook and the Severidge. Great Dickens (great diggings) was probably part of the lord's demesne. Linces, from linchets meaning ledges of ploughed earth gives us a clue as to how this land was traditionally

Medieval Life in Wolverton

used. Kent's Hook and Debb's Hook, meaning Kent's and Debb's corner respectively are also ancient Saxon names.

Nash Meadow, beside the river, was always pasture land.

The Lord's Demesne was probably the land that later became identified as the park, which was the land after enclosure that was reserved for the Longuevilles.

A lord was the pivotal figure in the manorial system which emerged after 1066. His wealth came from appropriating the best land for himself and requiring the peasantry on his manor to work his land for him. You could view this as a modified form of slavery or a version of tax in kind. In return the peasant got sufficient land for himself and his family and a certain security of tenure. Most scholars now believe that the so-called Feudal System never quite operated in the pure form I have described and that certainly after the plague years in the middle of the 14th century the old system gave way to one based upon money.

The first baron, Manno le Breton, established a motte and bailey castle near to the present site of Holy Trinity church and laid claim to the adjoining land for his demesne (domain). This would include the later named fields, Fiddler's Butts, Morter Pitts, Home Park, High Park, Park Meadow, Low Park, Kiln Close and Ludkin's Closes.

Fiddler's Butts was probably used for archery practice and Hyde suspects that Ratcliffe Close was also used for recreational purposes. The Morter Pitts would have been used to extract lime and Kiln Close suggests that there were once kilns on the present site of Wolverton Park House. Low Park was the original village settlement.

As I have already mentioned the great part of the manor to the south was not considered suitable arable land in earlier centuries. The Greenleys area, the Ardwell Fields (from OE aeord - meaning rough), the Furzes and the Bushy Fields were given over to pasture for the cattle and pigs. After enclosure these fields were used for sheep grazing, which was highly profitable when wool was about the only substance used for textiles.

While the open field system was still in operation this land would not have been enclosed and may have resembled a heath. It was probably known as Wolverton Common, but due to the early enclosure of these lands the name has been lost to history.

Manno's Manor

Aerial view of fields in Padbury showing the old medieval strips

You can see from this photograph of Padbury, not so far from Wolverton and in a similar landscape how strip farming shaped the land over many centuries, and because Padbury was a very late enclosure, the hedgerows visibly cut across what were once long continuous strips along which the peasants could drive their ox-drawn plough. The early enclosure of Wolverton land left a few centuries of variant cultivation between the old field system and a more recent aspect of the landscape. Dr Hyde's reconstruction of the early manorial landscape represents our best estimate.

A Walk around the Manor in 1307

It is very easy to telescope time when looking at the Medieval period, and particularly when looking at the uneventful history of Wolverton it is easy to miss the fact that 240 years had elapsed since the Conquest and the year that Edward II came to the throne. In the last chapter we looked at the

Medieval Life in Wolverton

change that was brought about by the development of Stony Stratford, so in this year let us do some time travelling of our own and see what the manor looked like in 1307. This is at the beginning of the 14th century when the population on the manor, without counting the Stony Stratford side, is at least double that of 1066. There will be no shortage of people as we walk around the manor. We are in the midst of one of those periods of global warming, which, in general, has led to increased food production. Men and women are more fertile and families are larger.

We can leave the high road at Stony Stratford where we have probably stayed overnight at one of its several hostelries. Stony Stratford is a newish town but it is already a place of some importance along the road. We will walk eastwards towards the village of Wolverton, just under a mile away. We will take the new road, Portfield Way, which cuts across the manor to Bradwell Brook and continues to Newport Pagnell. The growth of markets in both Stony Stratford and Newport Pagnell in the last century has led to increased traffic. The road, or rather track, is not in very good condition and carts have left deep ruts but if you walk or ride on horseback it is passable in good weather. As this is the end of June our problems are minimal. This road is slightly to the north of the present Wolverton Road and leads us directly to the village much closer to the mill.

While we are on this road we may as well take a detour to the mill, known as West Mill. As we walk down the track through the meadows there is a man in the meadow checking the height of the grass. He looks at us suspiciously. He is the Hay Ward, quite an important official in Wolverton, and his principal duty at this time of year is to organise the hay crop. He will organise the teams of mowers who skilfully swing their scythes back and forth in a long reaping motion. This is one of the critical crops of the year because it will keep the livestock fed during the winter month. At other times of the year he will ensure that animals do not stray onto the arable fields and issue fines to those who allow their animals off the commons. He is the man who make sure that the hay is properly stored and appropriately distributed during the winter months. The Hay Ward, as the right hand man to the Reeve, the village administrator, will most likely be assigned a number of duties during the year. As a village official he will certainly be keeping an eye on strangers like us.

Manno's Manor

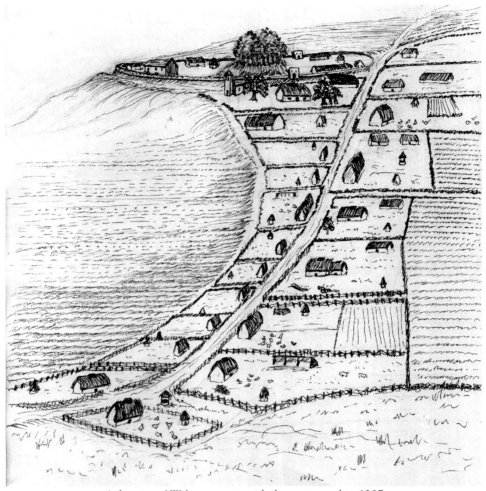

A drawing of Wolverton as it might have appeared in 1307

The mill, as we come to it, is probably the most sophisticated piece of machinery we will find on the manor. It has a huge waterwheel which is turning as we watch at a steady rate controlled by the mill race, a ditch dug beside the river. By means of a system of gears the power of the wheel turns a specially cut circular stone, which grinds the flour. the miller and his family are among the better off in the village. He has a good degree of control over prices and everyone has to come to him. At one time the Lord was in direct control of the mill but now he finds it more convenient to rent it out who can meet the annual rental. How much money he makes or loses is of little concern to Sir John de Wolverton.

Medieval Life in Wolverton

What will become quickly apparent to us as we walk back from the mill to re-join the road to the village is that there are none of the hedgerows or fences that we might expect to find in a farming landscape. The concept of enclosing fields has yet to be invented. Here are large open fields as we have come to call them, marked out in cultivatable strips, each tilled by one peasant family and separated from his neighbour by baulks, that is, raised furrows of earth. Each would be a furlong in length, although not necessarily the exact length which the furlong was later understood to be, but long enough. A furlong was later defined as 220 yards (just over 200 metres) but the very name would tell us that it was some distance to walk behind an oxen-drawn plough. The field picture would resemble todays allotments, but on a larger scale. Peasants are scattered across the manor.

We do notice that different crops are growing side-by-side in different strips. The old idea of everyone trooping off to one large field to sow barley has been replaced by a more sophisticated approach. Peasants now can farm their strips closer together in some cases. They are still practising crop rotation but within the limits of their own three strips rather than in a large communal field.

One area which is fenced off is the copse. These were small wooded areas which were vital for the community's supply of wood. We can see one example on the higher ground to the south in the area known as The Warren. There is a fence around it to stop deer from eating tree shoots. Not much of Wolverton is wooded at this time but what wooded areas are left are very carefully managed, under the strict control of the lord. Peasants are allowed to gather twigs and fallen branches for firewood but the cutting of trees is strictly controlled. Each year a coppicer will clear some of the undergrowth to allow the trees to grow to full strength and new saplings will be planted - hence the need for a fence. We will see several copses as you make our tour of the manor.

This last walk should bring us to the village settlement of Wolverton which straggles out for over half a mile along the road, with cottages built on both sides of the track. None of the cottages look very permanent, and indeed they are not. The low walls, about four feet high, are made of a mixture of clay, gravel and straw, using animal dung as a binder. We now see why the term housebreaking came into being, because any robber could easily break a hole in the wall in order to gain access. The cottages we see

Manno's Manor

vary from 16 to 20 feet long and are no more than 10 feet wide. They are single room dwellings without windows. Ventilation comes through the door and the roof, which is at a very steep pitch, so the whole dwelling might be as high as 25 feet. The steep pitch is essential to keep out the rain because these roofs are all thatched and our eyes will also notice that many of them are now green with moss. Thatch is common enough in these parts. It is a cheap roof covering and is easily repaired. It helps to keep the house warm too, although it provides that same service to a variety of animal and bird life who nest within it. Smoke from the open hearth fire inside the cottage escapes through a crude opening at the top. There is no chimney. This opening is covered by a louvre. The eaves also extend quite far out from the walls to protect them from rain. We will observe some variation in the size of the cottages, depending upon the relative status of the peasants within the community. Some, for example, may be able to afford a wooden sleeping platform inside the cottage.

The yards surrounding the cottages vary in size but all are fenced. This is because almost all of them keep some chickens and geese and they must be protected against foxes. Inside the yard, known as a toft, we can see an earth closet and further away from the cottage a mound of animal dung, destined for future use as a fertiliser. At this time of the year they can become high in both senses of the word and complaints about a neighbour's "mound" were common in these times. We also notice several crude clay pots under the thatch eaves' these are designed to collect the water run-off to meet immediate domestic needs, although there is a communal village well.

Some of the better off peasants have built byres for their livestock within their tofts.

As we go up the hill towards the church and the manor house the scene changes for the better. The church as we come to it far outstrips anything we have seen thus far in size and importance; however, it is still a simple 11th century building - rectangular, probably about 40 feet long and 25 feet wide. It has a tiled roof and the building is made of locally quarried stone. The church also boasts some expensive windows. Later in this century it would be extended with the addition of a tower and a chancel, but in 1307 we see only a functional and unprepossessing building.

Medieval Life in Wolverton

The vicarage, which stands nearby is larger and better built than the rough and ready structures we have passed in the village, but thatch again is the roof covering of choice.

This house is typical for the 12th century. The Wolverton Manor House may have resembled this.

Just to the north, we can see the huge earthworks which once held the keep of Wolverton's castle. Now that times are more peaceable it has been abandoned and there is no sign of the structure that must have been here when it was the residence of the baron. Even so, the earthworks and stone wall around the bailey remain and there are two gatehouses, one just ahead of us, and another north entrance. They are open during the day, although they are guarded. If we are challenged about our busienss we will say that we have a message for Sir John. Nobody in 1307 will understand tourism.

Once at the manor house and its related buildings we are left in no doubt as to the importance of the people living here. The house stands two stories in height and is built of quarried stone with a tiled roof. This is the great hall, presently occupied by Sir John de Wolverton and his family and servants. The main building is quite impressive and is about 50 feet long and 25 feet wide. The walls are built of stone brought from the quarry at nearby Cosgrove and the roof structure is an impressive piece of carpentry.

Manno's Manor

There is a huge fireplace at one end and a brick-built chimney. There are a a good number of buildings within the bailey, which is quite extensive.

The great hall itself is public and we will not be bothered if we wander in to take a look. People are always here on some matter of business or another. Everybody eats here and the servants work here and sleep on the floor at the end of the day. Sir John and his family have the luxury of a solar, a second storey platform that spans the hall and is reached by stone steps. The solar is the private area for Sir John and his family and only a privileged few have access. The family also has the luxury of a garderobe, a privy behind a screen at one end of the hall.

But this is not the only building here. there is a kitchen, separate from the main hall because of the risk of fire, stables of course, and a penned area for chickens and geese. We also find kennels for dogs, used mainly for hunting but also useful to warn against intruders, human or animal, at night time. Sir John also has a dovecote and many of these doves will grace the lord's table at one time or another. A huge barn will store grain from the Lord's demesne and the villagers' tithes.

Let's move further north, because the village continues. This landscape has no canal at this date. The road continues to a large barn known as the Grange. This is a barn for storing grain and is looked after by a granger who lives in one of the nearby cottages but this one does not belong to the manor. In fact this land has been acquired by the Priory of Chicksands, near Dunstable and the land here is worked for their benefit. Just on ourr left we can see a boundary ridge which has been dug to distinguish between the two manors. On either side we can see long strips of growing crops. Today, most of the villagers are out in the fields with their hoes removing weeds.

Ploughing in the 14th century - from the Luttrell Psalter.

Medieval Life in Wolverton

Directly north of the grange we can witness some new development. There are men at the bottom of the field digging a new trench or channel to cut across the great loop of the River Ouse. This new channel will become a mill race for a third mill in Wolverton. It is to be a fulling mill, planned by the Hastings family, well established in these parts, to ease the arduous process of fulling, that it is hammering the lumps out of the crude woollen cloth until it is smooth and wearable. If I said that the west Mill represented the pinnacle of mechanical sophistication in the village, that was true, but if we come back in a year's time we should see the fulling mill in action with a very complex mechanism of gears, levers and hammers. This mechanised process will make life much more bearable for those involved in the trade. Sheep farming, as we shall see, when we reach the commons, is becoming an important industry.

If we now rejoin the road we can proceed eastwards through some very good arable land. Furlong strips spread out on either side of the road and when the harvest is in next month will provide the bulk of food for the inhabitants of the manor. This road takes us along the valley for another mile or so where we rejoin the river Ouse as it meets a tributary stream known as Bradwell Brook. We will pass by the road to the north that goes to Wolverton's second mill, known as Mead or Meadow Mill. This mill is worked for the benefit of Bradwell Priory and the track to the south will take us to the priory itself, which was founded by the Baron of Wolverton in 1155. You can see the priory walls and building across the brook. It is not very grand. Its church, dedicated to St. Mary is quite a modest building and the priory does not seem to have made much progress beyond its original endowment 150 years earlier. The land across the brook was at one time part of the Wolverton Manor but it was granted to the priory by its founder Baron Meinfelin. Now this land feed the monks and earns some income for the priory. In addition the monastery was granted the income from Holy Trinity so one of their number is usually appointed vicar and the priory collects the church tithes from Wolverton.

This southern and eastern part of the manor is not well populated. We can only find the odd scattered cottage for shepherds and cowherds and woodsmen's cottages near some of the copses. But if we walk up to the old ridgeway, the old high trackway which crosses the manor from east to west, in later times known as Green Lane we find ourselves in the uplands of the manor above the valley. There is a good view to the north from here where we have a wide panorama of the cultivated lands by the river stretching up to the barley fields beside us. As we turn to face south we see mostly scrub lands and furzes. These are the great commons of Wolverton and here we can see the livestock of the manor grazing. We will of course be struck by how small the cattle are compared to what we see in the 21st century. The sheep too are much smaller animals than modern ones. The animals are all owned by various, but by no means all, members of the community. Livestock are costly to rear and maintain. Naturally, if one does own some livestock there are the benefits from the products of milk, wool or meat but the investment, and indeed the risks, are high. So, for the most part, the cattle and sheep we see grazing are owned by the more prosperous members of the community, including the lord.

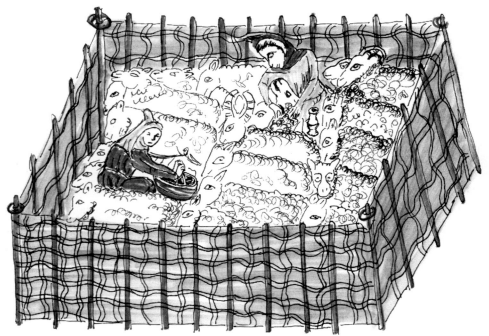

Sheep pen in the 14th century - from the Luttrell Psalter

Everywhere we go today we see men, women and children out in the fields. Children do not go to school; that activity is only available to a very few who may be sent to Oxford or Cambridge in their early adolescence to prepare themselves for a career in the church. So children, as soon as they are old enough, are given useful tasks. Everything in this world is done by hand and the days are long and arduous.

We can complete our circular tour of the manor by rejoining the Watling Street at Gallows or Galley Hill and then walk down to one of the inns for rest and refreshment.

The Early Church in Wolverton

We do not know when the first Christian Church was built on the Wolverton Manor. No archaeological evidence so far has been uncovered that might help to answer this question, and there are certainly no written records.

The larger picture tells us that the Christian mission from Rome began in 597 in Kent and it is probable that Christianity spread to Wolverton in the 7th century AD. The early establishments were minsters (from the Latin monasterium) which provided a base for monks to travel outwards on their missionary work. There is no evidence of a Minster near Wolverton. The nearest known minster in Buckinghamshire was at Wing. In Northamptonshire there was one at Higham Ferrers, although not, apparently, at Northampton and another was established in Bedford. The missionary work probably emanated from one or other of these minsters and served the spiritual needs of the converts until the establishment of a resident priest or church.

Saxon church foundations that do survive date from the 10th and 11th centuries, but it is likely that as Christianity embedded itself some sort of local building was erected to serve the needs of the population. The practice of the Norman conquerors was to replace Saxon churches with their own structures. Most were demolished and little evidence remains of their location or architecture. Even very substantial and important buildings were replaced. Winchester Old Minster, for example, was a large and imposing building, but once the new cathedral was built it was pulled down. As to small parish churches, they simply disappeared. In some cases the old building was a basis for the newer structure; in other instances the old building was pulled down and the materials reused in the new structure. Church building was a political statement by the Norman rulers. They were here to stay.

Manno's Manor

The general absence of Saxon churches has led historians to speculate that earlier Saxon churches were wooden buildings. In the case of Wolverton the best guess is that it was a wooden building and it is reasonable to assume that it was close to the present church of Holy Trinity. What the structure resembled is again pure speculation. Not all Saxon churches, for example, were complete buildings. Some merely provided some cover for the altar while the congregation gathered in the open air. Later buildings were more complete, but were usually modest buildings. I imagine that Wolverton's church, serving a population of no more than 200, was an unpretentious structure.

Church building started in earnest after the Norman conquest. The Normans were aggressive and ambitious church builders and most of the cathedrals and churches that we now recognise date from the post Norman period where grand impressive architecture was a manifestation of the ruling imperative. It was a matter of prestige for the new landowners, so it is probable that Manno, the new baron, built a new church once he established himself. There is however, no record that would confirm this.

Manno was succeeded by Meinfelin who was probably able to consolidate the wealth of the barony. In his will of 1155 he founded Bradwell Priory, as previously mentioned. Thereafter, until the dissolution, the Church at Old Wolverton was under the control of the Priory.

We can infer from this that there was an existing church at Wolverton, presumably under the direct control of the lord until 1155 and thereafter administered by the priory. No permanent priest appears to have been in charge until 1240, or thereabouts, when a man called Alan was Vicar. I assume that various monks or chaplains were appointed before that but with no specified living associated with the church. It is probably worth bearing in mind that although there was a settlement in the field to the south west of the church, there were probably families scattered across the manor.

The church of Holy Trinity was almost completely rebuilt in the early 19th century, leaving only parts of the tower as a record of its medieval past. William Cole, rector of Bletchley and a keen 18th century antiquarian, has left some record.

These notes, written 23rd April 1754, offer us a useful description.

Medieval Life in Wolverton

'Passing thro' this Parish in my way from the Archdeacon's Visitation held at Stony Stratford, I called in to look at the Church; which is a small building with the Tower, Cathedral Fashion, between the Nave and the Chancel; the last of which is tiled and the Nave and South Aisle leaded. It has 4 bells. The Chancel is very elegantly paved thro' out with black and white Marble. The Altar is railed in and stands on an elevation of 3 steps. On the North Side worked in the Wall is a very antique Altar Tomb of black marble but without arms or inscription to inform one to whom it appertains. The 2 Ends of the Arch and above it are adorned with very old-fashioned Carvings of Oak of Medallions of Men's Heads and old Shields. On the opposite side of the Altar against the south Wall is erected a very noble Monument of white Marble, having the Figure of a Gentleman in a Roman warlike Habit reclining on his left side, with his Eyes looking up to Heaven, and his right Hand laid on his Breast.'

The medieval church that was pulled down in the 19th century dates from the reign of Edward III, and is therefore of 14th century origin. Parts of the previous church were used to build the newer church. It looks as if the chancel formed the first church with a later addition of the tower. This was a conventional development of churches. The first small building became the chancel when the church was enlarged and was thus absorbed into the new building. The nave was likely a later addition and finally the crenellated south aisle. In the case of Holy Trinity, the almost total rebuild of the 19th century has left little of this evidence behind.

Someone had the foresight to record the old church before it was demolished so we do have some idea of what the new church replaced. Browne Willis made a rather crude sketch of the church in the first part of the 18th century and J Buckler made a fair copy of a drawing once in the possession of the Reverend Cook of Haversham which confirms the Browne Willis view. This drawing is reproduced here.

The church was a modest one but Cole indicates that some money had been spent on the interior.[2]

By placing the church under the jurisdiction of the Priory, Meinfelin met two objectives: to provide the Priory with income from the tithes, and to place the responsibility for the upkeep of the church upon the Priory.

Manno's Manor

After the dissolution of the monasteries the responsibility for the church reverted to the Lord of the Manor.

A drawing of the old Holy Trinity Church

The growth of Stony Stratford in the 12th and 13th centuries led to a need for a chapel of ease on the Watling Street. As noted on page 78 the earliest mention of any such place occurs in an undated document from 13th century, sometime during the tenure of William, son of Hamo, between 1214 and 1247, so the grant could have been made at any time during this period, but possibly earlier than 1238 when Hamo the Clerk was lodging in a house that formerly belonged to Richard the Weaver.[3] On this fairly thin evidence we could suggest that a chapel had been established in the first 30 years of the 13th century, and this is consistent with a foundation on the west side, made in 1203.[4] Both chapels succeed the formal establishment of markets at Stony Stratford and no doubt the increase in trade brought more travellers to the town and in those medieval times the need for a place to pray and make donations to the church.

Both new chapels, on both sides of the Watling Street, must have increased their congregations fairly rapidly in the thirteenth century as both were able to build full scale churches by the end of that century. The

Medieval Life in Wolverton

church on the Wolverton side, St Mary Magdalene, is thought to date from about 1290.

The tower was a later medieval development, from the middle of the 15th century, although there is no record of its building. Edward Swinfen Harris, the distinguished Stony Stratford architect, was impressed with the building and design. Writing at the end of the 19th century, he noted:

> "The tower of St. Mary Magdalene's church (though but a fragment of what must have been a very beautiful church) is a precious heritage, which we should all value very highly. It is the work of an able but unknown architect of the latter half of the fourteenth century, and has many features about it of a passing notice It has been illustrated in Parker's Glossary. Among these we may mention the almost Italian method of dispensing with buttresses, for those used are too shallow to deserve the name. Its belfry stage is of singular beauty and faultless proportion. The gurgoyles are full of quaint humour. The parapets form a beautiful compromise between the ordinary English embattled and the 'saddle-back' type found in Normandy and the Isle of France or rather they might well be described as a happy union of these two beautiful types. Its whole character is made up of exceeding delicacy, refinement, and reserve. It has been carefully repaired, and no more than was absolutely necessary had been done, in order to ensure the safety of a building, alas! too long allowed to suffer from past neglect."[5]

Records for the church are quite poor and early priests are largely unrecorded. This may have something to do with the fact that the Bradwell Prior regarded this as a chapelry and did not ever make a permanent appointment. Nevertheless, the quality of the building would suggest that the church was well-supported by the stony Stratford merchants on the Wolverton side.

Population Growth

The three centuries after the conquest became a period of growth and development in England. Once recovered from the initial ravages of the aftermath of the Conquest the country largely prospered under the new rulers. Several factors were at work here: some improvements in plough design which made the breaking of the soil easier and faster; a period of

Manno's Manor

global warming which extended the growing season, the breaking of new land and relative political stability.

Records specific to Wolverton that might tell us how the land was developed during this period are non-existent. There are modern scientific techniques which can discern soil movement and date from there, but techniques such as these have limited application to Wolverton where building over the past 170 years has destroyed such evidence. We can take information from the larger picture of England which has been developed by economic historians and infer some things about Wolverton's development.

Inevitably this growth in population must have led to a more complex society. The amount of land could not be increased and customary strips were probably tilled in much the same way that they always had. The difference may have been in the development of specialised trades. If less time was needed to work for food, surplus time was available for other activities. The 13th century deeds which make up part of the manorial documents deal with a number of transactions around Stony Stratford, which would suggest that the trade to the travelling public was well advanced. Inns would be found on both sides of the street, each with their own household and staff of servants. It is possible that specialised smithing trades could now be supported and the weaving and fulling of cloth and tanning of leather might earn enough to support a family without tilling the soil.

No estimates of population for these early centuries can be precise and we can only work with estimates from economic historians working from a variety of sources, but if the population of England was between 1.25 and 1.5 million in 1086, it was probably double that by the beginning of the 14th century. Estimates made from the Poll Tax figure of 1377 give a total population of 2.3 million living in England. If a loss of 40% as a consequence of the Black death of 1349 and its subsequent outbreaks is accepted, then there must have been 3.2 million in the country on the eve of the plague, double that of the 11th century. It took many centuries for the population to recover. This rise in population seems to have arisen through a period of global warming which had brought about higher food yields and enhanced by improvements in farming technology. Better fed people brought improved fertility and better chances of surviving infancy.

Medieval Life in Wolverton

Population estimates for Wolverton are complicated by the growth of Stony Stratford, which also had buildings on the Calverton side of the street. In the prime years of the coaching trade in the early 19th century the town had a population of about 1,500. The 14th century may have accommodated 3 to 400, although this is pure guesswork. But let us assume that, as discussed earlier, the manorial population doubled from 1086 to about 500 in 1349. A further 2 to 300 may have been making a living on the Wolverton side of Watling Street, giving a total population of about 800.

The Black Death and Wolverton

This growth might have continued but for the extraordinary pandemic known as the Black Death. Although we have no records from the time there is no reason to suppose that Wolverton escaped the affliction. We do know what happened at Bradwell Priory so there is no reason to suppose that the area escaped the impact of the plague. The numbers of monks at the Priory were greatly reduced after 1349, the year in which the Prior himself, William de Loughton, died and the fortunes of the Priory, never very well endowed, did not recover. Later they had to seek Papal dispensation to allow illegitimately born children to become monks, even the Prior – something that would not have been countenanced before the plague.

The plague was not a one-off; there were recurrences in the years immediately after 1349, and further devastating outbreaks in 1360-62, 1369 and 1375. The influence was profound.

We can begin to detect some of these changes in some of the deeds after 1349

1349 Stony Stratford

William Grik of Stony Stratford, chaplain grants and confirms to Roger Grocone of Calverton A MESSUAGE in Stony Stratford in the parish of Calverton between messuage of Henry Anketil and that once of Hugh Turnus & 10 acres arable at Calverton and 1 acre meadow in le Mulueholm. William's brother Thomas had held all those properties.[6]

Manno's Manor

We may deduce that Thomas Grik died in that year of the plague and possibly all of his direct heirs.

We find more women as heirs. For example:

1360 Wolverton

Alice, Elizabeth and Isabella Dikoun, daughters and heir of Elyas Dikoun release to John de Broughton and Eleanor his wife all their right and claim in lands, tenements and messuages in Wolverton next Stony Stratford which they had after the death of their father.[7]

These are some examples of how society was changing. In earlier centuries there were a small number of transactions either between the lord and his tenants or with a certain amount of hands-on involvement by the lord. The services were often specific. Here, and in other documents of the period, the reference to services has become formulaic and unspecified, simply noting It is probable that the services were acquitted on the basis of some agreed payment.

The years between the Black Death and the Peasants Revolt coincided with the end of the de Wolverton male line and the emergence of the de Longuevilles. John de Wolverton died in 1349, possibly a plague victim himself and his only son Ralph two years later. The barony was then divided between Sir John's daughters and their husbands. John de Longueville came into the manor in 1393 as the husband of John de Wolverton's granddaughter Joan Hunte. So it would appear that in the unsettled period of 1381 the manor was still in the hands of the established family and one might conclude that after three centuries the lords and the peasantry had settled into a comfortable relationship. Most people are inherently conservative; they only become radical when pushed too far. What would have mattered most to the majority on the Wolverton manor was that all their customary rights and practices were upheld and that they were treated fairly. Taxes were imposed from above, but if the tax gatherers were reasonable, then some accommodation would be found. What sparked the revolt and fed into accumulated grievances was the ineptness of the tax gatherers in Essex.

Social Change

The Black Death resulted in a serious labour shortage. A 40% reduction may have cut back the combined population of Wolverton and Stony Stratford to about 500. 14th century society was dependent on agriculture and it was the peasants who were engaged in actual production. Two segments of society, the nobility and the church, were entirely dependent on the work undertaken by the peasantry. Suddenly, there were not enough people to till the fields and harvest the crops. There was a slight shift in economic power. Lords who had hitherto been able to demand service and payment for the use of their land found themselves with 40% fewer bodies to undertake that service and a 40% reduction in output. Some began to circumvent to old system and offer wages and soon peasants, who had worked land for generations were drawn away to another village for the prospect of wages. This only deepened the plight of the lord who refused to adapt to changing circumstances. The result was a revolution as profound as what happened in the 19th century, when agricultural workers discovered that they could improve their income by moving from their traditional villages to the new industrial towns. And just as that change brought about later discontent in the form of campaigns for better wages and working conditions, so too did the changes of the latter part of the 14th century.

There were what we might call "working class" revolts in France and Italy during this period. Mostly they were led by members of the merchant classes. England came to its own version in 1381, known since as The Peasants Revolt. Although still an agricultural society (as it was to remain for a further 600 years) Wolverton, like most of southern England, had become more sophisticated in the diversity of trades. The care of a flock of sheep, for example, required a shepherd who might spend his days monitoring the sheep in the Stacey Bushes area and not have time to farm land for himself. He would be paid, probably by the lord of the manor, or he might earn a living from having his own small flock. The same could be said for a swineherd or a cowherd. With the growth of Stony Stratford on the edge of the manor, there would be sufficient work for thatchers, carpenters, masons, shoemakers, blacksmiths, tanners, fullers, weavers and dyers and carters. The River Ouse might also provide for the employment

Manno's Manor

of boatmen. The growth of Inns on the Watling Street opened up opportunities for ostlers and domestic servants. Most, if not all, these people would need to be paid in money rather than in kind. Tying people to service as a foundation for society was beginning to disappear, or at least become less central to the economy.

Wolverton was still a middling manor, not poor, but without a significant middle class. Those who might be considered an emerging middle class in Wolverton, were a few innkeepers in Stony Stratford, hardly a nucleus for rebellion. The unrest of the summer of 1381 passed Wolverton by.

Once again we have to observe that Wolverton was immune to another episode in English history. The uprisings came from Kent and Essex and East Anglia. There was also a brief uprising in Lincolnshire and there were signs that northerners were thinking about it, but these came to nothing.

There were some scary days for the government. The Kentish and Essex throngs raged through London, sacked John of Gaunt's Savoy palace on the Strand and executed Archbishop Sudbury, who was an unpopular chancellor. They were eventually persuaded to meet with Richard II at Smithfield, and planned or not, some of Richards men surprised and executed the leaders. The headless army was easier to deal with and the horde was dispersed with written promises of pardons - which subsequently were not even worth the paper they were written on. Once everyone had returned to their homes the government pursued and executed the ringleaders ruthlessly and the incident was over.

Wolverton people were on the sidelines. They may have heard some news and probably did from Watling Street travellers, but none were moved to take up arms.

240 years is not a negligible period and by the time Edward I's only surviving son came to the throne in 1307 this amount of time has passed on the Wolverton Manor since the Norman Conquest. The population had, as discussed in the last section, doubled, which meant that there were more people to work the land and there was a greater prospect of producing agricultural surplus. Slaves had disappeared from the economy and indeed many of the old feudal ties to the land had been weakened. Money was a larger part of the economy. Services to the lord, originally part

Medieval Life in Wolverton

of the feudal bargain, could now be excused for a cash payment or directly paid for in wages. This newish practice was accelerated by events of the 14th century.

In many respects the 14th century was a benighted century. Europe was in turmoil. Some serious weather problems caused famine in many years in Northern Europe. Political regimes were often unstable. England and France entered into a conflict in 1340 that was to continue for almost a century. It resulted in heavy taxation for the English and frequent ravaging of Northern France. The Papacy was in schism for much of the century, with one Pope in Avignon and another in Rome. The Iberian peninsula endured war between competing kingdoms and would be dynasties. The Italian states were at loggerheads and in frequent armed conflict. The great plague afflicted all of Europe in the middle of the century, and its aftermath was a restructuring of European economies.

It would be remarkable indeed if Wolverton was not affected by any of this.

---

1 Fullwell appears in Radcliffe Deeds
2 John Brushe. Holy Trinity, Wolverton, Buckinghamshire. p 8-9)
3 Close rolls 22 Hen III
4 Curia Regis. John 4. John de Calverton a "cotland and two messuages and appeurtenances in Stratford which he had receive from William the son of Alvric to Roger the clerk for the purpose of building a chapel."
5 Oliver Ratcliff. History and Antiquitiesof the Newport Pagnell Hundreds. Olney: The Cowper Press, 1900. p.376-377.
6 Bodleian. MSS. dd. Radcl. deed 262.
7 Bodleian. MSS. dd. Radcl. deed 114.

SIX

THE RISE OF THE LONGUEVILLES

While the de Wolverton family were in decline, the de Longueville family were on the way up. Manno le Breton, founder of the de Wolverton line, had acquired large estates after the Conquest which were later assessed at 15 knights' fees in service: that is he had fifteen principal knights under his patronage, each of whom would have had a manor or part of a manor to support himself and his family and indeed his ability to arm himself for potential combat – no mean expense.

The de Longuevilles by contrast appear to have started their life in England as knights but initially without any grant of land. They emerge on the record in the 12th century, a century after the Conquest in the Manor of Overton in Huntingdonshire, part way between Oundle and Peterborough. The manor only has one entry in the Domesday Book of 1086 but the holdings are shared between Eustace the Sheriff and the Bishop of Lincoln, Eustace having the larger share.

This quite large manor was divided into two parts, which later assumed the names of Orton Longueville and Orton Waterville after the holding families of the 13th century. It was subinfeudated, possibly by 1135, to Roger and John, both "men of Eustace". One or the other may be the ancestor of the de Longuevilles but there is no documentary evidence to make that connection. All we know is that the de Longuevilles hold this manor as one knight's fee to the Lovetoft barony. The Lovetoft Barony appears to have comprised the holdings of Eustace the Sheriff although in the murky world of 12th century records any lineage with Eustace is unclear.

This information does at least help us to place this de Longueville family. Their heritage was modest but over a period of centuries they appear to have established themselves as a middling rank family with some landed resources. The Orton Longueville family emerges from obscurity with Henry who held the fee in 1166. Henry had at least three sons of record but his heir was Reginald who died before 1219. His son John became the tenant and he died before 1265 leaving one son Henry as a minor. In the practice of the day Henry became a ward until he became of

Manno's Manor

age, under the protection of his overlord Roger de Lovetoft, who was then able to enjoy the revenue from the manor. Henry was married to Roger's daughter Petronilla and thus able to advance himself.

Some genealogists have tried to connect these Longuevilles with the great magnate, Walter Giffard de Longueville. There is no direct evidence for this although the name might offer some clue about the connection. Longueville was and is a village near Dieppe and Walter Giffard, who was one of William's great barons certainly originated from Longueville. It is a reasonable supposition that Walter Giffard brought with him several members of his extended family, but there is no evidence to allow us to conclude that our Longuevilles were in a direct line. It can be considered likely that the Orton Longuevilles came to England with the conquering army and were rewarded to a degree commensurate with their station. The assumption that they were descendants of Walter Giffard appears to have originated with an 18th century genealogy which confused Walterus de Longueville of Overton with Walter Giffard de Longueville, and may indeed have originated from the family itself in an attempt to burnish their lineage. Unfortunately more than a few genealogists have repeated this error.

Another coincidence that may lead to potential confusion is the presence of the manor of Newton Longueville some few miles away. This manor, originally Newton owes its appendage to Walter Giffard who assigned the income from this manor to the Abbey of Longueville. The name pre-dates the arrival of the Longuevilles in Wolverton and has never had any connection with the Wolverton family.

Exactly how and why part of the family moved from Orton to Little Billing is unknown. What we do know is that a John de Longueville acquired the Manor in 1301. At the same time, in 1302, a John de Longueville and his wife Margaret inherited the manor of Orton Longueville, but this couple had only a daughter for an heir and she married Gerard Braybrooke. Orton Longueville thereafter descended through this line. It therefore seems to me that the John de Longueville of Little Billing is a different person altogether, with no obvious connection to the Orton de Longuevilles other than a name. This does not mean that there is no connection, but simply that we do not have the concrete evidence to draw that conclusion.

122

The Rise of the Longuevilles

There are even hints that the de Longuevilles were already established in Northamptonshire. Prior to his acquisition of the manor in 1301 he granted some land in Little Billing to St John's Hospital in Northampton. This was not the action of a man without resources. Later in 1323 he founded the Austin Friars in Northampton. He could not be the John de Longueville who inherited Orton Longueville from his parents, Henry and Petronilla since he died in 1316. The Little Billing John Longuevile may not be directly descended from Henry and Petronilla.

It is possible, and even likely, that he descended from a younger brother of Henry and therefore both Johns share a common grandparent.

In the 14th century there were three, possibly four, ways to acquire land – through inheritance, though marriage and through service. The fourth possibility, through direct purchase, cannot be totally ignored, but in this case is less likely. The Longuevilles of Orton do not at this time appear to be that wealthy. The facts that we do know is that the title to the manor was transferred (alienated to use the terms of the time) to Sir John Longeville in 1301 and there was a so-called foot of fine to put this on record.[1] The rather odd name comes about because these transactions were usually recorded on a single sheet of parchment, on which three copies of the deed were made – one on the left, one on the right and one at the foot. Each part of the document was cut with wavy lines so that the originals could be matched without forgery. The two parties to the agreement kept the right and left hand copy and the court retained the foot. They are called fines because the agreement was a final concord – fine for short. Thus the court records, which are in most cases the only surviving records, became known as feet of fines.

The Manor of Billing was part of the small barony of Winemar the Fleming, the same man who held Hanslope in 1086. The descendants of Winemar, who took the name Preston, after Preston (Deanery) which they also held, appear to have run out of male heirs and in 1284 it was in the hands of the widow Alice de Preston. What happens after that is not altogether clear but Longueville may have come into the Manor through marriage to one in the female line of the de Prestons.

We know from record that Henry of Orton was put into wardship as a minor. He was the heir and there were estates to manage. A younger son with nothing to inherit may well have been given over to the custody of a

Manno's Manor

related family and it may have been this that brought the young John to Little Billing. There will have been no need for any record, which is why we have none, but he must have acquired some wealth somehow, possibly through a will from his relative but if no feudal holdings were involved there would be no need for royal intervention and a local deed would have been sufficient. We must assume that this was lost.

An 18th century genealogy traces the later Wolverton Longuevilles from a Thomas Longueville of Little Billing. The precise relationship with the John mentioned above is not recorded. He could have been either a son or grandson He married Beatrix Hastings and they had at least one son, Thomas. This Thomas married Isobel, and he died in 1361. They had a son John and his son, also John was the one who married Joan Hunt and thereby came into the Wolverton inheritance.

The de Wolverton line, as we have seen, produced no male heirs after the death of Ralph de Wolverton, then only a small boy, in 1351. At this point the great Barony of Manno was broken up. Chalfont St Giles and Padbury were settled on the four daughters of John de Wolverton's first marriage and Wolverton and Wyke Hamon (Wicken) divided between Ralph's elder sisters, Margaret and Elizabeth.

Margery married John de Hunte of Fenny Stratford, and gave birth to a daughter, Joan, who becomes important later. In the meantime, Elizabeth had married William de Cogenhoe

Margery outlived her first husband, then a second, Roger de Louth and a even third, Richard Imworth, but not the fourth, John Hewes, who after 1393 granted his interest to John de Longueville and his wife Joan.

This is the beginning of the Longueville story in Wolverton which was to last until 1713.

The de Longuevilles repeated the longevity of the first Wolverton ruling family and survived for over 300 years. Sir Frank Markham expresses the view that "successive generations of de Longuevilles followed two main lines of policy, first the acquisition of estates formerly held by priories, and second the enclosure of the common land of their manors." I will return to these two points later.

The Rise of the Longuevilles

The Longueville Descent from Orton Longueville

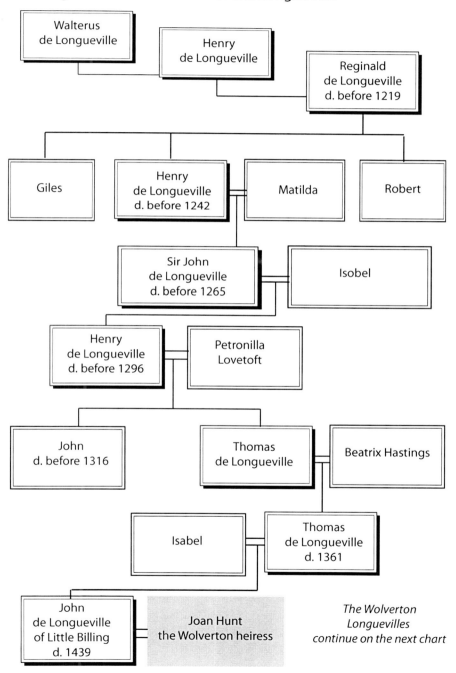

Manno's Manor

The Longuevilles of Wolverton

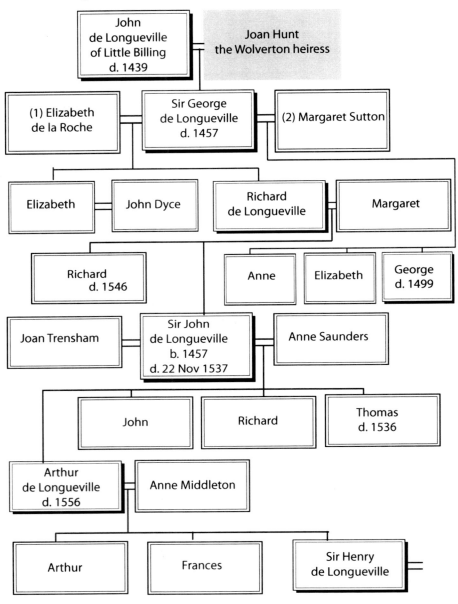

the line continues with the Longueville Baronetcy on page

The Rise of the Longuevilles

Sir John de Longueville, who had married Joan Hunt, the heiress of Wolverton, was born in 1351. In the succeeding years the division of the estates of the barony between the surviving daughters and their husbands led to some complicated dynastic settlements. The Wolverton estate eventually fell into the hands of Joan and her husband John de Longueville, probably after 1393. The new Lord of Wolverton moved there upon his wife's inheritance while continuing to maintain the Little Billing manor, which they passed on to their eldest son. The house at Wolverton however became the chief seat of the Longuevilles from this time forth.

We have no idea what sort of building was there in the 14th century, but we can assume, given the relative wealth of the de Wolvertons, that it was a splendid enough manor house for the period. From surviving knowledge of domestic architecture of that time, the house at Wolverton probably had a great hall, where all the activities of the house took place, including sleeping places for the servants. By the end of the 14th century the house could have been enlarged by at least one wing to give the family more privacy. At this time the house may have been "L-shaped". Kitchens were usually housed in a separate building set away from the great hall, as a precaution against the all too frequent risk of fire. We do not know if this house was of timber or stone construction; all we can presume is that there was a house there and it was of a standard befitting its occupants.

Sir John was energetic in seeking office. He was Sheriff of Buckingham in 1394 and no doubt took the opportunity (as did all holders of this office) to enrich himself and his family. His son George served as a member of Parliament for Buckinghamshire and was Sheriff of Northamptonshire in 1430. If we accept John's date of birth as 1351, then this John de Longueville lived a very long life, dying as he did in 1439. In any case his presumed father, Sir George Longueville, was murdered in 1357, so the birth of his son would have to be before that year. But his longevity meant that his heir, Sir George was already advanced in years at the time of his inheritance. He in turn lived to 1457. The succession once again becoes involved and difficult to unravel.

He had two sons - Richard, the eldest, by his first wife Elizabeth, and a younger son, George, the issue of a second wife, Margaret. Richard must have died in the some years earlier, but he already had a son, Richard, who by rights ought to have inherited according to the rules of the age.

Manno's Manor

However, this Richard also died before 1458, possibly before his grandfather, and Sir George made his younger son George, heir before he died in 1458. The younger Richard had a son, John, who was an infant at the time and this may explain why the old Sir George bypassed him in favour of his second son, George. There would have been sound motives for this. As a minor John would automatically become a ward of the king who could then sell the wardship to someone who would take responsibility for the upbringing of the boy, and, more attractively, enjoy the revenues from the estates. Sir George's manoeuvre may have been a tax avoidance scheme, because by naming his second son, who had already achieved his majority, he would only have to pay a fine of a fixed amount to the crown. Wardship was a much more expensive proposition and carried the risk of someone else plundering the estate for twenty years. Accordingly George was confirmed in the livery of his estates by Edward IV in 1461. The disinherited John did not at all subscribe to the notion that he should accept his lot and upon obtaining his majority began to pursue his rights. He must have had a clear case because on October 14 1479 the king's court made this order at Woburn.

> **licence for** John Longvile son and heir of Richard Longvile, esquire, tenant in chief, to enter freely without proof of age into all castles, lordships, manors, honours, lands, fee- farms, annuities, reversions, farms, rents, services, hundreds, offices, fees, views of frank-pledge, courts, leets, sheriffs' turns, liberties, franchises, fairs, markets, jurisdictions, stews, fisheries, warrens, knights' fees, advowsons and other possessions and hereditaments in England and Wales and the marches of Wales of which his father or any other of his ancestors was seised and which should descend to him on their death, saving to the king homage and fealty.[2]

He is still treated as a tenant-in-chief, even though the barony had lapsed for over a hundred years. The ancient rights established in 1066 prevailed.

A court order was one thing, but displacing the incumbent was quite another. George was unwilling to move and must have resolved to ignore the order because in 1485 John, probably in exasperation, made a forcible entry to the Manor and asserted his rights as he perceived them. It had

The Rise of the Longuevilles

taken him six years since his majority to get to this point; George was intractable, having the confidence that possession was nine-tenths of the law. What sort of menaces were involved we can only imagine but John must have made his point successfully, because upon George's death in 1499 John had in his hands a document renouncing any claims by George and his heirs on the manor. The probable agreement that they reached in 1485 was that George could enjoy the manor until his death provided that everything came to John and that there were no further claims from George's heirs.

This John, who was knighted, lived to the good age of 83 (although in one place he is accorded the great age of 103) and took the family into the 16th century. He appears to have behaved somewhat like Henry VIII but without the ability to divorce his wife. His first wife bore only one surviving child, a daughter Anne. With no prospects for a son Sir John took up with Anne Saunders who produced no fewer than four sons - Thomas, Arthur, John and Richard. Thomas pre-deceased his father and Arthur was named as his heir. His illegitimacy was apparently no bar to inheritance although it was noted by contemporaries:

> Langeville an 103 yeres old made his landes from his heires general to his bastard sunne Arture. The yonger bastard is now heir.[3]

The one legitimate child, Anne, married John Cheyne of the Chenies manor in Chalfont St Giles from the family that had already established close connections with the de Wolvertons and the prospect of uniting the two manors, which were once part of the Wolverton barony must have been considered; however, Sir John de Longueville decided to will everything to his illegitimate son Arthur, who accordingly inherited in 1541. In the following year he secured himself from any claim by his half sister and her children and descendants.

Arthur Longueville was the one who acquired Bradwell Priory, which had been originally endowed by the Baron Meinfelin in the 12th Century. It had latterly been the property of Cardinal Wolsey but after his downfall it reverted to the crown. From here it was sold to Arthur Longueville.

The "younger bastard" died in 1557 leaving his widow Anne to manage the estate until his son Henry came of age. Henry died in 1618.

Manno's Manor

The period was a momentous one for the Manor because land enclosures were largely effected during this century - a policy instigated by Arthur and pursued more assiduously by his son Henry.

Wolverton in the 15th century

The 15th century in Wolverton and Stony Stratford can be set against a rising background of nationalism. England was in the middle of a protracted and almost perpetual war with France that came to be known as the Hundred Years War. In these circumstances some people seem anxious to shed their French connections. One example we find in the Wolverton Deeds (which are now written exclusively in English) is of one member at least of the Vis de Lou family changing his name to Oxe.[4] The Vis de lous were an early family prominent in the 13th and 14th centuries, as described earlier. At one moment they appear to have died out, perhaps as a result of the Black death, but one member at least shows up in 1431 in a land transaction. He is recorded as John Oxe, alias John Vydeloue of Wolverton. He also appears as witness in later documents as John Oxe. This was at a time when the English were still fighting in France and one suspects that anti French sentiment was running high so it appears that the once proud name of Vis de Loup which used a wolf's head as its seal in the 13th century is now lost to history.

New houses were developed on either side of the Watling Street during the 14th century, growing the town into a notable economic unit. Most of the land close to Stony Stratford tended to be used for pasture and was lost to arable production.

In the second half of the 15th century new enterprising families moved to the town and developed some wealth and prominence. Surviving deeds and records introduce a lot of new names during this period: Edys, the Braysers, the Tailours, Rokys, Hayles and Lawes. It is not known how and why they came to the town but possibly marriage to a line that had run out of male heirs would be one means of entry.

The Edy family, who became prominent in the early part of the 15th century, can illustrate this rise of new families. Wool was the great raw commodity that made England relatively wealthy in the middle ages and the Edys were amongst those who learned how to profit from the trade. They emerge as wool merchants, men who could buy raw wool from the

The Rise of the Longuevilles

primary producers and bundle it for sale to Flanders where it would be turned into quality cloth. English wool had certain qualities that made it prized above other sources and therefore commanded a good price. The Edys quickly became prosperous and although they were not large landholders they did not need to be. They were classic entrepreneurs with the intelligence and resources to organise the gathering of wool. Once sheared, the wool was bound in bales and carted to Buckingham by Woolmen. From there the wool was transported to Bristol for shipment abroad.

We first learn of the Edys through taxation rolls where they were regularly assessed by the monarchy. It is a mark of their prosperity that they were taxed. The monarchy in medieval times only bothered to tax the landed and merchant classes and left it up to them to extract whatever they could from the peasantry. At this stage we must assume that the Edys were already prosperous and perhaps it had only taken a single generation. Then they start to do what nouveau riche have done in all ages - acquire land and the accompanying status. In 1445 John Edy junior acquired the land around Stony Stratford which later became known as the Mallets. Another John, who died in 1487 held land in Cosgrove and had acquired the manor of little Loughton. Further, by his marriage to the heiress of Beachampton he had garnered this estate into his landholdings.

Medieval Industry In Wolverton and Stony Stratford

For almost the entire period covered by this book Wolverton's major industry was agriculture. There were of course blacksmiths and braziers working with metal, tanners with leather and fullers with wool, malt makers with barley and brewers of ale. In all cases these were cottage industries, worked by one man with assistants perhaps and few buildings with the possible exception of an isolated tannery would be distinguishable.

The buildings that did stand out were the mills which were built along the Ouse to harness the power of the stream. Each manor in North Bucks had at least one mill - Passenham, Calverton, Haversham, Stantonbury - Wolverton had two, and at one time a third mill.

Two mills were recorded at Domesday in 1086. It is thought that one was located in the east and was later known as Mead Mill; the other, the

Manno's Manor

West Mill, was on the site of the present Wolverton Mill. In one form or another this mill had a history of at least 1000 years.

Mead Mill was close to the present railway viaduct along the road to Haversham. Until the dissolution it was the mill for the Priory and old maps show a direct road from Mead Mill to Bradwell. The mill survived there until 1837 when the viaduct was built. This viaduct required that the course of the river be diverted and the Haversham road being moved a little to the east. This left the mill isolated but it was probably decided at the time that local milling needs could be met by the surviving mills in the district, including the relatively new Bradwell Windmill. The buildings there were occupied as residences for a couple of decades but were then pulled down.

The West Mill, latterly known as Wolverton Mill continued to function until the 20th century when it was eventually made obsolete by larger centralised milling facilities. It was last used for milling in the 1940s. The present structure was built in the 18th century.

There was once a third mill in Wolverton. There are documented references to it in 1464 and 1465 and indeed there are traces of a building on the site. It was certainly not functioning as a mill in 1710 when detailed records of the manor occur so we must assume that its life was not extensive or especially productive. Given its location you could guess that the channel cutting across a bend in the Ouse and bordering Colts Holm, was dug as a mill race.

From the surviving deeds it would appear to be in the hands of the Hastings family. The Hastings name appears early in Wolverton and is still prominent in the 15th century so it is probable that their ancestor was one of Manno's retainers who was granted some land on the Wolverton manor. The first of these 15th century documents is a letter of attorney that defines the lifetime interest of one Richard Savage of Kings Norton in these properties which had come to him through his marriage to Alice Hastings, the heiress of John Hastings. Alice had recently died. Several properties in Wolverton, Stony Stratford, Bradwell, Wicken and Padbury were noted, and most of these manors were once within the barony of Wolverton, but our interest here is Terle Mill. The date of this letter is 9th April 1465. There is a second deed, dated 19th April 1465, which releases Richard Savage's interest to John Hastings and John Hayle. We might assume that

132

The Rise of the Longuevilles

John Hastings was a brother of Alice and John Hayle another brother in law. Probably these two had completed a monetary settlement with Richard Savage for his lifetime interest. Then in a third deed, John Hastings grants his interest to John Hayle. The date of this last document is 12th June 1465.[5]

Through this series of documents we can attach a narrative for family settlements. The mill was a small part of the deal but its mention does provide us with proof of its existence.

We cannot know when it was built but one is drawn to the idea that it was a late medieval venture. There can scarcely have been a need for a third corn mill in Wolverton so it might possibly have been a fulling mill. Mechanised fulling mills start to appear in England in the very late 12th century but the absence of any mention of a mill in the 14th century, while not proving anything one way or another, might lead us to believe that it was a 15th century foundation. The location, with its flat land on the meadow would certainly lend itself to stretching out the cloth to dry, As far as the name is concerned it may derive from twirl which was simply descriptive of the action of the mill. There is a Turl Street in Oxford which derives from twirl.

In the end there may not have been as much demand for the fulling of cloth locally, and plainly the mill was not a long term success, The process of fulling was hard and required a good source of green earth, the nearest local supply coming from Woburn Sands. Any number of factors may have contributed to its demise and we have so little to go on. Wolverton men may have preferred to raise their sheep, shear them, bundle up the wool, takes their comfortable profits and buy the finished cloth from elsewhere. Certainly it was abandoned before 1700, and possibly much earlier.

There is a sunken track leading directly north from Manor Farm to what was probably the site of Terle Mill on the channel that was at one time dug for use as a mill race.

The soil on the manor is largely clay which tends to favour its use for pasture rather than crops such as wheat and barley and as generations gradually overcame the capital requirements of raising livestock Wolverton folk increasingly turned their efforts to animal husbandry. In consequence, as Hyde shows in his analysis, pasture land began to outstrip arable land in

Manno's Manor

price.[6] By the 15th century Wolverton manor was predominantly given over to the breeding of sheep, cattle and horses. One reason why the enclosures were so fiercely fought in the 16th century was that so many had a high stake in the common pasture land. This story will wait for a later chapter.

There were even those who resorted to cattle rustling in order to acquire livestock. In 1350 the earl of Warwick brought proceedings against John le Warner and others of Stony Stratford who raided his close at Greens Norton (at the time known as Norton Davy) and drove away twelve horse, six mares, forty oxen and twenty cows. The value of this haul was £60 - a large sum of money.[7] One imagines that John le Warner expected to get away with it in the confusing aftermath of the Black Death mortality.

By products of animal husbandry were the cloth making and leather industries. Weavers and dyers were natural cottage industries that attached themselves to the ready availability of wool and fulling of cloth, although it could be accomplished by hand, may, as I have suggested above, have been done by a mill.

The treatment of leather, known as tanning, was a complex process of several stages to make the leather supple and durable. Unfortunately in medieval times the chemicals necessary for the processes, apart from lime, were dung and urine, which together created a high noxious environment. Therefore tanneries were always consigned to the edge of town. The tannery in Stony Stratford was most likely at the end of Church Lane in medieval times.

In 1436 Simon Rook, born in the town of Gilder (possibly Gouda) in Gilderland, was given royal permission to settle in Stony Stratford. He was one of a considerable number of Flemish immigrants to this country, neither the first nor the last, but this influx coincided with yet another period of disruption in Flanders. In 1435 the duke of Burgundy, a long time ally of England turned and mounted a siege of Calais. The ensuing disruption of war harmed the economy of Flanders and a considerable number sought to re-settle in England. Simon Rook was one of a very long list. We are not told his trade but it is almost certain that he brought skills with him and was able to work for his own livelihood. In all probability he was a weaver, but he could have been a lace-maker, and if so, this would have been the earliest introduction of a skill that was to become a staple industry of North bucks until machine made lace put them out of business in the 19th century.

Three Kings and Stony Stratford

Medieval kings did not travel light. Wherever they went within the realm they had to carry all the machinery of government with them. Over time it became necessary to anchor the machinery of government in London but this really did not take full effect until the reigns of the Tudors. The problem with this mobile government was to find sufficient accommodation for the king's retinue. In this regard Stony Stratford, with its plentiful supply of inns and its location was a useful stopping point.

Most medieval kings from John onward, recorded a stay at Stony Stratford and usually this fact was recorded by a royal document of some kind relating to a matter of small importance. The three Yorkist kings however were connected with Stony Stratford in events which were indeed momentous for the crown.

On April 30th 1464 King Edward IV and his party stopped overnight at Stony Stratford. We don't know which Inn the king himself stayed at but it is likely that the king's entourage was a large one and they probably used up all the inn space at Stony Stratford between them. So far nothing remarkable, but the following day Edward quietly slipped away and rode out to Grafton where the Woodvilles or Wydvilles had a house. His objective was the beautiful widow Elizabeth de Grey (formerly Woodville) and apparently that day they were secretly married. The King returned to Stony Stratford and said he had been hunting, that he was tired and went to sleep. The following day he returned to Grafton for three days and each night he and Elizabeth came together for a secret assignation.

This is about the only fact we have although as one would expect there is a great deal of legend. It has been said that he first encountered her at the "Queens Oak" in Whittlewood forest while hunting. It is also said that she had resolved to approach the king over the forfeited estates of her previous husband. There may be some gain of truth here but it leaves room for questions. Had the king encountered Elizabeth Woodville while hunting it would have happened in a very public environment with the likelihood of other observers and reporters on the meeting. There are however none, and the marriage itself was kept secret for 6 months. It is of

Manno's Manor

course possible, given Edwards established womanizing reputation, that his courtiers paid no especial attention to his apparent fling with the de Grey widow.

On balance I am inclined to take this view. Kings led very public lives and were rarely out of sight of anybody. Any dalliance with Elizabeth de Grey would have been noticed. However if it were thought no more of than an affair nobody would have paid much mind to what was going on. The announcement on October 4th that he was married must have been a sensational revelation.

These details come from a contemporary chronicler, Robert Fabyan.

It was a marriage that astonished his contemporaries and historians have generally been at a loss to explain Edward's choice other than sheer impetuousness. It is not even clear when Edward first met Elizabeth Woodville and became enamoured of her. He did spend three days in Stony Stratford in 1461 when he pardoned Lord Rivers and this has been suggested as a time for a first meeting, but if so one wonders why it took three years for Edward's passion to incubate.

The point is that Edward could have, should have made a marriage which was more dynastically important. In fact, even after the secret marriage negotiations continued for a French marriage. Edward must have been conscious that his marriage would cause dismay, to put it at its mildest, amongst the English nobility, because he kept his secret until October when the French marriage plans had reached a point of decision.

And what of Elizabeth Woodville? She was a beautiful woman and at the time of here marriage to Edward a 27 year-old widow with two young sons. Her fist husband was Sir John Grey of Groby who had been killed at the Battle of St Albans in 1461 fighting on the Lancastrian side. As a widow she was relatively impoverished which might in part explain why men were not lining up to marry her. The usual tale that is told of the whirlwind pursuit by Edward is that she virtuously resisted his advances and the only way of breaking down her resistance was to propose marriage. This may be so, although we simply have no way of knowing.

Elizabeth Woodville brought with her a set of difficult problems for the monarch, partly through her own rather icy personality and partly through the preferment of her family. Elizabeth, although beautiful, lacked warmth and generosity of spirit. She bore grudges for a very long time and

The Rise of the Longuevilles

worked tirelessly and often unscrupulously to enrich her own family. And that family was very large. She had 11 brothers and sisters and waged a constant campaign to see that they married into money or were given honours that brought in great wealth. A certain amount of self help in this area was to be expected and tolerated, but the Woodvilles were greedy and resentment gradually increased to the point where the Yorkist regime was fatally undermined. It was as much the prospect of Elizabeth Woodville and her family running the monarchy that shifted significant support to Edward's brother Richard of Gloucester. It can be argued that were it not for the Woodvilles sudden rise to power, the Yorkist dynasty may well have continued and the Tudor name would not have come into our history.

Edward IV died after a short illness a few weeks short of his 41st birthday. The date was April 9th 1483. The cause of his death is still a matter of some speculation. Some contemporaries hinted darkly at poison but modern assessments conclude that he was a victim of his gargantuan appetites and taste for a debauched lifestyle. He left behind two sons, twelve year-old Edward and his brother Richard, just over two years younger.

The succession should have been secure; the concept of a regency was not unknown in England and it has worked well through the minorities of Henry III and Henry VI. However, the position of the potential young monarch unravelled very quickly and the arrest and subsequent murder of these two potential heirs quickly led to the doom of the Plantagenet dynasty.

At the time of his father's death the young heir was at Ludlow castle with his uncle Earl Rivers. They delayed their departure for London until April 24th, probably believing their position to be impregnable, and indeed it was very strong. The Marquess of Dorset, Earl Rivers brother, was in London and had secured the Treasury in the Tower. Richard, Duke of Gloucester, was in York. At this point Dorset overplayed his hand and began to issue orders in the King's name. This at once awoke all the simmering resentments against the Woodville family whom many regarded as upstarts. If the Woodvilles had one quality, it was their ability to breed large families, and the patronage and preferment of Edward IV had seen to it that many of them enjoyed positions of wealth and authority. The situation was not unlike a small minority political party enjoying and

Manno's Manor

exercising power while the majority could only sit and helplessly watch. In hindsight, the seeds of the revolution that was about to take place had been lying there for years waiting for the right growing conditions.

The Woodville's naked attempt to grab power left an opening for Richard, which he was clever enough and ruthless enough to exploit. Within seven weeks of his brother's death he was crowned king, a situation probably unimagined on April 9th.

Edward V's party made its way from Ludlow towards London and reached Northampton on April 29th. Gloucester and the Duke of Buckingham reached Northampton the same afternoon, intending to rendevous with Rivers' party but Rivers, having the custody of the princes, and possibly doubtful of Richard's intentions, had already made haste to Stony Stratford. However, on hearing that Richard had reached Northampton, Rivers rode back with a small party to try to assure Richard of his good faith

When they did meet both parties were on their best behaviour and acted with great civility towards one another. They spent the night together in 'friendly cheer' and 'conviviality'.[8] But after Rivers had retired, Buckingham and Gloucester stayed up planning their coup. At dawn they mustered their men, obtained the keys to the inn where Rivers was staying and locked all the outside doors. They also set up road blocks on the road to Stony Stratford. Richard then arrested Rivers and accused him of trying to turn Edward against him.

Once that had been effected Richard and Buckingham rode on with their retinue to Stony Stratford where they were able to catch up with Edward. Richard knelt and acknowledged him as king and took him inside with Buckingham to communicate certain matter in private, where he outlined the various charges against Rivers and those other Woodvilles whom he regarded as a corrupting influence on the boy. He moved swiftly and ruthlessly. Edward's chief guardians were sent to Northampton under armed guard. The rest of his retainers were dismissed and replaced with Richard's own trusted people. After a good morning's work Richard and Buckingham returned to Northampton for a self-congratulatory dinner.

Richard's actions were initially very popular. He was seen as the protector of the king who had successfully removed the malign and

The Rise of the Longuevilles

grasping influence of the Woodvilles. Subsequent events were to change his standing in public opinion, but at this moment he was riding high.

The events at Stony Stratford on April 29th and 30th 1483 were therefore at a pivotal moment in history and it has always been of interest to historians as to where these happenings took place. There has been a tradition that the inn where Edward stayed was the *Rose and Crown* and indeed there is now a plaque on the wall of the present house proclaiming that "fact". There is, however, no surviving document that can corroborate or disprove this assertion. All we can take as evidence is that the building certainly dates from the late 15th century and that its name might lead us to infer some royal connection. Browne Willis, writing in the 18th century, was of the opinion that Edward stayed at *The Swan,* more to the centre of the town and one of the larger hostelries. *The Swan* was almost certainly one of Stony Stratford's premier inns at the time and would probably rival the Cock as such but it was destroyed in the great fire of 1742 and there are no medieval remains to inspect.

I am inclined to support Browne Willis in this. The royal party accompanying Edward must have been large. Contemporary estimates talk about 2,000 men, and even if that was an exaggeration the retinue would need plenty of accommodation. It is possible, probable even, that the retinue was accommodated in several inns, but one feels almost certain that the head of the party, the new king in waiting, would not be shunted off to a smaller minor inn up the street. He would have to be at the centre of things. Therefore it makes better sense to believe that he stayed at one of the larger hostelries. It may have been *The Swan.* Of course a plaque on the wall of a 15th century building looks much more attractive than a plaque on the ground marking the approximate spot.

Archaeology will probably help us, when and if the work can be done. Dendrochronological analysis on timbers in the building can give us an earlier date, and deeper excavations across Stony Stratford may unearth some medieval foundations.

Manno's Manor

1 Feet of Fines Northants. 30 Edward I, no. 415.

2 Inquisitions Post Mortem 19 Edw IV m. 17. Oct 14 Woburn

3 Lucy Toulmin Smith. The Itinerary of John leland in or about the Years 1535-1543, Vol II, p.23

4 Bodleian. MSS. dd. Radcl.. Deed 270

5 Bodleian. MSS. dd. Radcl.. Deeds 345, 148, 499

6 F.E. Hyde. The Growth of a Town, Part II

7 Patent Rolls, 24 Edw. III.

8 Desmond Seward. Richard III, England's Black legend. Country Life Books, 1983. p. 93.

SEVEN

THE LONGUEVILLE ASCENDANCY

1485 is generally taken in England to mark the end of the middle ages. The year marked the end of the Plantagenet dynasty and founded a new one with Henry Tudor. It also suited Tudor propaganda to present this as a new age, and beneath the propaganda there was a germ of truth in the idea. There were currents of change in western Europe, in Italy in particular, but these were slow to reach these shores and it was not really until the reign of Henry VIII that England began to shed the intellectual encumbrances of the middle ages. Henry himself and many of his ministers had been schooled in the new Humanism and were themselves beginning to think in new ways. Scholasticism, the name given to the medieval application of reason and logic to explain the ways of God to man, was now beginning to share the intellectual stage with Humanism which sought to explain the role of the individual within God's universe.

The upshot was to encourage a new spirit of enquiry and in this period, now known as the Renaissance, people embarked on voyages of discovery, undertook scientific enquiry and challenged the established way of doing things. In this new age a man like John Leland, who visited Wolverton on his travels, wrote down his observations (scant as they were) whereas men of earlier generations had not thought to do so. Geoffrey Chaucer, for example, who travelled widely in France and Italy, learned a great deal but it did not occur to him for one moment to keep a record. Travel in this new century could be undertaken for its own sake, as indeed it was in later centuries.

These currents trickled down to Wolverton and as we shall explore through the dissolution of the monasteries, the Reformation and land enclosure. The former left the English treasury considerably richer, but it also opened up possibilities for a rising middle class who could, within a generation, become wealthy and powerful.

The End of Bradwell Priory

For almost 400 years Wolverton had its own monastery. Baron Meinfelin had parcelled off one hide of the manor and given it to the Black

Manno's Manor

Monks as a foundation for the priory that would take the name of Bradwell. This Priory, as we have seen, was never a very rich or great establishment but it did have its influence on Wolverton. It had been given the living of Holy Trinity Church quite early in its history, which meant that over this entire period it was able to use the tithes as revenue and appoint the vicar. The Priors probably had some moral influence in the community.

Outside the manor there may have been little interest. Bradwell produced no saints and apparently owned no relics to attract pilgrims. It was off the beaten track and there may have been no demand for its use as a hostelry, which was customary in those days. The growth of Stony Stratford with its cluster of inns made it unnecessary to make a detour to nearby Bradwell, so revenue which might have typically gone to the monastery was diverted to the commercial sector. In summary the handful monks at Bradwell priory were probably pursuing their vocation, uninterested in the needs of the outside world.

There are no reports of corruption at Bradwell at any time in its history. Priors were occasionally chided for ineffectiveness or poor leadership but there was never at any time criticism of the kind that was sometimes applied to other monasteries - operating brothels, exploitation of the peasants, or of abbots and priors amassing personal wealth.

Nevertheless Bradwell, despite its blameless existence, was caught up in the great wave of reform that took place in the 16th century which resulted in the evetual dissolution of all monasteries. Much blame has been heaped on the heads of Henry VIII and his ministers by supporters of the church who have tended to represent their actions in extreme terms, but a more sober assessment 500 years after the event might lead us to the view that monasteries had lost their usefulness to society. Certainly many contemporaries thought so because Henry and Thomas Cromwell acting alone would never have pulled it off. It was certainly a bold move and masterfully executed by the brilliant Thomas Cromwell, but it could not have been achieved without a groundswell of support across the land. There were pockets of resistance of course and the default position of most people when confronted with change is to resist it, but on balance, the generality of opinion, at least amongst those who mattered, was that it was a necessary reform.

The Longueville Ascendancy

Bradwell's fate was sealed somewhat earlier that the general dissolution of 1536.

In 1524 the priory lands and revenues were granted to Cardinal Wolsey to help him in his great project of building Christchurch College, Oxford. This probably did not contribute very much money but Wolsey was scratching around for every source of available cash for his ambitious and expensive undertaking. This would not be the last time Wolverton had contributed to an Oxford institution. Sir John Longueville, who made the grant, did so *in jure fundator* provided that a chaplain said a mass for himself and his ancestors, either at Bradwell or at the new chapel at Christ Chruch. Obviously this was an undertaking that could be freely given and accepted by both parties, but when it came down to it the transaction was about money. Wolsey acquired some income and Sir John kept the church at Wolverton and its tithes. At this time this not only included Holy Trinity but also St Mary Magdalene at Stony Stratford. Sir John was probably quite pleased with the transaction; he had improved his income and at the same time had embellished the credentials of his immortal soul.

The priory therefore was suppressed in 1524 because after this date is no longer functioned as such. The Prior and monks were either pensioned off or found a living elsewhere. It was a small manor of about 400 acres. After Wolsey's death it fell into the hands of the crown and in 1531 was granted to the Priory of Sheen in exchange for the manors of Lewisham and Greenwich. At this date Thomas Rowse was the tenant and his annual rental was £24. After Sheen was suppressed in 1539 the Bradwell estate once more reverted to the crown, who administered it for four years until 1543 when it was granted to Arthur Longueville, son of Sir John, who had died in 1541. After this the priory was converted into a house and it became known as Bradwell Abbey.

A paragraph or two here should be applied to the Priory of Luffield which also has a Wolverton connection. It was founded in 1133 and thus the first monastic foundation in Buckinghamshire. Robert de Bossu, Earl of Leicester was its founder. Hamo, the son of Baron Meinfelin, took an interest in this Priory and made an endowment of one hide in Thornborough in the reign of Henry II. This was confirmed by his grandson William in 1242.[1] A few months later in October, William's son Hugh quitclaimed his interest forever for the sum of 5 marks of silver from

Manno's Manor

the Prior. By 1279 the Priory had 5½ hides (about one third of the manor) and the church at Thornborough, so there were probably some later bequests.

The Luffield Priory was also Benedictine and was senior to Bradwell, so when the Bradwell Priory got into difficulties it was taken under the wing of Luffield. However, even Luffield had difficulty making ends meet and its suppression preceded that of Bradwell by 30 years. The last prior left in 1494 for Abingdon.

The priory of Chicksand at Dunstable also had a Wolverton interest which can be noted here. The priory itself was founded in 1150, about the same time that Meinfelin founded the Priory of Bradwell. Here the similarities end, for while Bradwell was never well-endowed and limped along as a small impecunious priory until the 16th century, Chicksand was large and wealthy, at least in its first century. The institution supported as many as 100 canons, nuns and lay brothers until 1250 when it got into financial difficulties and was forced to scale down its operation. Somewhere during this period it acquired some land in Wolverton. There are some 13th century deeds which refer to lands next to or abutting the land of the Prior of Chicksand. These are all in the east of Wolverton so exactly where it was located or how much land was taken is hard to say, however there is some evidence that the place known as The Grange (now Manor Farm) was in the hands of a religious house.

What we do know is that this manor was redeemed by a merchant of Genoa in partial repayment of a debt. The priory had overreached itself in its borrowings and in 1325 had to find ways of meeting its obligations. What happened to it after the merchant of Genoa got his hands upon it is unknown, or at least unclear. There are several 14th century deeds which make reference to land "next to the Prior of Chicksands" that are dated well after 1325, so it may be that the Priory was able to redeem the debt from the merchant of Genoa, or the locals had become accustomed to referring to this land in this way long after it had been sold. At any rate It is likely that it was sold back to the de Wolvertons since the east side of the manor appears to be intact in later centuries when records are more coherent.

The Longueville Ascendancy

Chicksand Priory was dissolved quite late. It held on until 1538 and was sold by the King in 1540 to Richard Snowe and it had a long afterlife as a large country house.

The priory at Snelshall occupied part of the land around Tattenhoe. It was also Benedictine but not a Wolverton foundation. There are some Wolverton deeds surviving which made some small bequests to this Priory. It was, as it turned out, even poorer than Bradwell. Bishop Burghershe, visiting in 1321, described the priory as so poor that it barely had the necessities of life. It seems not to have supported more than three monks. Oddly enough, or perhaps because of its poverty, it never got into debt like some of the richer monasteries. It may have found other ways of getting by. In 1529, another Bishop's visitation found several "irregularities" and commanded the Prior to dismiss all women from the precincts of the monastery. The Prior probably cleaned up his act because in 1535, the year of dissolution, no immorality was noted. The buildings were described as "wholly in ruin" but the priory had no debt. The Prior, William Maltby, was given an annual pension of £5, a comfortable figure in those day. The other monks were provided for.

Snellshall seems to have had no future after 1535. The land must have had some value, but the buildings were not worth saving and in time they disappeared.

The Reformed Church

The last fifteen years of the reign of Henry VIII instigated a long period of social upheaval that was to last until the closing years of the Longueville's tenure on Wolverton. The axis of discord was religion which swung from conservative catholic to reforming protestantism and occasionally reached some tolerable equilibrium. Like several other country families in North Bucks the Longuevilles remain staunchly Roman Catholic. Certainly they were sensible enough to keep their heads down and it was the policy of Elizabeth's reign to tolerate catholic practice by the gentry as long as it did not lead to sedition. On practical advantage of this policy was that spymasters like Sir Francis Walsingham could keep an eye on potential dissidents.

Common folk had no choice in the matter. Once the common prayer book was officially adopted and the catholic mass made illegal, those who

Manno's Manor

attended Holy Trinity and St Mary Magdalen were presented with the official state version of Christianity. The Longueville family may have attended these services as part of their public duty and arranged a private mass for themselves. Since there is no record of recusancy or transgression, we must assume that their policy of lying low and avoiding troublemakers was successful The Digbys, living nearby in Gayhurst, would have been well-known to the Longuevilles but there is no evidence they were tempted to join the disastrous Gunpower Plot of 1605.

The fortunes of Holy Trinity Church were tied to the priory until its dissolution. After the Priory was acquired by Arthur Longueville the church was reunited with the Wolverton Manor for the first time since the 12th century.

The vicars appointed by the Longuevilles during this uncertain period show a remarkable stability. George Turner was appointed in 1546 and remained until his death in 1587. He was succeeded by Ralph Langford until his death in 1596 and the next incumbent, Robert Reynolds lasted until 1631. So for almost 100 years the vicars must have satisfactorily met the needs of the congregation and the Longuevilles.

The church, and the income associated with it, had a different and slightly more intricate history of ownership. It came into crown ownership in 1531 and was leased to various parties. The rectory was granted to Sir John Spencer in 1599. His daughter and heir, Elizabeth, married William Compton who became Earl of Northampton. The lease of the property was sold back to Sir Henry Longueville in 1601. The Earls of Northampton retained this interest until 1737, when it was sold to Brazenose College, Oxford.

The 16th and 17th centuries may not have been prosperous ones for the vicars of Holy Trinity with revenues from the rectory and the church being siphoned off by other interests. Some attempt to simplify matters was agreed in 1656. The Earl of Northampton assigned his rights to the Lord of the Manor in return for a perpetual rent charge of £100 per annum. The Lord of the Manor allotted land to the value of £50 to the Vicar in exchange for his abandoning rights to the tithe. Six years later, the Longuevilles, in their continued zeal for land enclosure, went back on the agreement and appropriated the land allotted to the Parson and paid him instead £40 per annum. The vicars were now entirely dependent for their

The Longueville Ascendancy

income on the Lord of the Manor. This income was reduced to £30 when Thomas Evans became incumbent in 1702. In the meantime, the Lords of the Manor, the Longueville family, were busy enclosing land and depopulating Wolverton Manor.

We can also see the disruption of the 17th century Civil War in the dates of the vicars. In 1645 the incumbent was Robert Ladbroke, who was replaced in that year by Gilbert Newton. Newton, presumably, was acceptable to the Puritan regime, but not to the High Church Anglicans, or perhaps even to the Longuevilles, because he was replaced in 1660, the year of the Restoration, by Robert Bostock. Wholesale turnover was common enough amongst priests at this time and some who had been dispossessed in 1649 were returned to their former benefices. Bostock only lasted a year due to some unwise remarks about MPs , apparently calling them "precious rogues".[2] Such remarks, however near the truth they might have been, were not acceptable and he was dispossessed. Robert Duncumbe, his successor, held the position until he died.

The Longuevilles were known Royalist supporters, although Sir Edward's wife, Margaret, was from the Temple family of Stowe, and they were Parliamentary supporters. and indeed contributed large amounts of money to the doomed cause of King Charles I, but these dates suggest that they yielded to puritan pressure on matters of religion during the Commonwealth years.

The Enclosures

When we last looked at Wolverton's medieval landscape we saw very different agricultural patterns. Medieval agriculture was undertaken in open fields where each peasant had traditional rights to grow and harvest crops in strips. The fields were "open" in the sense that they were not enclosed by hedgerows, but there was in no sense a free-for-all. Strips of land were passed down through generations, usually on payment of an entry fine. Thereafter the peasant was entitled to make use of the land allotted to him by custom and everyone knew where the boundaries were. Some peasants had acquired more land rights than other over centuries and some were landless labourers working for day wages. Sheep and cattle were driven out to graze on "waste" (land that was hard to cultivate), sometimes

Manno's Manor

known as common land. Common rights were critical to the peasant economy; without them it was hard to maintain livestock.

The Tudor period witnessed the beginning of land enclosures which continued to the 18th century. What we now see as a familiar pattern of fields and hedgerows in the countryside was developed during these centuries.

In the 16th century common rights were held by all the residents of the manor, that is the inhabitants of the village of Wolverton and outlying cottages and the fifty or so dwellings on the east side of the Watling Street. Every level of the economy was dependent on agriculture and there was probably nobody on the Wolverton manor who was not in some way connected with agriculture. Even the vicar had to depend on growing some of his own food and the field known as Parson's Piece is an indicator of that. The Cock Inn, as another example, had, like the other inns, land stretching for a few acres to the east behind the inn and effectively ran a smallholding which could be used to supply food for the travelling public.

Enclosure began very early in Wolverton, probably to the lasting infamy of the Longuevilles who were assiduous in using their power to bring about this change. Because of this there were no parliamentary survey of the land as there were for manors that brought about enclosure later in the 18th and 19th centuries and as Hyde has pointed out, this has made some difficulty for our understanding of open field and common land usage in Wolverton prior to the 16th century enclosure. It is difficult to generalise from so little information but the situation at 1500 was probably a mixed picture. Over the 400 years following the Conquest parcels of land had been granted under varying conditions. The use of the word sale in this context is difficult because all land technically belonged to the king and was granted to his tenant in chief in return for future military service. The tenant in turn had granted certain rights to land in return for services that he required and that was the basis for the so-called feudal system. It was a system that required very little money to make it work. But land transaction since that time had become as complex as the different people engaging in the bargain, as has been described in the earlier chapter. Without knowing the exact distribution of land and right we can infer that most of these parcels clustered on the east side of the Watling Street, in use by the commercial establishments there.

The Longueville Ascendancy

Besides these pieces, which might be grouped as Stony Stratford Townlands, the open field system which had developed in the middle ages spread itself across the manor, leaving the marshy land by the River Ouse and the higher scrub land as commons.

The enclosures began in a tentative manner. George Longueville tried to annex a piece of land towards the end of the 15th century which "had long been within the custom" of the villagers. The piece of land is not specified but it was probably contiguous to the lord's demesne. His kinsman and successor Sir John Longueville began in a more determined fashion by enclosing 8 acres from Barr Piece, 10 acres from Barr Close together with an additional 7 acres. The intention behind this land grab was to make a park to hunt in. There were subsequent complaints about later annexations, "taking an acre of land lying at Mile Bushen in the field of Wolverton." And then another acre of meadowland adjoining the mill "which land has been time out of mind lying to the said house until Sir John Longueville took it and withheld it." In another report of 1530 he enclosed 10 acres around the present site of Bushfield School. These were small encroachments compared to what was to happen later.[3]

When his sons came of age they too continued the policy. Thomas, the eldest, enclosed 32 acres in a field called the Diggins, but he appears to have had an attack of conscience and revoked the action on his deathbed. But when his brother Arthur succeeded to the estates in 1541 he promptly re-enclosed the land and in 1554 enclosed another 50 acres in the Stacey Bushes area. However, he also relented and re-opened that field.

His son, Henry, was more determined. In 1566 he enclosed those lands that had formerly been enclosed and in 1579-80 enclosed a 158 acre tract of land known as the Furzes, some part of which was used for Wolverton housing in the 20th century. Furze Way, for example, takes its name from that ancient tract of land. These combined actions took some 250 acres out of common usage, to all intents a complete farm.

Clearly exasperated at losing their commons rights some of the inhabitants of Wolverton and Stony Stratford petitioned the Lord Chancellor in 1584. Three men had the courage to make the petition, Thomas Furtho, John Hinders and Christopher Carne. This event is also important in the history of Wolverton because it marks a significant change in the demographic; people who in the past would not have been listened

Manno's Manor

to now had a voice, and the resources to pursue their grievance. Men like Furtho and Hinders style themselves "esquires", almost certainly landholders, but of a lesser degree to the ancient family of Longueville. Christopher Carne was an innkeeper. They were men of some standing who could afford to register their complaint in law.

This petition provides us with the history of the earlier attempts by the Longueville family to annexe land. Folk memory lasted a long time in these pre-industrial communities and in this document they were able to remember the first enclosure some 56 years before the petition.

The complaint recounted the history of the land, its first enclosure, the death bed repentance of Sir Thomas Longueville, the reclaiming of this land by Arthur Longueville, "being moved by the sinister persuasion of certain evil disposed persons", his retraction for 14 years and the to the substance of the suit.

After presenting these early incursions on the commons as acts which their perpetrators later repented he petition goes on to outline the particular encroachments of Henry Longueville in detail. Sir Henry was quite unwilling to listen to reason and had resorted to bullying tactics to enforce his will. Collectively the commons had been able to feed 200 cattle and allow 1000 sheep out to pasture and the area of land was able to sustain this number. The consequence of Sir Henry's action was to restrict them to 400 sheep and 50 cattle at the maximum. This had a serious affect on their livelihood. One family, if they could afford it, might own a cow which could keep them supplied with milk butter and cheese and cash for the surplus. The more important people heading the petition presumably had more at stake but it is safe to say that everyone would be affected.When reasonable persuasion was closed to them they broke down fences to allow their animals access to the former common land. Sir Henry responded by hiring thugs ("unknown or poor persons") to drive off and harass the cattle and make threats against the cattle owners and indeed kill those cattle found on Sir Henry's newly annexed land.

Appeals to local justice were of little avail as Sir Henry, as Justice of the Peace, was the law in those parts. The petitioners were helpless, and in many ways desperate.

They also describe Sir Henry's action in raising the banks of the millrace, causing flooding of 30 acres of meadow land, the result of which

The Longueville Ascendancy

was to either ruin or deplete hay crops and, because of the soggy nature of the ground, made it impossible to take a cart into the meadow.

The petition speaks to us clearly after 400 years with the voice of men who were conscious of their ancient rights and who were desperately worried about the economic impact of Sir Henry's unilateral actions. It tells us about a society where power was still invested in the hands of a few and that the right of men of lesser status in society could still be ignored. The petitioners, who were not as we have noted common peasants, had obviously reached a point where there was no alternative but to try to get the ear of a higher authority.

It appears that their complaint was upheld, one assumes at some cost to the litigants. Justice always came at a cost. There are no follow up documents to make clear how the judgement was enforced, but we can assume that some kind of equilibrium must have been restored because no issues surface until 50 years later. At this time the enclosures were finally and ruthlessly effected. It does appear that Christopher Carne at any rate was compensated.[4]

Christopher Carne was granted by Queen Elizabeth I, a messuage in Stony Stratford called the White House, near the Butts with a piece of ground adjoining.[5] A further description of this property is given in a deed dated March 10th 1595, by which Carne leased to George Clark 'a parcel of ground in Butt Close with a hay house of two bays, bounded by the Queen's highway in the east and by Thomas Swain's land and new house on the south, together with common rights in Calverton at a rent of 4 marks a year.' In 1664 this property was sold to Thomas Rabone who in turn sold to James Mansell in 1623.[6]

Before I go on to the next phase which is usually presented as a dramatic picture of mass evictions from the land we should take note of a kind of census that was undertaken in Elizabethan times. In 1563 Lord Burghley charged the bishops with the task of recording information about their parishes. The number of churches and clergy were recorded along with the number of household in each parish. In this year Wolverton had 31 households and there were a further 30 recorded in Stony Stratford East. To put this figure into perspective, Loughton had 29 households, Calverton 26 , Bradwell 16 and Great Linford 31. In other words the rural population of the Wolverton manor was about the same as several other

Manno's Manor

manors in the area. If we apply a multiplier of 5 per family this yields a population of about 150 - a figure not too far off the population estimate of 200 in 1086, which most likely included families living along side the Watling Street. Should this surprise us? I think not. Agricultural technology had improved little over five centuries and even with additional land brought under cultivation there was a limit to the numbers that could be supported by a manor. There had been a great increase in the 14th century due to the warmer climate in those year, but the sudden and unexpected arrival of the great plague of 1349 reduced the population by as much as 40% in some places. Economic historians estimate that it took until 1700 before the population recovered its 1349 level.

What we can take from these figures is that Wolverton village population and the east side of Stony Stratford were roughly equivalent. When we next get figures in 1801 Wolverton had 238 recorded inhabitants and 67 families living in 46 houses. The east side of Stony Stratford had doubled in the meantime with 528 inhabitants made up of 104 families living in 104 houses.

We might deduce from this that the agricultural activity of 1801 still required a similar number of people as in 1563, before enclosure. Enclosure certainly had a disruptive effect on the way people farmed the land, but it may have made little difference to the numbers. We should bear in mind that the technology of farming had made little progress in those 150 years.

The final phase of the enclosures occurred around 1654 when Sir Edward Longueville was Lord of the manor, chiefly, it appears from report, at the instigation of his wife Margaret. At this date the Longuevilles abandoned their policy of incremental enclosure and annexed all of it, with the exception of those parcels in Stony Stratford which had already been enclosed and had defined leases. The inhabitants of the village were ruthlessly deprived of their livelihood, with the exception of the few who could continue to work as labourers for the Longuevilles. The medieval settlement in low park was demolished and all that remains on the site are the ridges and furrows that indicate the earlier presence of a settlement. We should perhaps bear in mind that the Longuevilles were at the time in somewhat straitened circumstances due to their heavy commitment to the royalist cause in the Civil War and may have acted with more ruthlessness

The Longueville Ascendancy

than they might have in more affluent times. Not a bit of this mitigation would have impressed the villagers who were uprooted from their homes, and in some cases from their traditional livelihoods. There was probably some compensation, although this is unrecorded, and was probably little enough. Some may have found employment on the manor for low wages, but many would have had to find new ways of making a living in Stony Stratford. Dame Margaret's name was infamous in the popular mind.

If we now take the longer view we can see that enclosure had its advantages. Strip farming had come into being because of the limitations of the plough, a simple wooden mold board drawn by oxen. Turning was difficult, so the idea of ploughing square fields developed only from the combination of the iron plough share and the breeding of horses to draw a plough. Once these two came together a plough team could be much more manoeuvrable. In 1500 strip farming was still the norm on the Wolverton manor, with the higher ground and some of the ouse meadows being used for pasture. Strips were wasteful of land because each strip required a division between neighbours which essentially took land out of production. The idea of using the land more efficiently took a long time to bring into practice.

By itself this knowledge was not an impetus for change. If the old ways could continue to support the population adequately then there would be no compelling reason to modify agricultural practices. However, there were external factors which drove economic change. Prime among these was inflation. The import of plentiful supplies of gold into Spain from the Americas, starting as a trickle, but by 1530 becoming a flood, had the overall effect of devaluing gold in Europe. Prices started to go up as more gold (and silver from German mines) purchased less. The classic laws of supply and demand operated except that no government at the time had any mechanism to control inflation. Goods and services cost more, therefore more money was required. Governments responded (and certainly the government of Henry VIII) by debasing the coinage, that is by adding a greater percentage of base metal to silver coins. The effect was devaluation.

The consequence of this was most keenly felt by the lord of the manor who was the prime purchaser of manufactured goods. His need for more money resulted in increasing rents where he could. Eventually these

Manno's Manor

pressures trickled down to the peasant working the land. His costs went up while his productivity remained the same and this last fact placed limits upon the rent that could be charged.

The idea of enclosure must then have seemed like an inspired solution to the Longuevilles and others like them. They may have been better placed than many rural manors by having the trade of the Watling Street, but there must have been a limit even to that source of income. The 16th century enclosures were mostly about pasture land. The principal reason for this was that more money could be made from grazing sheep than by tilling arable land. Arable farming, although essential, was subject to the arbitrary whims of the weather, and when harvests were poor, and therefore prices high, the government would not allow corn to be sold abroad. Farmers and landlords were therefore restricted to a fixed income from their crops. Wool, on the other hand, could be sold in any year at the prevailing price and was a dependable source of income regardless of the weather. The Spencer family of Northamptonshire built their great fortune on sheep farming.

The temptation for the Longuevilles was obvious. Enclosing the higher ground in Wolverton, the Furzes, enabled their tenants to rear sheep on what was hitherto unproductive land and make a good deal more money into the bargain.

The enclosure of the Wolverton manor proceeded at a stuttering pace throughout the 16th century and one might deduce that the Longuevilles were not so hard up that they could not afford to relax their land reform. It was only after the civil war of the 17th century when Sir Edward Longueville, who had invested a considerable amount of money in supporting the losing cause of Charles I, took stock of his situation and realised that enclosure was the only way forward that the action became irrevocable. Sir Edward was out of favour after 1649 and had no scope for enjoying the proceeds of some lucrative office of state, even at the county level. Those perquisites were snaffled up by the supporters of Oliver Cromwell. It took them five years to realise that this policy could rescue the family; they could have had no way of knowing in 1654 that the monarchy would return.

The Longueville Ascendancy

Farms

The tenant farmer was from this time a new and important figure in Wolverton. Probably these tenants emerged from some of the larger smallholders on the estate whose families had acquired more land over the centuries and who already employed men to work their land. The difference in 1654 was that they took on contiguous blocks of land which could then be enclosed by hedgerows. Most of the later farms still functioning in the twentieth century date from this time.

Sir Edward retained the low park around the old manor house for himself. This was most likely the old lord's demesne and there is still today a long bulwark of earth dividing the low park from the northern farm now known as Manor Farm. This land also contained the old village and he probably retained some families to continue labouring on his land.

The old grange became the basis for Manor Farm, and one would guess that it only acquired the name Manor Farm after the old manor had gone in the 18th century. This farm had all the choice arable land and meadows in the north. Stonebridge House Farm, with its house beside Bradwell Brook emerged as a farm on the east side of the manor. Stacey Farm, which originally had a farm house and buildings beside Bradwell Brook on the north side, was most likely a new farm with most of the land given over to sheep pasture. From the 18th century papers we learn of at least two farm houses on the Watling Street, one of them later known as Brick Kiln Farm and there were three or four farms in the middle, one with a farm house and buildings where Wolverton Park house is now located, another near the old rabbit warren, another based on a site later taken by the railway works and possibly another on or near the site of Wolverton House.

These new farmers rented each rented between 100 and 400 acres so there were disparities of income, but between them they formed a middling group in the social structure of rural Wolverton with only the vicar and the lord above them in social status. They had to find large rents each year for Sir Edward and they all appear to have held long leases. Until the coming of the canal and later the railway this was the biggest change to the Wolverton landscape.

Manno's Manor

Michael Hipwell's Will

In the meantime a newer type of man was emerging in Stony Stratford. The entrepreneurial Edy family, whom we touched on in the previous chapter, created their wealth from the wool trade, which was still an agricultural product. However, Michael Hipwell, who drew up his will in 1609, was a different sort altogether. While he owned some land his principal earnings came from the inn trade and the properties he owned in Stony Stratford. It was a long and difficult document, but in it he made a number of bequests that were significant for Stony Stratford, in particular founding its first school. Michael Hipwell was a successful businessman who owned several hostelries and properties on both sides of the Watling Street. We would place him as a member of the rising middle classes of the 16th century. What is most remarkable about his will is that he takes it upon himself to act as a public benefactor and this marks a change from the period when the old knightly class were expected to perform such functions and the new mercantile class who were able to fulfill this role.

The tenor of the bequest changes too. Whereas 13th century men like William Vis de Lou and Hugh of Stratford made their bequests to the church with the assumption that all good would flow from this source, and 15th century figures like John Edy were similarly motivated, Michael Hipwell assumes direct responsibility for social improvement. He founds a school and allows income from some other properties to be used for the upkeep of Buckingham gaol.

It is perhaps also noteworthy in a negative sense that the Longuevilles do not make bequests of this kind. In the 16th and 17th centuries they are consumed with their own affairs, with land enclosure and consolidating their wealth. There were no (as far as I am aware) public bequests or charities of any kind. A lot of money was squandered in support of King Charles during the civil war and much after that by the last of the line, Sir Edward Longueville in the losing cause of James II. Not to be too unkind about it one would be hard pressed to think of a single legacy to Wolverton and Stony Stratford from the Longueville tenancy of 300 years.

Hipwell owned the *Rose and Crown* and some fields behind it. He also owned three houses on the west side including *The George*. He also held a lease on *The Swan* which he had re-named *The Swan with Two Necks* after he

The Longueville Ascendancy

became a member of the Vintner's Guild. He had an extensive family which he appears to take care of in his will

Hipwell was a man who had the confidence to think far into the future. His *Rose and Crown* charity was to employ the rental income from the inn and adjoining lands to employ a schoolmaster of good Christian standing and maintain a grammar school in the barn at the back of the *Rose and Crown*. His vision was justified, although it has to be noted from very scarce records that it was never as well funded as it needed to be, because in 1819, when the National School system was in place, it became the foundation for Stony Stratford's Church of England school.

The Longueville's Last Century

The 17th century witnessed a rise in the Longueville fortunes and a tragic collapse. Since the introduction of Sir John Longueville to the manor through his marriage to the heiress, the family had enjoyed a steady rise in fortune. Notwithstanding some of the economic difficulties of the 16th century the family faced the 17th century with only prosperity ahead of them Henry married Elizabeth Cotton from a family that made a rapid rise during the early Tudor period. They had lands in south east Hampshire and Huntingdonshire and were by this time quite prosperous. From the Longueville's perspective this was a good match.

Elizabeth was a healthy young woman who gave birth to at least seven children. Several of them made good marriages which brought the family powerful connections across the country. His eldest son Henry married Catharine, daughter of Sir Edward Carey of Aldenham in Hertfordshire. Thomas married a daughter of Leonard Sarjant of Cookham in Berkshire, Michael married into the Grey family who had established themselves as earls of Kent in the 15th century. Francis married a daughter and co-heir of Edward Furtho in neighbouring south Northamptonshire, which brought Cosgrove into Longueville hands and the sole daughter, Elizabeth, married Sir Nicholas Gascoigne of Huntingdonshire. This new network of marriages made the new century very promising.

The next generation, led by Sir Henry took them through the relatively placid years of the early 17th century until the civil war which was to engulf the nation, That had no small impact on Wolverton's leading family. Sir Edward, his son and heir, was a Roman Catholic and a staunch

Manno's Manor

The Longueville Baronetcy

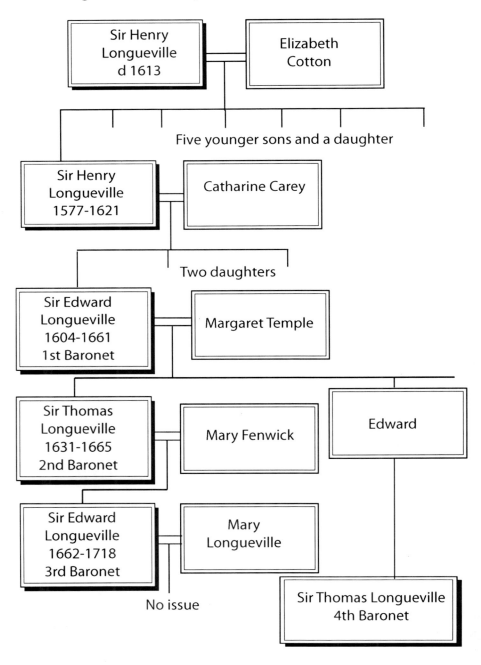

royalist who committed himself fully to the king's cause. His support was not merely ideological, but he went as far as to make monetary commitments. Raising arms for the king was expensive but it was probably even more expensive to be on the losing side, not only in fines and penalties but also in lost income. In 1643 he was captured and imprisoned at Grafton House and assessed a fine of £330. In 1646 he was fined £800, a large sum for those times. In 1650 he sold Bradwell Manor to pay the fine. And as noted in the last section it was probably the financial strain that impelled him to force the enclosures of 1654.

Sir Edward was made a baronet of Nova Scotia by Charles I in 1638. The baronet was at the time an entirely new creation and as the name suggests was low down in the order of precedence amongst the titled. It was James I's idea to create these baronetcies in the newly acquired territory of New Scotland, Nova Scotia, as a means to raise revenue, but it was not implemented until later in the reign of Charles I. The premium paid to the king was 1000 marks and there was a grant of land, at least up to 1638, so that the recipient could, in theory, recover his premium. The land grant ceased in 1638 and I am unclear as to whether Sir Edward got his baronetcy before the cut-off. It may have been an empty title.

This apparently made no difference to Sir Edward's zealous loyalty. Perhaps he hoped for preferment, and it might have come after the Restoration but for Sir Edward inconveniently dying in 1661 soon after Charles II came to the throne.

His son Thomas succeeded to the reduced estate. He had married an heiress, Mary Silvester of Iver in Buckinghamshire, which must have helped him to maintain some sort of style. However, there is no record of him as an office holder and he appears to have lived a quiet life, that is until he was thrown by his horse about a half mile away from his house. The exact spot is unknown, but the fall was fatal to the unlucky baronet who died from his injuries. The year was 1685.

The young Sir Edward, who was his only son, proved himself to be a man who preferred to spend rather than earn and he gradually dissipated the wealth of the Longuevilles. In addition he shared his grandfather's instinct for backing the losing side. The Longuevilles had retained their adherence to the Roman Catholic faith and the young Sir Edward was no less committed. In James II he would have seen a soul mate. In 1688 he

Manno's Manor

impetuously sold the manor of Little Billing to raise money for the king. It was a noble and generous act but it was part of his bad luck that the sale was immediately followed by James' army deserting him at Blackheath. James II was finished as king of England and Sir Edward Longueville was a poorer man. Over the next twenty years the estate drifted into decay.

The Manor House

Of the earlier buildings we know next to nothing. It is probable that the Longuevilles improved and enlarged the earlier medieval property during the 15th century. The only reference we have to the building is from the Tudor traveller and writer John Leland, who was passing through around 1540.

> The Langevilles of later tymes hath lyen and bilded fairly at Wolverstun in Bukinghamshie (nere Stony Streatford).[7]

We can only interpret "bilded fairly" as that the house was of sufficient size for Leland to take notice.

Later in the century Sir Henry Longueville decided to embark on his own building project at a cost of £12,000 - a very significant sum of money. This was in 1586. Once again we are short of any drawing or description until Thomas Hearne, writing in 1711 tells us this much:

> It stood near a large mount, thrown up East of the Church, & it was a magnificent Edifice, being 145 Feet in length & built with good Free-stone. It had 9 large transome windows in the Front, of good polished Free-stone which was very regular; it had in the first Range a spacious lofty Kitchen, Buttery, Hall & Great Parlour, in which last room were painted in the large Escucheons (sic), the Arms of the Longueville Family with their matches quartered & impaled. There were also some arms in the windows of painted glass; particularly of Wolverton & Roche: the first of which bore, B. an Eagle displayed A determined by a Bendlet G. K. the other, viz. Roche, gave G. 3 Roaches A. This front part, as seems to me, built by Sir Hen Longueville in Queen Elizabeth's time: and Sir Henry & his lady Elizabeth Cotton's Arms, being placed there in 2 Shields, with this date, 1586, seems as if they were the builders, and that it was begun to be built then; it cost, as I have been informed, above 12 thousand

The Longueville Ascendancy

pounds in those days. At each end were several Rooms of an antient tower structure, which were chiefly made use of, & particularly those on the south wing, by Sir Edward Longueville. I visited him in 1711: & several rooms in the new building were never finished, or properly furnished, as appeared to me.

There is also a document in the Nottinghamshire archive which was prepared about the same time for a sale prospectus. It is able to offer us some supporting (although in places conflicting) detail.

The House is 60 yards in front with two Wings about 15 yards in lenght (sic). Built of Stone is very Strong & in perfect good repair. The Gallary which is a very noble one, the floore was never layed down, all offices that are necessary as Wash houses, Brew house, dary house, larders, Granarys, Wood Barns, Stables for 20 horse, Coach House with 20 Bay of Barning with a Worke House, two Duffcoates & several Houses very necessary for any use in good repair.[8]

We can read from these two accounts that the house was stone built with a frontage of 180 feet (Hearne says 145) with two wings at each side of 45 feet. It is not clear which of the "offices" are included in the wings of the great house but it is probable, given the size of the stables and coach house, that these and almost certainly the dovecotes are separate structures. From Hearne's description we might infer that the kitchen and buttery (larder) made up one wing of the building. I am guessing that a second floor gallery was designed around either the hall or the "great parlour" but that this floor was never completed, although this phrase never layed down is open to different interpretations.

Hearne's observations are probably accurate but his interpretations can be modified. The window displaying the date of 1586 is more likely to have been the completion date rather than the date building began; windows are usually the last part of house building. His observation that the greater part of the building seemed unfurnished may have more to do with Sir Edward's straitened circumstances than the fact that the building was not completed and that he had been selling off furniture to pay debts and was confining himself to one wing of the building. £12,000 was an enormous sum of money to spend on a house in Elizabethan times, and even if that sum had been exaggerated, there should have been plenty of

Manno's Manor

money to complete the building to the satisfaction of Sir Henry and his wife.

The sketch below is a representation of the architecture of the period with only Hearne's notes as a guide. We do not know the placement or orientation of the building but as Hearne writes of a south wing one would guess that the western aspect overlooks the valley. It was probably built to the west of the old motte, but within the bounds of the Norman bailey.

Possible appearance of the 1586 Manor

We are told in the Nottingham Archive document that the building was strongly built, which doesn't quite square with the fate of the building in 1726. It is impossible to say who wrote this document. If it had been prepared by one of Sir Edward's men as a prospectus then a certain amount of puffery might be expected. In any event, only a few years later, the Radcliffe trustees took a different view. In a letter dated 24th October 1715 William Bromley (one of the Trustees) wrote in a letter that "the Great House was: very ruinous, & since it is now never likes to be used as a Gentleman's Seat you'll consider whether it may not be advisable that it be taken down, & the materials disposed of."[9]

Many of the buildings on the estate were in poor state of repair and when it came time to rebuild the Vicarage this course of action

The Longueville Ascendancy

recommended itself to the Trustees. Parts of the old mansion can be found in the Vicarage which is still standing today.

The following year, 1712 he sold the entire manor to Dr. John Radcliffe for £40,000. It was the close of another 300 year chapter in the history of the manor. Having paid off his debts Sir Edward carried on with the cash he had left, and presumably did not hold back on his taste for the pursuit of pleasure.

He had six more years to live. Unluckily, he met the same fate as his father. He was thrown from his horse during a race at Bicester and thus met his end. The date was 28th August 1718.

The 17th century, which had begun so promisingly for the Longuevilles, thus petered out in a run of bad luck. Sir Edward had no children to succeed him and the baronetcy passed to a cadet branch of the family and it appears that even this baronetcy has become extinct once male heirs dried up completely.

With his debts paid off Sir Edward was able to embark on the next phase of his life with sufficient funds to see out the rest of his days in some comfort. He settled in Fritwell in Oxfordshire, some 10 miles west of Buckingham. Fritwell kept him close to his old haunts and lifestyle and enabled him to live comfortably within his means. Most of this manor had been parcelled into smaller estates, which probably meant that there was a reasonable supply of fair size but not grand houses which could be managed with a small number of servants.

One might also assume that Sir Edward sold a lot of his house contents prior to his move to Fritwell. Again no record of this survives. So either these records went with him or were left in the house, only to be disposed of a few years later when the house was torn down.

Sir Edward married a cousin Marie Longueville. It appears to have been a loveless marriage. There were no children from the marriage and it seems likely that after the Wolverton estate was sold the two of them parted company; he to Fritwell and she to Aspley in Bedfordshire. I assume that he made some settlement with her because she is not mentioned in Sir Edward's will. Instead, after making some bequests to some cousins, he left everything to his companion Dorothy Godfrey who was living with him at the time at Fritwell.

Manno's Manor

His widow remarried a year later to a Mr John Lawton of Lawton in Cheshire.

The documents inherited by Dr John Radcliffe and his Trust after 1713 provide us with a lot of useful information about the Wolverton Manor stretching back to the 13th century. In one respect however they are the wrong kind of documents. Those that were passed on or kept by the Trust are all legal documents, together with the occasional letter. There are no household or estate account books that survive from the 17th century or earlier. We must assume that either they were kept by Sir Edward, or, if they were passed on, were later destroyed.

This is a pity. Household account books, even from the 17th century, would have given us some idea of the staff that the Longuevilles retained in order to manage such a large house and estate. Estate rental books might have added some flesh to our description of the Wolverton estate in the time of the Longuevilles. Bills for the repair of the house and outlying properties may also have told us more about the house itself.

---

1 Feet of Fines Bucks 26 Hen III, 2.

2 Mentioned in Oliver Ratcliff. History and Antiquities of the Newport Hundreds. Olney: Cowper Press, 1900

3 Summary and quotations taken from the 1580 petition to Sir Thomas Bromley, Lord Chancellor.

4 See Hyde Town Development II p 195n

5 MSS in Aylesbury Museum Nov 1584.

6 The land and house are identifiable in Radcliffe MSS Dep. D (521) 1638,

7 Lucy Toulmin Smith. The Itinerary of John leland in or about the Years 1535-1543, Vol II, p.23

8 Bodleian. MSS. dd. Radcl. c. 15. (This document is a hand written copy made by William Cole a century later.)

9 Bodleian. MSS. dd. Radcl.. c. 66 Letter, 24 October 1715

EIGHT

THE 18TH. CENTURY AND THE RADCLIFFE TRUST

In 1713 Dr John Radcliffe, the most eminent physician of his day, purchased the Wolverton Manor from the extravagant and hard-up Sir Edward Longueville. The sale marked an important transition for Wolverton, because for the first time ever, the manor had a non-resident landlord, and within a year that non-resident landlord had died and the manor thereafter was managed by a Trust.

Radcliffe became very wealthy through his fame as a doctor and by the time of his death had amassed a large fortune. In the last few years of his life he started to spend some of it and the purchase of the manor for £40,000 not only enabled him to make a shrewd investment with a good return on capital but also to re-enter Parliament as an eligible MP for Buckingham.

Sadly, years of heavy drinking with his cronies had taken its toll on his physical health, and at the time of the purchase had not very much life left in him. Within a year of the purchase Dr Radcliffe died and as far as we know had little to do with his new manor but in his will he set up a Trust that still bears his name and which had a long term impact on Wolverton. After Radcliffe's death this Trust used his bequest to build several institutions at Oxford where Radcliffe studied for many years. These were the Radcliffe Library, the Radcliffe Infirmary and the Radcliffe Observatory.

The library, which is still a prominent landmark off Oxford's Broad Street and Catte Street, and now known as the Radcliffe Camera, was built between 1737 and 1749. It was designed by the architect James Gibbs. It is a circular building placed in a quadrangle, designed so that the windows at all times during the day could admit light for reading. It is still in use today. £40,000 was allocated to the cost of construction and the Trust maintained the library for 178 years, both provisioning it with books and staffing the institution. In the mid-19th century the original building was having difficulty coping with the expanding number of volumes, so when the University was able to build a new museum along Parks Road both parties agreed to relocate all the scientific books and journals to the new building, which henceforth became the Radcliffe Science Library. The old building, now used as a reading room for arts books, became known as the Radcliffe Camera. Eventually the management and funding of libraries exceeded the Trust's ability to continue its support and in 1927 an agreement was made with the University to transfer the freehold of the Radcliffe Camera, although the Trust continued to contribute £1500 a year towards the cost of operation.

The Radcliffe Library in 1755 - engraving from a drawing by John Donowell

The second project, more modest in cost, but equally far reaching in its impact, was a new hospital, The Radcliffe Infirmary. It was built on donated land about half a mile out of Oxford as it then was for a total cost of £12,791. The original estimate was £4,000, but as is the case with all building projects the budget ballooned. The Radcliffe Trust took on the responsibility for repairs and building additions while the operating costs for the hospital came through donations and through free services given by Oxford physicians. Modern medical practice has far outstripped the relatively modest provisions of the 18th century building and even in the early 20th century the Trust was hard pressed to keep up. They were to some degree saved by the timely intervention of William Morris who had made

The 18th. Century and the Radcliffe Trust

an enormous fortune in the early motor industry. He was able to contribute substantially to the infirmary and when a new hospital was built at Headington, this was given Radcliffe's name while the old infirmary became the Nuffield Institute for Medical Research.

The Radcliffe Infirmary 1821, watercolour by J.C. Buckler

The last of these great Oxford institutions was the Radcliffe Observatory, built in the grounds of the Infirmary a few years later. This project was probably not in Dr. Radcliffe's mind but the trustees identified a need and had the resources to build it. The observatory continued to be used until 1934, when the problem of light pollution made it impractical. The building was sold and a new observatory built outside Pretoria, South Africa.

What is all this to do with Wolverton? Well each of these institutions, and indeed the Trust itself, was funded from the income from the Manor. In 1713 annual income from rents was £2,187 2s. 4d. A high figure in its day which rather underscores the last Sir Edward Longueville's inability to live within his means. The money came from about 50 tenants on the Manor, six farms, two mills, and most of the properties on the Wolverton side of Watling Street in Stony Stratford, then made up of coaching inns, other commercial establishments and houses. The total rent was a 5%

Manno's Manor

return on Dr. Radcliffe's investment and sufficient to maintain these important Oxford institutions for over 200 years.

The Radcliffe Observatory: engraving by J.C. Stadler from a watercolour by William Westall

The Radcliffe name was strongly associated with Wolverton until the remaining farms were sold to the Milton Keynes Development Corporation in 1970. The Trust, as landlord of the Wolverton Manor, had a dominant influence until the coming of the Railways, after which it slowly declined The Trust still retains its interest in Wolverton Mill.

The memory of John Radcliffe is tenuously preserved in the street named after him and the secondary school which was founded in 1958. Radcliffe Street was opened during the 1860s phase of development to connect the Stratford Road with the newer streets to the south that became part of Wolverton's later 19th century expansion. It is now a rather nondescript street of two sections after town planners decided to block it off in 1980 with a new building called the Agora.

The 18th. Century and the Radcliffe Trust

A Brief Life of Doctor Radcliffe

Portrait of Dr. John Radcliffe by Sir Geoffrey Keller, 1712

John Radcliffe was born in Wakefield, Yorkshire at the end of 1652. He was the third son and fourth child of George and Ann Radcliffe. There were two other sons to follow but John was the only boy to survive infancy; however he had three sisters as companions when he was growing up. As to his exact date of birth there is no record. Parish registers during the Republican period were often either poorly kept or not at all and in some instances actively discouraged by the new authorities who wished to

Manno's Manor

undermine the established Church, so it is not surprising to find no record, even though his father was a relatively prominent citizen.

George Radcliffe was an attorney at law and himself the son of a country vicar. As a supporter of the Parliamentary cause he was rewarded with the post of Governor at Wakefield's House of Correction, only to lose this to the previous incumbent after the restoration of the monarchy.

John's background therefore was solid provincial middle class. The Radcliffes were not wealthy but neither were they poor. John attended the local Grammar School and showed himself to be a bright pupil and in 1666, when he was just 13 years old, he was sent to University College, Oxford. He graduated with a B.A. in 1669 and then embarked upon studies in anatomy, chemistry and botany for an M.A., which he was awarded in 1672. Following this he was able to begin his proper medical studies. He obtained a licence to practice medecine in 1675.

From the start he appeared to have an intuitive gift to diagnose illness and prescribe novel and effective treatment. For example, his treatment of smallpox, then a common enough scourge, used cooling emulsions on the skin, and giving instructions to his patients to get plenty of fresh air. The conventional treatment was to bleed the patient and to confine him to bed in a dark and stuffy room. It did not take too long for the word to spread about the effectiveness of Radcliffe's treatment and prospective patients were soon lining up outside his door. And as these matters often run it took the cure of one celebrated patient to cement his rising reputation. A certain Lady Spencer had been ill for years and the ministrations of successive doctors had made no impression. After three weeks in Radcliffe's care she was up and about looking better than she had in years. The word quickly spread and Radcliffe could now command high fees from the well-to-do and well-connected.

In 1682, after completing his Doctor of Medicine degree he moved to London where he found a house in Covent garden, strategically placed between Westminster and the city. As his fame grew so did his fees and by 1690 he was charging 20 guineas for a consultation. He was patronized by the Royal Family and by much of the Aristocracy. With the exception of his drinking habit, which I will come to, he tended to live frugally. He had no wife or children and there was very little that he wanted to spend his money on with the consequence that over the years his wealth

The 18th. Century and the Radcliffe Trust

accumulated. Later in life he began to invest money in various speculative ventures. Usually these paid off, leaving him more wealthy than before.

In his day John Radcliffe was a "personality". His fame was initially based upon his medical skill but his no-nonsense, blunt speaking also attracted attention and possibly made him more celebrated.

He liked to talk; he liked male company; he liked the ale-house; he did not care very much what he said to people and to whom. He was able to maintain good friendships but he was often arrogant and unsparing in his criticisms of some of his colleagues. Needless to say this did not go down well with the medical profession of the day.

He was no less gentle with his patients. One peer, apparently something of a hypochondriac, came to him to complain of singing in his head. He was dismissed with the advice that "you should try wiping your Arse with a ballad." Radcliffe was probably insensitive to the concept of a gentle bedside manner; nevertheless he was effective.

Even the Royals were not immune to Radcliffe in one of his arrogant moods. Princess Anne (later Queen) sent a summons to him one evening while he was drinking in a tavern. He replied that he would be along shortly and carried on drinking. An hour or two later a second messenger was sent when Radcliffe was even more comfortably ensconced. The Princess's symptoms were described and Radcliffe reacted, "By God! Her Highness's distemper is nothing but the vapours, and she is in as good a state of health as any woman breathing, could she but give in to the belief of it." It would not surprise you to learn that Anne never called him again.[1]

But his commanding and bullying manner was no doubt part of the attraction. Patients generally appreciate forceful advice, even if they do not always act upon it. In 1697 he was called to King William, who was then suffering from dropsy. Radcliffe told him that the best he could expect was another three or four years of life, but only if he followed Radcliffe's orders. "If Your Majesty will forbear making long visits to the Earl of Bradford (the kings drinking companion), I'll try what can be done to make you live easily."[2]

Radcliffe showed little interest in women, although there were some reported dalliances, and even less in marriage. He therefore found himself towards the end of his life with no heirs. In his last decade he began to acquire property - the Wolverton Manor being the chief, and a smaller

Manno's Manor

estate in Yorkshire. In the last year of his life he bought a large house at Carshalton in Surrey.

His own health problems started to appear when he was fifty with a serious attack of pleurisy in 1703. He recovered but the years of overindulgence in red wine began to catch up with his health. He began to go to places like Bath and Tunbridge Wells for recuperation, but the decline had set in. He was still practising in his last decade but increasingly his thoughts turned to his legacy. He did provide for his sisters and their families and make some other bequests, but the main endowment went through his Trust, to his first college, University College, Oxford.

He died of a stroke at his house in Carshalton on November 1st, 1714.

Managing the Manor

The Wolverton Manor is our interest and the circumstances of the purchase meant that a very detailed picture of the manor, and its tenants survives in documented form.

The immediate effect of Radcliffe's acquisition was to bring the estate under more responsible management. Radcliffe hired a man called John Battison from Quinton whose father had been estate manager under the Longuevilles. For this service Battison was paid £40 a year. Battison knew the manor and its tenants inside out and his presence on the spot probably became more important after Radcliffe's death when the estate was left in the hands of busy men of affairs in London. He was not perhaps the best man for the task of reporting to a distant board through the intermediary of a secretary and he was found wanting on more than one occasion. Nevertheless he prevailed in the position for 26 years until he was dismissed in 1740.

The transfer of ownership did mean that documents detailing the tenants holdings were prepared and there are four surviving documents that for the first time in history provide great detail about how the post-enclosure manor was managed. One set of documents, prepared for the Duke of Newcastle, ended up amongst the papers of the Duke of Portland. These were prepared in 1710 for the Duke who was interested in purchasing the estate. They were carefully analysed by the Duke's own people who came up with a valuation of £30,200. This was probably the Duke's first

The 18th. Century and the Radcliffe Trust

offer in 1710 and this may have led to further negotiation, but as the Duke died in 1711 one assumes that there was no further interest in the purchase. Three years later Sir Edward was able to get £40,000 from Dr. Radcliffe. The next three sets of papers, headed "A Particular of the Manor" confirm the information in the 1710 set and add some details. They are each undated, but the inferred dates are 1713, 1714, and 1716.[3]

Two of Radcliffe's trustees, Sir George Beaumont and William Bromley, visited the estate early in 1715 and again in 1716. Some £1400 was spent on building repairs, although not on the great house itself, which was too far gone. They appear, from William Bromley's letter to his fellow Trustees, to have been quite satisfied:

> "You would have the satisfaction of seeing a noble Estate, & the management of it such that I think there is little cause to complain of."[4]

I suspect that the inhabitants of Wolverton and Stony Stratford regarded their new administration in a kindly light. The Trustees were all very successful and well-to-do in their own right who had nothing personal to gain and collectively they seem to have taken the view that as long as the rents were paid they should discharge their duties to their tenants in a responsible fashion. They were obviously interested in sufficient income from the rents but this need was generally tempered by sympathetic understanding of the circumstances of their tenants. The Trustees took the long view. Misfortunes such as bad harvests, flooding and even insolvency were met with tolerant arrangements to reduce, defer, or even forgive rents. There were several instances in both the 18th and 19th centuries where successively poor harvests led the trustees to approve rent reductions and their benign approach even extended to some of the landlords on Stony Stratford's High Street.

Christopher Carter was the innkeeper of the *Three Swans* in the early part of the 18th century. The Wolverton Estate owned and leased several of the major inns on the Wolverton side of Stony Stratford - *The Bull, The Red Lyon, The Horseshoe, The Three Swans* - and two smaller ones - *The Queen's Head* and *The Nag's Head*. Of those *The Three Swans* was considered the premier inn. It was located on the site now occupied by 92-94 High Street.

Manno's Manor

In 1726 Christopher Carter was not a happy man. Part of his inn was falling into disrepair and despite promises made to him 12 years earlier the work had not been remedied.

According to his account, Dr. Radcliffe visited the inn and ordered that a dilapidated part of the building be torn down so that it could be replaced by a new building. One assumes that this was in 1713, just after Radcliffe had made his purchase and one might guess that there was a certain amount of persuasion by Carter that this work, probably neglected by the hard up Sir Edward Longueville, was essential.

However Dr. Radcliffe died the following year and this may have left Carter in limbo. His Trustees needed time to organise and familiarise themselves with the manor and establish priorities. Since they only met twice a year on the average it was probably difficult to get decisions in those early years. Christopher Carter may have been living in misguided hope.

Eventually, after 12 years he submitted this petition to the Trustees which was, to judge by the neatness of the script and the language, drawn up by a lawyer. The Trustees were minded to listen and allowed him some relief on his rent. It was probably too late to revive his fortunes because in 1730 he was facing insolvency.

That the said Doctor Radcliffe soon after the purchasing of the said manor came to the Three Swans in Stony Stratford (being the Inn your petitioner lives inn) and ordered part of his house to be pulled down and to be new built again and accordingly the same was pulled down and continued for about twelve yeares before the same was rebuilt and the new buildings are not yet finished.

That the buildings that were taken down consisted of six bay containing a shuffleboard room and severall other chambers and their not being built up again was a very great damage and disadvantage to your petitioner the buildings being demolished in such a manner as did not only render the said roomes useless but gave the inn such an ill report that Gentlemen and Travellers who were Strangers would not come to itt and severall Gentlemen after they had turned into the yard and saw in what condition the inn was in have went out again and gone to other Inns.

The 18th. Century and the Radcliffe Trust

And that the brewhouse which was under part of the said roomes was so bad and ruinous that your Petitioner could not brew therein without great difficulty and hazard and oftentimes had his drink damaged by mortar and other rubbish falling into it from the walls of the said brewhouse.[5]

One can easily imagine the reaction of customers who found clumps of mortar in their ale.

Christopher Carter had been the innkeeper of the *Three Swans Inn* on Stony Stratford's High Street since 1705. He claimed in the letter of 1726 that his business misfortunes arose from the demolition of part of his building 12 years earlier and a failure to make it new. It is hard to estimate at this distance in time how much of Christopher Carter's business losses were due to this factor or his own mismanagement.

Anyway, by 1730, Christopher Carter was facing insolvency and was unable to pay his rent. The Trustees received a desperate letter from Thomas Chapman, who I take to be a Stony Stratford solicitor. Mr. Chapman comes across as a reluctant advocate who is not terribly sympathetic to Christopher Carter.

Upon the continued and pressing entreaties of poore Mr. Carter of Stratford, I am prevailed upon (very unwillingly) to give you this trouble,[6]

The tenor of the letter, although couched in very deferential terms, is that if Carter could be forgiven his arrears he would be able to leave quickly so that a new tenant could come in. Sir George Beaumont, one of the trustees, was inclined to take an understanding view:

"I shall always be of Opinion that if we can preserve our tenants from impending ruin, it will be charity well applyd."[7]

The outcome was that the Trustees did give the man relief from his debts and immediately took on another tenant - R. Wilmer in 1730.

The tone of the letter is interesting. Chapman is doing his duty by his client (who is presumably paying him for the letter) but he is clearly anxious not to offend anyone as mighty as a Radcliffe Trustee.

The Three Swans would have been caught up in the great fire of 1742 and was presumably rebuilt. It stayed in business until about 1785 when it was converted into a residence.

Manno's Manor

The manor, which the Radcliffe Trust took over in 1713, was still largely an agricultural estate, as it had been for at least 800 years. Change there had been: the growth of commercial activity at Stony Stratford in the Middle Ages, and the forced abandonment of the old Wolverton village in the 16th century - but agriculture remained at the core. Parcels of the land abutting Watling Street had been granted or sold over the centuries but these had been transacted in a piecemeal fashion and even though Stony Stratford had later emerged as a parish, considerable parts of it were still the property of the Manor of Wolverton and therefore still paying rent to the Radclffe Trust. *The Cock Inn* and its adjoining lands, for example, had probably been under separate ownership since at least the 13th century (possibly earlier), but *The Bull* and the other large inns were still on manor property.

Surveys of the manor at this time can provide some insight into the way inns were managed. They were in essence small farms which had to produce food for their guest's table and provide pasture and fodder for horses. The transportation of food (at least over any distance above a few miles) was unknown at this time and all hostelries depended on local produce. The larger inns were clearly self sufficient. The *Particular of the Manor*, drawn up by Thomas Battison, showed the Bull was renting 52 acres of meadow and pasture land. *The Three Swans* has an orchard and gardens and 36 acres of pasture and meadow. *The Red Lyon* also had an orchard and gardens and rented 42 acres of pasture. There was another 73 acres of meadow and pasture and a further 24 acres of arable land described as Red Lyon Leys, farmed in this case by another farmer, but the description would suggest that it had once been under the tenure of *The Red Lyon*. *The Horseshoe Inn*, another big hostelry had a combined total of 74 acres. As these were mainly pasture lands the inns clearly had an interest in keeping livestock which could be butchered locally and served at table, not forgetting the teams of horses that scampered up and down the Watling Street. It is interesting to note that even in the 19th century when the railway came to Wolverton, the Refreshment Rooms acquired land for growing vegetables and maintaining a piggery. I will come to the inns later but for now it is enough to note that these inns were still very much intertwined with the agricultural economy. The smaller taverns, such as the *Nags Head* and the *Queens Head* were without any land holdings.

The 18th. Century and the Radcliffe Trust

Dr. Radcliffe assumed several major farm tenancies, which were more-or-less based upon farms which were founded after enclosure. The boundaries changed as some farmers prospered while others fell back but in the early 18th century snapshot we can recognise a broad division of land use. The largest tenant was Richard Wodell who held about 550 acres in the north of the manor, probably with his house at Manor Farm. Stonebridge House Farm, in the north eastern corner, was held by Thomas Scott whose son some years later was dispossessed for non-payment of rent. He had 147 acres which included Brook Field. Post Hill Ground and Deans Close. In the south east, from Green Lane to Bradwell Brook, William Harding farmed 289 acres. This was known as Stacey Bushes Farm and the farm house and buildings were beside Bradwell Brook, not on the 19th century site at Stacey Hill. Further west, extending over the Furzes, James Brittain farmed livestock over these pastures, totalling 276 acres, Further west still, mostly taking in Greenleys to the Watling Street, William Swannell rented 243 acres, mostly pasture but with 25 acres of arable land. Since he also rented 30 acres in the Low Park and 5 acres at Kiln Close, it is likely that his farm buildings were to be found around the site of the later Wolverton Park house. In between these were some other farmers. William Lucy held land in Ardwell Field, Carter's Leyes and Brick Close amounting to 172 acres. His farm may have been the basis for the later Brick Kiln Farm. The Widow Durrant held land in the Fullers Slade area, probably with a farm house and buildings at the Gib Lane corner and her son held land which may have been the basis for the later Warren farm.

The Widow Bryant held a lease over 128 acres mostly on either side of the Old Wolverton Road. Her land included Roger's Holm, the Lower Slade, part of the Diggins and Barr Piece. There was also a house and orchard which may have been located in Rogers Holm.[8]

The fields by this time had all acquired names. Some were quite old. Ardwell, Barr Piece, Rylands, Stacey Bushes are all Anglo-Saxon in origin. Fullers Slade can be found in 13th century deeds as Fullwell's Slade and Grindley's or Greenleys also seems to date from that time, as does the Severins, which was probably Severungfurlong in the 13th century and was also described as the Severidge. Most of the closes, as their name suggests, were more recent in the 17th century. Ludkins Close may have taken its name from a 16th century innkeeper. Red Lyon Close was probably attached

Manno's Manor

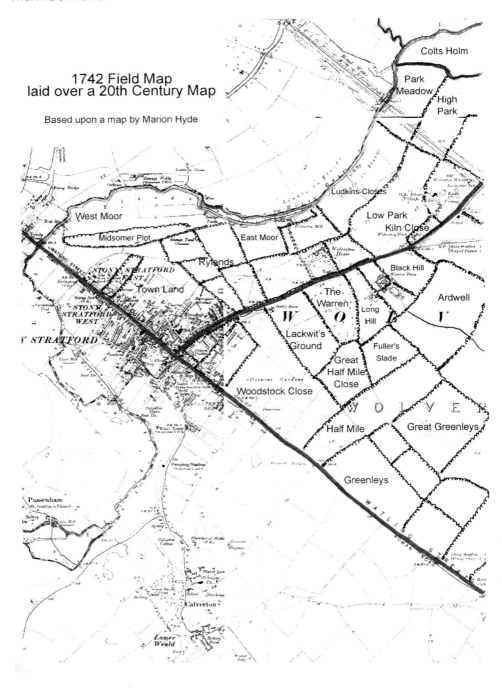

The 18th. Century and the Radcliffe Trust

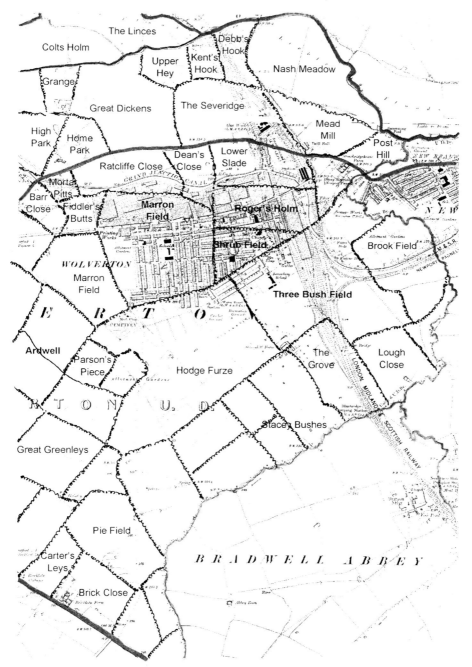

The 17th Century Field enclosures overlaid on an early 20th century map.

Manno's Manor

to the *Red Lyon Inn* when it was first enclosed, although it was not attached to the hostelry in 1710. Carters Leyes we might imagine took its name from the family that leased *The Swan Inn*. In the dying years of the tenure of the Longuevilles and the early years of the Radcliffe Trust we come across some very detailed descriptions of land use after enclosure. We cannot be totally precise because some of the field names used in 1710 may have been subdivided and given another name in 1742; however we can agree that the Longuevilles had successfully enclosed all the land and distributed it among a limited number of tenants.

There was at one time a field map dated 1742 which was in the possession of the Trust's land agents. It was certainly seen by Professor Hyde in the 1940s and his wife made a copy which was reproduced in his *Short History of Wolverton*. Unfortunately the original map has disappeared in the intervening years and we are now left with the copied version. To a great extent, with the exception of those fields which had been cut through by the canal and the railway and later eaten up by town development, many of these field boundaries remained until the Milton Keynes development started in the late 20th century.

The two mills also rented some land, although not a great deal. Both Mills were operated by the Perry family. Thomas Perry had Mead Mill and William Perry the West Mill, later known as Wolverton Mill. The rest of the estate was made up of houses and small properties, mostly on the Watling Street. There were also a number of smaller holdings - mostly closer to Stony Stratford.

Farm rents were quite hefty. Wodall was paying £270 a year, Brittain £210 and Swannell £225. Between them they accounted for one-third of the estate income, which gives some indication of the importance of farming. The Inns also paid a high rent. *The Bull* contributed £94, *The Three Swans* £67, *The Horseshoe* £107 and *The Red Lyon* £55. *The Queens Head* paid £5 10s and *The Nags Head*, which must have been very small, a mere 17s. Both were probably no more than alehouses.

Most of these larger farms did quite well, but the Scott farm at Stonebridge House got into difficulties in the 1720s. At least that is what we can infer from the arrears of rent. Robert Scott, presumably the son of Thomas, was described as "a very troublesome fellow"[9], and he set about trying to develop legal arguments to justify his withholding of the rent.

The 18th. Century and the Radcliffe Trust

These proved to be of no avail and in 1722 the Trust evicted him from the farm and gave the tenancy to Thomas Ratcliffe, whose descendants were active at this farm until 1884.

The main farm was held by Richard Wodell and his father, 418 acres mostly in the northern part of the estate. It is described as "The Capitall messuage of Wolverton with the Outhouses, Barnes, Stables, Dovehouses, Orchards, Fishponds, Royalty of Fishing in the River Ouse for near Five Miles, Cherry Garden of Twenty Acres, Stone Pitts, Gravel Pitts and Sand Pitts, Timber not valued, and the Lands in the Parishes of Wolverton and Stony Stratford Tythe Free and other Hereditaments, therewith held and enjoyed" and then goes on to list the fields with their acreages. We must conclude that the Wodells were farming part of the old Lord's desmesne, together with the northern farm. It is less clear whether or not they took over Sir Edward's house, the old mansion. Describing it as a messuage would suggest so, but obviously they could not have been living there while Sir Edward was resident, so we should assume that they were living in the farmhouse as the location now known as Manor Farm. Aside from the extensive prime arable and pasture land they could enjoy income from fishing rights and from the gravel and sand pits. The Wodells were plainly the premier farming tenants.

And they knew it. They were farming the "capital messuage" and its adjoining lands and most likely considered themselves in the position of the lord of the manor recently vacated in person by Sir Edward Longueville and replaced by a London-based committee. On the ground, at the manor, they were the biggest fish in the tiny pond of Wolverton. Consequently they were not inclined to be pushed around by Battison on his occasional visits. It is quite possible that the Wodells got a bit above themselves but Battison obviously did not handle them well and appears to have made an enemy of Thomas Wodell.

The dispute had its origins in the ploughing of Brook Field, in the east of the manor. Battison felt that it was being ploughed and cropped too much. Wodell argued that he had been permitted to plough it by Sir Edward Longueville in return for a rent increase. Wodell was leaving the field fallow for some years, but not enough in Battison's mind. The dispute rumbled on for some years and was brought to the Trustees who ruled that if Wodell did not obey Battison he would be deprived of his tenancy. This

Manno's Manor

was in March 1726 but it appears that the matter was still unresolved in 1729 and like so many of these issues, whatever resolution there may have been has disappeared or remains unrecorded.

Thomas Wodell was clearly a man to nurse a grievance and a decade later, in 1739, wrote to the Trustees to inform them that Battison had rented some woodland without reporting it in his accounts. The Trustees met in March 1740 to consider this and wrote to Battison asking him to explain what appeared to be a £25 discrepancy. This was not a small amount of money; for many people in the 18th century this represented a healthy annual income. Battison appears not to have faced up to this and Ivor Guest concludes in his book[10] that he either resigned or was dismissed.

Nevertheless, despite being less than assiduous in pressing for arrears from tenants, and sometimes being late with the preparation of his accounts the Trust stuck with him John Battison for 26 years and until Thomas Harrison, whom we will meet later, was the longest serving land agent.

The word about John Battison's financial difficulties had got around, because George Gill, who was to succeed him in 1740, wrote to the Duke of Beaufort in the summer of 1739 putting himself forward "if the Fraud which will be laid before the Gentlemen at their next meeting shou'd occasion his Discharge.[11]"

Gill had some virtues, although accounting was not one of them. He did succeed in drawing up a plan of the estate in 1742 which was mentioned earlier.

Gill was the agent during two great crises - the great fire at Stony Stratford in 1742 and an outbreak of cattle distemper in 1746. The fires will be discussed below.

The cattle distemper was ruinous for the farmers on the estate. Herds were lost and the Trustees had to give relief on the rents in order to allow the farmers to recover.

Gill died in 1749 and when the Trust's Secretary, Charles Pryor, visited the estate office in Stony Stratford he found the accounts in a state of confusion. This was obviously not the kind of paperwork that George Gill wished to confront. What became clear after careful inspection, was that a fair sum of money was owing to the Trustees and that there were not the funds there to repay.

The 18th. Century and the Radcliffe Trust

It is not altogether evident how he got into this pickle but it might be suspected that the aftermath of the Great Fire of 1742 resulted in considerable loss of rent, and perhaps due to the stress of these events he neglected to account for this properly.

George Gill's son and widow were approached to make up the losses and eventually, when it was clear that they were unable to do it the Trustees went to court to recover the debt from George Gill's sureties. The sureties were guarantors of the land agent and in this case it cost them money. We can see this process at work when Richard Harrison was appointed to succeed his father. He had to find guarantors (in this case his older brother John Harrison and a man called William Grant) to stand for £7,500, about two years rent, in case he should default in any way, and a legal document was prepared to that effect.[12]

In the case of the Gill default it took until 1757 before the trustees were able to recover the debt. The amount was huge - £818 17s. 1½d. During this time the next land agent, Joseph Stephenson held a brief tenure until he unfortunately died "of a Jaundice & of a Dropsy".[13] This was 1753.

In March 1754 the Trustees appointed his successor, Thomas Quartley, who was already steward of an estate at Wicken. Quartley proved to be meticulous in sharp contrast to the lackadaisical approach of George Gill. It also has to be said in his favour that his stewardship, which lasted until his death in 1766, was entirely uneventful and the only conclusion one can draw from this is that Thomas Quartley was a good manager who took care to address the concerns of the tenants before they became issues and ensured that rents were collected on time. There was a crop failure in 1757 and suitable relief was given to the poor by the Trustees through the medium of the vicar.

The Trustees next appointed Henry Smith from Bicester in 1767 and he served a similarly uneventful period until his death in September 1772. In the absence of information to the contrary, one must assume that his stewardship was as efficient as Quartley's. The next land agent, who was a very considerable figure, began his tenure in January 1773. He was Thomas Harrison and there is much more to say about him in the next chapter.

The Stony Stratford Fires

Fire was not uncommon. Heating and cooking depended on open fires. Ceilings were low. Rooms were often crowded. Most buildings still used thatch covering for the roof and were thus especially vulnerable. The inns were especially vulnerable and *The Horseshoe*, an inn for the wagon trade, had experienced fire outbreaks in 1703 and 1729. After the 1729 fire the Radcliffe Trust decided to take out insurance on the four major inns - *The Bull, The Swan, The Red Lyon* and *The Horseshoe* - for a total annual premium of £3 12s. 6d. It was a wise precaution. The tiled buildings were covered for £1,251 and the thatched buildings for £450 1s. These were high premiums, but necessary as the Sun Fire office faced a large payout in 1742.

In 1736 an accidental fire brought the loss of 53 houses, mainly on Church Lane.

Six years later there was a much bigger fire and we have a reported account from the Northampton Mercury of May 1st 1742.

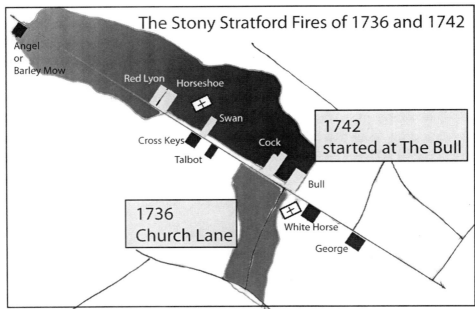

Showing the areas of devastation in the 18th century fires

The fire originated at The Bull Inn with a servant girl who was drying sheets before the fire place. One of them caught fire and instead of

The 18th. Century and the Radcliffe Trust

smothering it she panicked and stuffed the sheet up the chimney, hoping not to be found out by her mistress. This action compounded her problems. the chimney caught fire and then the roof. There was also a high wind on this day and the fire leapt from one building to another, not simply on the one side of the High Street, but also crossing the street, hitting a thatched roof on the other side and relentlessly catching other houses in its destructive path.

The church of St Mary Magdalene, built about 1280, was completely destroyed. It was never rebuilt, apart from the Tower, which the MP Browne Willis generously funded. There may have been good intentions to rebuild the church but the enthusiasm probably melted away when the citizens of Stony Stratford discovered that St. Giles was adequate for their needs.

The paper also reported that the fire crossed the River Ouse and even caught some houses in Old Stratford with airborne fiery debris. 146 buildings were destroyed and the majority of Medieval Stony Stratford with it.

If you take a look at Stony Stratford High Street today you can find surviving Medieval buildings to the south of the Bull on the Wolverton side but nothing to the north.

The fire was a disaster for Stony Stratford, but the precaution of insurance allowed the inns to rebuild and resume their trade during the boom years of coach travel. George Gill must have been very busy during this time.

Clergy at Wolverton in the 18th Century

18th century Wolverton was a flattish social pyramid. At the top was the Lord of the Manor, Sir Edward Longueville, who was quite rich. Below him were a few well-to-do businessmen in Stony Stratford, possibly inn-holders and and about three or four tenant farmers. There was the vicar, and then the rest of the population, from labourers to artisans and small trades people, none of whom had much in the way of income and resources, nor did they have much of a voice in the affairs of the community. The vicar in Wolverton occupied a unique place in society. He usually came from a middle class background and had been educated at either Oxford or Cambridge. In return for his incumbency he was provided

Manno's Manor

with a residence and an income. It was for good reason described as a living, because it was just that, you could not become wealthy. Some had resources of their own.

The divine at Wolverton was a vicar, that is a substitute. Unlike rectors, who had land and tithes at their disposal, the church at Wolverton had been given over to the Priory at Bradwell, and from then on they received the tithes and the income and provided the vicar with a living. After the dissolution of the monasteries the advowson was retained by the crown and then sold in 1568. From there it was subject to some complex changes with a part of the income coming to the Longuevilles in 1601.

In 1702, Thomas Evans was appointed the incumbent at a stipend of £40, not a bad income for those days and certainly better than the average worker. Before too long he discovered that his predecessor had been paid £10 per annum more and he felt much aggrieved. Unluckily for him, he came into the living at a time when Sir Edward was much pressed for money and he did not get a sympathetic ear from his lord. Undaunted he assiduously sought evidence to support his case and eventually he had found a rent roll that he claimed proved that the tithes in the 17th century did indeed amount to £50, and that in lieu of those tithes he was entitled to that sum of money. Even so, he made no progress with Sir Edward but as soon as the Trust was established in 1714 he re-launched his grievance with them. The Trustees were prepared to listen but felt that the case should be presented in a proper legal context. Proceedings were instituted at Stony Stratford in 1718 and witnesses were heard who testified they they or their fathers paid tithes to the Vicar at one time. However, the case foundered because the Deed of Composition from 1656 (which described these financial arrangements) could not be found. It had been lost and the court was unwilling to pass judgement on the hearsay of a solitary and very old witnesses. The case petered out. The unfortunate Evans died in 1720 - apparently destitute.

The trustees then appointed a young clergyman by the name of Edmund Green. He was of a more humble disposition and was prepared to accept the £40 without dispute - and there the matter rested for some years.

In the meantime, the church and the vicarage were in extremely poor condition and these matters had to be addressed. In 1724 he asked the Trustees to repair the chancel, to add rails round the communion table and

The 18th. Century and the Radcliffe Trust

seat for communicants. While he was doing this, the virtuous Reverend Green was trying to live with his family in a rectory that was liable to fall down. He tried to effect repairs out of his own limited income but by 1727 the condition of the rectory was desperate and the Bishop's Court declared it a ruin.

Green approached the Trustees for help. The Longueville Manor had been partly demolished in 1720 but there were materials that could be used to build a new rectory. However, this was as much help as the unlucky Reverend Green got because the Trust at this time was committed to building the Radcliffe Library at Oxford and had no funds to spare. The poor man was obliged to build the new rectory out of his own resources. It cost him:

> "the full sum of £300 which was the whole fortune I had with my wife & which has obliged me to Preach at two places more to enable me to support myself and my Family with dignity as a clergyman."[14]

Only in 1750 that the Radcliffe Trust, free of its own projects, were able to help the Reverend Green. They paid £200 into the Queen Anne's Bounty fund, which was matched by an equal figure by the Bounty. This investment enabled an improved income to Reverend Green in his last years, which were under four. He died on 11th April 1754.

It would seem that Edmund Green was a genuinely humble man who sought to practice the gospel he preached. As a consequence his wife and family may have indeed been disadvantaged.

The stipend limped along at this level until 1770 when the Trust raised the stipend to £50 per annum - the level at which it had been reported 110 years earlier.

His successor, Edward Smith, benefited from Green's efforts and self-denial. He was able to inhabit a newish rectory and enjoy an improved stipend. He was also made Vicar of Stantonbury, which must have increased his income. He died in 1782 and his successor was Samuel Hale. Their combined years, which took up the last half of the 18th century were quite uneventful. This 18th century placidity changed on the arrival of the thrusting Henry Quartley.

Henry Quartley was a nephew of their former land agent. He was a man of some energy, although his approach to the ministry was closer to

Manno's Manor

that of an 18th century squire rather than a 19th century churchman. He enjoyed hunting and sat on the bench as J.P., where he was fairly unforgiving in his sentencing of the miscreants brought before him.

He re-opened the case for the lost tithes in 1797 and put his case that the living had no glebe to produce income nor tithes. The Trustees were again willing to listen but would not take the matter further until there was proper documentation. Accordingly they authorized the secretary to the Trust, Thomas Wall, to inspect the ancient documents held in the Radcliffe Library. As a goodwill gesture, they doubled the stipend to £100.

The tenant farmers on the estate were less happy. What they foresaw was the likelihood of any imposition of tithes for Quartley as an additional tax on their own earnings and accordingly, when the matter was considered by a court it was expressed as a complaint between Henry Quartley and the principal farm tenants, Thomas Battams, Thomas Gleed, Thomas Ratcliffe and William Wilkinson and the Trustees as lay rectors. The case was eventually heard on August 20th 1805 before a panel of 24 jurymen.

Quartley had argued from an old document of 1209[15] which he claimed represented an endowment to the vicar. The Trust's lawyer, Edmond Escourt, was quite scornful of this ploy and explained that this so-called endowment was nothing of the kind but merely a memorandum "without date or title, and by whom made, on what occasion, or when did not appear", in other words, he argued, not a meaningful document at all. In addition he pointed out that since the dissolution there had been no evidence of any endowment to the vicar apart from depositions "two old men had *once* paid *some* small tythes to *a former* vicar."[16] He also pointed out that the tithes in question would have, as estimated by Thomas Harrison, amounted to about £200, a sum of money completely out of proportion to the vicar's status. Accordingly the jury decided that there was no case for Quartley. They decided against the complainant and ruled that Henry Quartley was not entitled to receive any tithes.

This was, after 150 years, the end of the matter.

The episode tells us something about Quartley's character which certainly contrasts with the meek and accommodating Edmund Green.

In addition to the Wolverton post he was also Rector of Wicken and in 1832 became Vicar of Stantonbury. The last-named parish was very under-populated but still had the church of St Peter at Stanton Low.

The 18th. Century and the Radcliffe Trust

Presumably this extra benefice brought additional income to the Reverend Quartley without too much extra work.

On the other side of the balance sheet, Quartley did spearhead the building of the new church which will be described in the next chapter.

Parish Welfare

For most of the centuries in this narrative the poor are unrecorded. In the 16th century, with the beginnings of a national system for recording births, marriages and deaths, we begin to learn something of their lives, but in the 18th century, where these records survive, we can begin to acquire a greater understanding. There are a set of books recording the churchwardens accounts for Holy Trinity from the late 17th century to the early 19th century. From here we can learn a little more about life at the bottom of the social pyramid in Wolverton.

The responsibility for social welfare in those days rested with the Parish and the Churchwardens took over the task of raising money from those who could pay and disbursing funds to the sick and needy throughout the course of the year. The churchwardens were usually the farmers and some of the more substantial citizens of the parish. In Wolverton they appointed one or two of their number as overseers of the poor for that year. These nominees administered the fund and each year the churchwardens as a committee approved the accounts.

There seem to be a variety of ways in which people were helped.

In April 1717, to take one year of many, the churchwardens appointed Samuel and Thomas Durham as overseers. During that year they raised £35 3s 8d through levys but had to spend £38 14s 0d, an overspend, which was either made up from the previous surplus or from the following year's levy. As far as I can tell the Overseer could be out of pocket in some years. There were a variety of calls on the fund. The widow Barber was paid 1/6d per week for 49 weeks for a total of £3 16s 0d. This money was presumably sufficient to help her get by without any other income. The general payout to widows was 1/- per week as in the case of Widow Manweel. George Henson was paid 2/- to go to the doctor and 2/- a week for 38 weeks while he was sick. He must have been in a bad way.

Manno's Manor

A page from the Churchwarden's Accounts

People were helped in other ways. Henry Smith was given 10/6 "for a new coat and waistcoat" and his shoes had to be mended at a cost of 8d. James Morton got a considerable handout that year. The parish paid for '14 yards of fine fustian at 1/3d per yard" 1/-. There was a further 2s for trimming, 2s for a pair of shoes, a further 2s for a hat and comb, 2s for two neckcloths and an astonishing £20 4s for two new shirts. This was more than half the budget for the year. This must have been a highly unusual circumstance as we note further down the ledger that James Morton was paid 4s to travel to London. I guess that he was sent to London to conduct some important parish business and that the new clothes were supplied to

190

The 18th. Century and the Radcliffe Trust

ensure that he made a good impression. One also suspects that James Morton was not one of the poor and needy of the parish.

But it is mainly the long term sick and widows that receive the handouts. Henry Smith and George Henson are still receiving payments in the following year and there is an additional payment for the care of Henry Smith's children. Occasionally payments are made to repair the houses of the poor - 5/- for a load of straw and a further 2/- for the thatching of Widow Barber's house.

But in all years it is a small handful of people who receive assistance from the parish. There is no evidence of people being paid for short term illness and I draw the impression that only those in desperate straits receive money. The fund was clearly only used in exceptional circumstances.

Not all of the churchwardens were literate. The signed accounts for 1719 show the mark of Robert Scott, a farmer. Yet he was nominated as one of the overseers for the following year. Presumably he had some help. Similarly Richard Wodell senior was also illiterate, yet in the years after enclosure his family took up over 400 of the best acres and at the time Dr Radcliffe bought the estate was the largest farmer on the manor.

One cannot doubt that the fund was set up for and to some extent met the needs of the destitute within the parish. The churchwardens were no doubt convinced that they were doing their best for the community, yet, with a slightly cynical 20th century eye one cannot help but note that the professionals are appropriately paid from the fund, and the churchwardens extract their due expenses, such as a carriage to Newport Pagnell. When lawyers prepare indentures they are paid their fee.

18th Century Buildings in Wolverton

Sir Edward's prospectus for the sale of the estate to the Duke of Newcastle in 1710 was probably subject to the gloss of estate agents today or perhaps of all time in that the virtues were magnified and the faults minimized. There is no doubt that when Dr. Radcliffe and subsequently his Trust started to look at the issues facing them they probably had to face the consequences of two decades of neglect.

The manor house itself, built or substantially rebuilt in 1586 was by 1720 in a poor way. From the trust's perspective it was a bit of a white

Manno's Manor

elephant. There was no resident lord on the estate and William Bromley saw quite early that it would be a problem:

> "Very ruinous, & since it now never likes to be used as a Gentleman's seat, you'l consider whether it may not be advisable that it be taken down & the materials disposed of." [17]

These issues were serious for the trustees. Some £1400 had been spent on repairs and new building in the first two years, some authorized by Radcliffe himself, and there was a sense that this was getting out of hand. Christopher Carter, whose story we told earlier, may have been somewhat of a victim of the new policy, as William Bromley and Sir George Beaumont, after a visit in December 1714 told Battison to put all expenditure on hold until he received further instructions from the Trustees.

The great house was a major issue but one which the Trustees deferred for a few years while they attended to more important business. However, in 1720 most of it was demolished. John Battison reported:

> "The great house is pulled down & the materialls Thomas Durrant hath carryd to his yard in order to help build his house." [18]

Some of the materials probably disappeared over the years for various building projects. I have been told that pieces of carved or dressed stone, obviously from another building, can be discovered in the Manor Farm Cottages dating from that period. Locally, they call it "castle stone" but these materials must have come from the late elizabethan mansion. However, there was still sufficient stone left in 1727, particularly some of the finer stonework elements to contribute to the rebuilding of the Vicarage.

Fortunately we have surviving documents which relate to the building of Thomas Durrant's house. It is possible, drawing inferences from the land that Durrant farmed, that this house was on the site of Warren Farm. Durrant was a sheep farmer who leased about 100 acres in "the sheep walks", on the higher ground above Warren Farm. He also leased Nash Meadow "fore crop" on the north east edge of the manor and 18 acres of "meadow next the house" plus another 3 acres which included an orchard and Holme Close. This latter reference might equally lead us to believe that it was on or close to the site of the later Wolverton house. It is difficult to

The 18th. Century and the Radcliffe Trust

imagine any meadow land in the Warren area, whereas the land lower down at the Wolverton house location is exactly that. We know that Thomas Harrison built onto an existing building when he built his large house in the 1780s. It would be interesting to discover how much of the Durrant House (if any) forms part of the present Wolverton House.

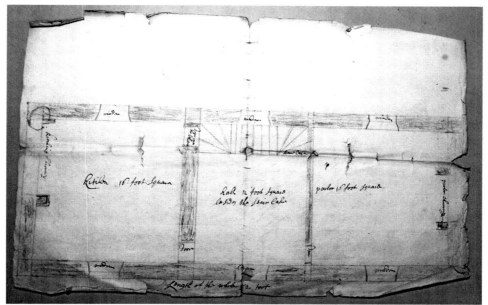

Plan for the "Durrant House."

The design of the house was a simple rectangle, "48 foot long at the front, 16 foot in width and 18 foot high above the ground." It is not clear from this description if the height of 18 feet is to the top of the roof or to the eaves. I would guess the former, since the roof would have a high pitch to include space for sleeping quarters above. There were two partitions to provide for a 16 foot square kitchen, a 16 foot square hall in the middle and a 16 foot square parlour. Upstairs there might be an equal number of bedrooms.

Mr. Durrant (sometimes written as Durham or Durrain) was paying £91 a year to the Trust and was therefore one of the more prominent people living in Wolverton in those years. If this was middle class accommodation one can make a good guess at the living conditions of the labouring poor.

Thomas: Durrants house 48 foot long in the front 16 foot wide within
18 foot high above ground

	£ s d
mason worke in the Case and Sollar 16 perchat 1:5 per perch	20:00:0
Chimneys and oven — — — — — — —	05:00:0
diging the Sollar 120 yards att 4 per yard — — —	02:00:0
for diging 200 load of Stons att 8 per load — —	05:00:10
for diging 70 loads of Morter att 2:4 per load — —	00:14:17
Carpenter worke in the roofe floos partittions 44 squars att 8:8 per squaid — — — — —	18:14:0
for cutting out the timber and making the Stairs out of the Sollar & 2 Story above — — }	03:00:0
laying the floor 20 squares att 3 per squears — —	03:00:0
for making the windows 4 lights att 1 per light —	01:00:0
for making the doors & door cases laying the lintolls over the windows ant laying the Mantle trees and Sawing out the timber for them and the windows }	03:00:0
for straw and thatching the house — — —	05:00:0
for lath & lath nails — — — — —	02:00:0
wall plastering 300 yards att 4 d per yard — —	05:00:0
lath plastering for partittion & ceiling 280 yards att 8 d per yard —	09:00:5
600 foot of timber att 1:2 per foot — — —	35:00:0
loads 2600 foot att 15 per hund — — —	19:10:0
brick for the oven Chimneys & floos 3500 att 15 per thousand	04:07:5
lime for the walls & Chimneys 20 quarters att 4 s per quarter — — —	04:00:0
nails & Iron worke — — — — —	10:00:0
for Scuttles Saaffold coards and other Small materialls that will be wanting —	02:00:0
	157:06:7

The 18th. Century and the Radcliffe Trust

The estimated cost of this building was £157 6s 7d. - a not inconsiderable cost. Timber, at ½d. per foot appears to be a high cost, presumably reflecting the labour of sawing everything by hand, and amounted to about ⅓rd of the total. "Nails and ironwork" adds up to £10 - another high cost. Bricks were used for the chimney and floor; they appear to be relatively cheap. The timber-framed walls were filled with lath and plaster and the roof was thatched. Possibly the stones from the old mansion were used to fill the walls between the timbers and then plastered.

The remainder of the agricultural population (where they were not living in the farmhouses) had to make do with simple hall type houses, with low walls and steep thatched roofs. Cottages by this time may have had two rooms and possibly a sleeping loft, but other than that there may not have been much improvement from the middle ages.

In Stony Stratford, many of the buildings would have been of 16th and 17th century construction, with some perhaps dating to the late 15th century. *The Rose and Crown*, a survivor from the 16th century may give some idea of one of the more substantial buildings from that time. Equally *The George*, *The White Horse* and *The Cross Keys* offer good examples of buildings which would have been prominent in the early 18th century.

By the middle of the 18th century the Wolverton Manor was showing signs of improved prosperity. The manor was under good management. The farms were doing well in the good years, and the rapidly improving state of the roads gave Stony Stratford an increased importance.

The Radcliffe Trust

In 1714 the manor entered a very distinctive phase in its history; for 650 years it was under the control of a single person; after the death of Dr. Radcliffe its future management lay in the hands of a committee. The Wolverton Manor would not be the only example of a manor being used for the benefit of an institution. There are plenty of other instances where manors were used to provide income for the crown or the church or university colleges, but in many of these instance the power could be traced back to an individual. The Trust that Dr Radcliffe set up before his death was a rarer beast - a group of men, more-or-less equal in status, who could come to collective decisions about the manor.

195

Manno's Manor

I remark on this because there was a spirit of disinterestedness about the Trust's decisions. The Trustees were selected because they were very distinguished men. It began its life with men who had been Radcliffe' friends but as time went on dukes, earls and barons typically graced the list. Well known 19th century Prime Ministers like Henry Addington, Robert Peel and William Gladstone also served their time. In the 20th century the Trust drew upon the services of eminent men of letters like Sir Geoffrey Faber, Sir Fred Hoyle and Sir Edgar Trevor Williams. The general picture, throughout almost 300 years is that the Trust attracted men who were only willing to serve the public benefit of the Trust's purpose and had no personal kites to fly. The only possible exception to this was the enthusiastic promotion of the young architect Henry Hakewill by the Earl of Aylesford to rebuild Holy Trinity. The initial proposals for some modest repairs to the old church were scrapped and the rather extravagant new church was built in its stead.

That aside (and it was not an entirely unmixed blessing) the trustees maintained a fine record for looking after their tenants, safeguarding the long term interests of the Wolverton Manor, and of course, taking care of the purpose of the Trust.

Most of these trustees may never have visited Wolverton in their life and depended upon their secretary, based in London, and the land agent on the ground to properly administer the estate. They appear to have been mostly judicious in their choices and this must have been another factor in the smooth running of the estate for 250 years until it was surrendered to Milton Keynes. They were inclined to encourage family inheritance of tenancies, keep up repairs and maintain reasonable, if not low, rents. In terms of community life, they rebuilt Holy Trinity Church at the huge cost of £7,793 and contributed £2,629 for the church and vicarage at St George's. They granted land for the school at Wolverton Station and built the Old Wolverton School House in 1856 for £600. Over the years they made various donation or repairs and additions and paid all or part of the stipends for the Rector at Holy Trinity, the Vicar at Wolverton and the curate at Wolverton St Mary's.

The 18th. Century and the Radcliffe Trust

1 Ivor Guest. Dr. Radcliffe and his Trust. The Radcliffe Trust 1991, p.17.

2 Ibid. p.18

3 The dates can be inferred from an assumption that the first document is 1713 and the length of leases. For example, in the first document Richard Woodall and his father have held the land for 25 years; in the next it is 26 years, and in the third 28 years.

4 Bodleian MSS. dd. Radcl., c.66. Bromley to Keck. 20 Oct. 1716

5 Bodleian. MSS. dd. Radcl. c.16. Letter to Trustees.

6 Bodleian. MSS. dd. Radcl. c.16 The letter to William Bromley, one of the original trustees and dated March 30th 1730.

7 Bodleian MSS. dd. Radcl. c. 66 Letter from George Beaumont 25 Apr 1730.

8 The 1830 OS map shows buildings with a road leading to the Old Wolverton road, over a canal bridge. Since the house looks isolated I would infer that this was tehn, and previously a farm house. It is on Roger's Holmes.

9 Bodleian MSS. DD. Radcl. d 36 Porter to Battinson. 14 May 1723.

10 Ivor Guest. The Radcliffe Trust.

11 Badminton archives. 508.12.1. Lord Noel Somerset to Gill. 15 July 1739

12 Bodleian MSS. dd. Radcl. c.23.

13 Badminton archives. 508.12.1. Tynte to Duke of Beaufort, July 1753.

14 Badminton archives. 508.12.1. Green to Lord Noel Somerset. 18 February 1743.

15 The whereabouts of this document is not known.

16 Bodleian MSS. dd. Radcl. c.18.

17 Bodleian MSS. dd. Radcl. c. 66 Letter from Bromley to Keck 24 october 1715

18 Bodleian MSS. dd. Radcl. c 16 Battison to Singleton 9 April 1720.

NINE

THOMAS HARRISON AND THE CANAL AGE

The late 18th century brought the first stirrings of the Industrial Revolution. Those areas close to natural resources were the first to benefit and small towns like Birmingham and Sheffield were beginning to develop product manufacturing industries which catapulted them into major towns and cities. North Buckinghamshire did not have any of the natural resources that fed the new industrial economy and largely had no choice but to continue on its customary path, which indeed it did. But there must have been growing awareness of change as many of the products made in Birmingham and Sheffield were finding their way into Stony Stratford by the end of the 18th century. In the early 19th century you could, for example, discover shops in Leighton Buzzard and Stony Stratford selling china and glass. That was probably unthinkable a generation or two before.

In 1800 Wolverton still depended upon agriculture as it had for over 1000 years. Stony Stratford, on the fringe of Wolverton, enjoyed commercial opportunities from the traffic on the Watling Street and road improvement throughout the 18th century. Change, if it had been noticed at all, was gradual. At the very dawn of the 19th century change became remarkable with the cutting of the Grand Junction Canal and the first transformation of the Wolverton landscape. From this point on Wolverton was in direct contact with the products of the industrial midlands and north.

As can be seen from Jeffrey's 1770 map of the area on page 223, the roads and trackways followed slightly different paths than they did after the Industrial revolution. A route from Haversham to Bradwell, for example, follows a trackway alongside Bradwell Brook - a natural and direct route that probably fell into general disuse after the construction of the canal and the Newport Pagnell branch line in the 1860s. The road from Calverton to the west, the old ridgeway, was also undivided by canal or railway.

Sometimes men appear who are apparently made for the times they live in. Such a man was Thomas Harrison who made his first appearance in 1773 and whose presence in Wolverton may have had a pivotal impact on Wolverton's transition to the industrial age. Harrison's origins are obscure in the sense that we cannot easily discover a record of his birth. At least I have not been able to discover his parentage. Possible lines of enquiry have

Thomas Harrison of Wolverton 1734-1809

been pursued, each starting out with promise but ending without being able to make a positive connection. He had a sister, Jane, who married a man called Samuel Exley in the Halifax area. This might point to Yorkshire

Thomas Harrison and the Canal Age

origins but, although there are many Thomas Harrisons to be found, none quite match the known dates with certainty. During his dealings with the Copper King he used the services of a lawyer named Harrison from Daventry in Northamptonshire. A relative perhaps? Unfortunately, another cold trail. There is a St. Albans connection. Earl Spencer had property there and Thomas Harrison's son John certainly lived at St Albans. London is another possibility. A search of online marriage indexes for a marriage between Thomas Harrison and a woman named Elizabeth yields some possibilities but nothing that prompts a confident identification. In every place mentioned there are Harrisons, but the connection proves elusive. Ironically, it would be easier to trace the lineage of a family of farm labourers in Wolverton throughout the 18th century than a middle class family like the Harrisons who had mobility. With a name like Harrison he could have come from anywhere.

From his stated age on his tomb we know that he was born circa 1734, probably to a well-connected middle class family. This is a fair assumption; he was certainly educated and probably had some legal training which qualified him to become a land agent. Indeed a Thomas Harrison can be found in the admissions registers of the inner Temple.[1] We learn from this that he was the third son of Sir Thomas Harrison and that his call date was in February 1757, just before Thomas Harrison is known to have arrived in Stantonbury. Coincidences like this are not proof but there are some elements of the Thomas Harrison at the Inner Temple and the Thomas Harrison of our knowledge, and that may add up to something.

We know from the Stantonbury parish registers that he and his wife Elizabeth baptized five children - John, 20 Nov 1757, Elizabeth, 4 Feb 1759; Mary 28 June 1761; Thomas, 18 May 1763 and Jane, 27 Jan 1765. So from at least 1757, when he was in his early twenties, and possibly recently married, they were living in Stantonbury. Since there were no more than four houses in Stantonbuy at that time[2] and as he was employed by Earl Spencer as a land agent, it is a fairly safe assumption that they were living in the Wittewronge mansion.

This particular house has an interesting, if brief history. Sir John Wittewronge, a Hertfordshire baronet, came into possession of the Stantonbury manor in 1658 and settled it upon his eldest son John in

201

Manno's Manor

1664. At this time building began on a new mansion which probably, as at the Wittewronge mansion at Rothampstead in Hertfordshire, incorporated pre-existing buildings. Documentary evidence suggests that the building may have been L-shaped, with a main hall and a "return". The building is known to have been built of brick with some stone embellishments. It was probably completed in 1668 when the last payments were recorded.

The village around Stantonbury was at this time quite small. Lipscomb mentions that in 1736 there were only four houses. This probably should be interpreted as the manor house, the rectory and two farms. The cottager's "tofts" would not be counted. Of these there may have been no more than six at this time, and by the end of the century this number had dwindled to four. The enclosures of the 16th century had led to a concentration on sheep farming, so the manor still had good value when Wittewronge purchased it. The deed of settlement on the younger John Wittewronge and his wife in 1664 describes:

> "All that cappital messuage or mansion House of and in the said manor now or late in the possession of the said Sir John Wittewronge . . . And of all and singular Houses, Edefices, Buildings, Barnes, Stables, Dove Houses, Courts, Yards, Orchards, Gardens and Backsides thereunto belonging, and also all those three Water Milles under one roof, and the Millhouses thereunto belonging."[3]

The Wittewronges at Stantonbury had a colourful history which involved the murder of a man in Newport Pagnell and the flight of Sir John Wittewronge from the country, rather like Lord Lucan 250 years later, and this essentially led to the end of the Wittewronge interest in Stantonbury and in 1727 the manor was conveyed to Sarah, Duchess of Marlborough who willed it to her grandson after her death in 1744. He became the first Earl Spencer. The previous year, in 1743, there had been a fire in the house which caused some damage. With the transfer of the manor to the new earl it may have been some few years before the house was made habitable again and it is quite possible that its readiness coincided with the need for appropriate accommodation for the newly married Thomas Harrison.

Thomas Harrison was not solely concerned with managing the Stantonbury manor, which alone would be unworthy of his undoubted skills. The earl now had wide-ranging holdings, from around St. Albans,

Thomas Harrison and the Canal Age

Northamptonshire certainly, and estate in other parts of the country. The Wittewronge mansion at Stantonbury, while of no particular use to the earl for himself, possibly recommended itself as an ideal location for Harrison who would have to travel extensively in the course of his duties. At any rate it must have been home for the Harrisons for about twenty years until Harrison himself was able to build his own mansion at Wolverton in the 1780s. He retained some affection for Stantonbury for he chose to be buried in the church there after his death in 1809. The church is now a ruin and all of the interior has either been removed or destroyed but the inscription stones inside the church were recorded by Lipscomb in the 19th century.[4]

Of this first family only John and Jane are subsequently heard of. John is one of the executors of his father's will and Jane it appears, predeceased her father but is mentioned in the will. Of the other three nothing is heard. Thomas must be presumed to have died young or in infancy. There is no burial record so it may be that he died shortly after baptism. The other two daughters may have married, or they may have died in childhood.

The fate of his wife Elizabeth is also a mystery but one must conclude that she died after 1765. There is no evidence of her being buried at Stantonbury, so it is possible that she was buried somewhere else, perhaps at the place of her birth. But since we have no apparent record of her marriage any search in that direction is a stab in the dark.

At any rate, Thomas Harrison re-married, and this time there is a record. His new wife was Catharine or Caterina Drayson and the marriage took place at Brownsover near Rugby on October 21st 1769. He now began a second family with her. I have an inkling that the family were of Germanic origin. They appear in Brownsover, which may have had little more than a large house standing there at the time but there is no indication as to why they might be living there. Caterina was baptized there in 1745. Quite who or what the Draysons were can only be guessed at; certainly they would have matched all the social criteria that Thomas Harrison would need to consider.

Thomas Harrison was appointed Land Agent for the Wolverton estate in January 1773 and held that position for the Trustees until his death in 1809. At the time nobody could have suspected that his tenure

Manno's Manor

would be any different from his predecessors but, it can be argued, that Thomas Harrison was instrumental in bringing Wolverton into contact with the first phase of the industrial revolution. He brought to the Wolverton estate a high level of competence and new energy. Naturally enough he applied his attention first to the agricultural estate. One of his early reforms was to subject the rents to a thorough review, which may not have happened since Dr Radcliffe purchased the manor 60 years previously energy, and concluded that an increase of 24% was warranted. This was a substantial increase and it speaks to the power of Harrison's persuasion that there is no evidence of any complaint from the tenants. Everyone paid up; there were no defaults. It is possible that by making himself one of those tenants that Harrison was able to bolster his argument amongst his fellow farmers.

One of Harrison's early steps was to turn himself into a substantial tenant farmer on Trust land, taking up eventually over 400 acres. A tenancy became available in the low park and Harrison put himself forward. Over time he added to his holding. It is thought that he employed a steward or bailiff to manage the day-to-day affairs of the farm and housed him at some farm buildings in The Warren, later to be known as Warren Farm. Harrison was, as we shall see, a man of many parts, but the role he created for himself was that of a new breed of farmer emerging in the late 18th century - the gentleman farmer.

Part of his motivation must have been to enhance his social status. A man's standing in society was usually measured by land and even in the 19th century you can witness the new industrialists, having established their wealth, seeking social approval by buying country acres and a country seat. A decade after coming to Wolverton Harrison was in a position to afford to build a large house and have it surrounded by farm land. Even though he did not own any of it he could enjoy the appearance of a man with a country seat. He liked to style himself Mr. Harrison of Wolverton.

Thomas Harrison and the Copper King

If we only paid attention to Thomas Harrison's activities on the Wolverton Manor his story would not appear remarkable. His wider story is more interesting and does indeed have some bearing on Wolverton. Harrison had his fingers in many pies, some of them very lucrative indeed.

Thomas Harrison and the Canal Age

And his administration of the Wolverton Estate may have taken up the smallest amount of his time. His income of £40 a year for managing the Wolverton Estate was not much better than the annual stipend of the Vicar of Holy Trinity and could not begin to cover the lifestyle he evidently enjoyed. One can only assume that it suited him to live at Wolverton because of its proximity to the Watling Street, the major highway that connected him to his business interests in London, the West Midlands and North Wales.

In 1773, when he became land agent for the Radcliffe Trust, he was already the principal agent for Earl Spencer. The Radcliffe Trust job gave Harrison the opportunity to move to more habitable accommodation and live close to, if not actually on, the Watling Street.

Somehow, possibly through the Spencer association, he came into contact with the Paget family, Earls of Uxbridge and later Marquesses of Anglesey. The Paget family were an old family with their seat at Beaudesert in Cannock Chase in Staffordshire, and Thomas Harrison was first employed to look after these interests. Caroline Paget was the last of this line and she had married Sir Nicholas Bayly, an Anglesey baronet, and it was this connection that brought everybody in this story into the new world of the industrial revolution.

The Baylys owned half of a mountain in Anglesey which, in this new age that was hungry for metal, was found to have an extremely rich and accessible seam of copper. However, the seam of copper was no respecter of surface land boundaries and inevitably disputes arose with the owner of the other half of the mountain, the Reverend Edward Hughes. The struggle between them was fierce and litigious.

At some stage after Hughes had established his own mining company he engaged the services of one of the sharpest and most enterprising minds of the new industrial age, Thomas Williams. Williams was an Anglesey lawyer without any great prospects ahead of him until he came to represent Edward Hughes in the dispute with the Baylys. From here he was able to use his agile mind and tough bargaining credentials to build up his own industrial empire. He later became known as the Copper King and rubbed shoulders on equal terms with the likes of Matthew Boulton and James Watt. Williams was easily able to bring about beneficial deals for Edward Hughes and himself and leave Sir Nicholas Bayly and his agent Hugh Price

Manno's Manor

puzzled and discontented, and it was probably in an attempt to bring the contest to more equal terms that Henry Bayly (Sir Nicholas's son and heir and the future Earl of Uxbridge) brought in Thomas Harrison. Harrison was up against a very considerable opponent.

The discovery of the copper seam was dated to March 2nd 1768, long before Harrison became involved, and was initially worked by Roe and Company, a firm of Chester mining engineers, with Bayly taking a 1/8th share. Sir Nicholas later had regrets about the arrangement, believing, with some justification, that he had less than he deserved. Issues were further complicated by interventions by the Reverend Edward Hughes, who owned the other half of Parys mountain and there were several legal proceedings during the 1770s.

During this period the Hughes family had engaged the services of Thomas Williams. Williams was an opportunist of the first rank and subsequently parlayed his role in this local dispute into a very considerable fortune for himself and an almost monopolistic control of the copper industry in late 18th century Britain. At his death in 1802 his many companies were valued in total at over £1 million – a huge sum in those days. Williams was clever and probably unscrupulous but clearly had the personality and charm to convince a number of hard-headed businessmen to enter into deals and partnerships with him.

One early sign of his method of operating emerged in 1778 when he persuaded Sir Nicholas Bayly, by then worn down by years of litigation, to lease his share of the mine to John Dawes, a London banker, for 21 years. With the ink scarcely dry on the agreement, Dawes then formed a new mining company with Hughes and Williams, thereby bringing the Parys Mountain mining enterprise under the control of one company. There is little doubt that Williams was behind this move and he became the powerful figure in the partnership. Sir Nicholas Bayly's share of the lease to Dawes was for 1/3rd of the production. A month later the terms were changed and agreed as a fixed sum of £4000 per annum. In retrospect, not the best deal for Sir Nicholas.

Thomas Harrison entered the picture in 1782 when he was asked by Sir Nicholas's son and heir Henry to compile a report on the mining operations in Anglesey. Harrison had no background in mining but would have been known to Henry Bayly through the Pagets at Beaudesert in

Thomas Harrison and the Canal Age

Staffordshire. Sir Nicholas's land agent at Plas Newydd, Hugh Price, was obviously being outfoxed by Williams and a sharper brain, one more attuned to the times, was needed. Henry Bayly was concerned about his inheritance but since Sir Nicholas was still alive he had to tread carefully. So by asking Thomas Harrison to compile a report Henry Bayly hoped to gather intelligence without outflanking his father or his agent Hugh Price. Price was undoubtedly worried by this intervention and tried to counter any potential criticism by insisting at the outset that he had "repeatedly requested" a copy of the lease between Sir Nicholas and Charles Roe, but that the baronet had kept all negotiations secret. Whether this was true or not Price was obviously sensitive to the inadequate terms of the agreement with Dawes.

Thomas Harrison could not but note the desolate landscape of the mining operation:

> Not a blade of any sort can live where the Smoke reaches as is evident from the burning of Ore which destroys and has destroyed every thing of the Vegetable kind within its reach, and such is the stench of it, as well as its tendency to suffocation, that no mortal being can think of living near such works, but those who are employed in them.[5]

It was a startlingly different environment from the gentle Cowperian landscape of the Ouse valley.

Harrison then proceeded to describe the mines and the port of Amlwch together with the smelting works in Lancashire and Swansea, which he presumably visited, and their operations. It is not until 1784, after the death of Sir Nicholas, that he was able to report on the accounts. The news was not good. In a letter dated 19th January 1784 he sends a warning to the earl of Uxbridge, "to my great Mortification, I have already proceeded enough to put me in a cold Sweat." He warns that expenditure appeared to exceed income (albeit a huge figure of £14,000 for December and January) and he could see no immediate solution to the problem. He complained to Paget about the amount of time he was spending on this work. He wrote that his son (presumably John Harrison, then about 24) had "not spent a day in any other Business since the 25th December" and he had spent three-quarters of his time on this work, which was a long way from being finished.[6]

Manno's Manor

This work brought him into regular contact with Thomas Williams who was angling to increase his control of copper production by acquiring the Cerrig y Bledda mine, a smaller mine, still in the hands of Uxbridge with the lease to Roe and company expiring in 1786. Harrison met with Williams in August 1784 to discuss irregularities in the accounts for the Parys mine, and at this time Williams broached the subject of taking over the lease for the Cerrig y Bledda mine. Harrison wrote to Paget on August 21st 1784 to ask if his lordship wished to work the mine himself or lease it. Paget firmly replied firmly that he wished to retain the mine and work it directly.

This determination may have been prompted by Harrison's investigation which revealed that Roe and Company had been taking £15,000 a year in profit for the previous three years, although he may not have heeded the caveat that because of the poor drafting of the lease "they could take all the ore they cared to at the least expense and leave the more difficult to a later date," meaning that the most accessible ore was taken first. In retrospect these were the most productive and profitable years for the mine.[7]

A deal was concluded that involved the ambitious Thomas Williams. On 11th October 1785 Harrison recorded, "We yesterday took possession of the Cerrig y Bleidda Mine being first agreed with Roe and Co. for all their engines, stock of coal, utensils, implements and iron at the sum of £2,013 6s. 0d.[8] The possession of this work by Lord Uxbridge and Mr. Williams as joint adventurers in the proportion of ¾ to His Lordship and ¼ to Mr. Williams commenced on 10 October 1785."[9]

Something must have happened between September 5th when Uxbridge was minded to take no partners and October 10th when the new company was founded. What convinced Uxbridge to change his mind we do not know, but plainly, Williams had got his way.

Williams was nothing if not determined to get a share in the new mining company and had several meetings with Harrison in London and Anglesey to pursue his case, and one can only conclude that Harrison's recommendation had some bearing on Uxbridge allowing Williams a quarter share in the new venture, since as late as September 5th 1785 the earl was determined to go it alone. At some point in these negotiations

Thomas Harrison and the Canal Age

something happened that made Harrison more amenable to Williams involvement and he was able to persuade his lordship to acquiesce.

Harrison could have advanced good reasons for the earl to take Williams into partnership. The best parts of the mine were depleted and Roe and Company had left the mine in a poor state with a lot of clearing up to do. Lord Uxbridge knew very little about mining and with the example of his father before him he may have been reluctant to get into a protracted legal battle with Williams, who was a master of that game. Even so, at least one writer suggests collusion between Williams and Harrison to achieve an outcome desirable to Williams.

> One need not look too far to discover Harrison and Williams working together behind the scenes, in part evidenced by Harrison's inclusion in one of the manufacturing partnerships.[10]

This is difficult territory for the historian because there is absolutely no proof one way or the other of any impropriety on the part of Thomas Harrison but some of the circumstantial happenings around this time should raise some questions.

We can note the following. The Stanley Smelting Company, which had works at St Helens and Swansea, was half owned by Lord Uxbridge and a quarter owned by Thomas Williams. The remaining quarter was shared between the ironmaster, John Wilkinson, the works manager, Michael Hughes, the London banker and investor, John Dawes, and Thomas Harrison. Another company, the Greenfield Copper and Brass Company in Flintshire was another Williams company and Harrison appears about this time as a minor shareholder. And finally there was the Flint Coal Canal company, founded in 1784, which included all the players in the Parys Mountain mining drama, Edward Hughes, Thomas Williams, John Wilkinson, Edward Jones, a lead mine owner at Wepre, Flintshire, and Thomas Harrison.

Unfortunately we still do not know enough about Thomas Harrison's background to properly assess his wealth. He was certainly well-to-do at his death in 1809 and he was able to make good the damages assessed against him for the failed Wolverton aqueduct, a sum of over £9,000, without significant impact on the family. A few years later his son Richard was able to meet the demands of creditors on the failure of the Stony Stratford Bank without falling into bankruptcy. So the Harrisons had resources, although

Manno's Manor

notably not in land, which would lead me to conjecture that Thomas Harrison did not himself inherit any land and had to make his way in the world without significant assets. Did he have sufficient cash resources to invest in these companies in the 1780s, and if so, where did the money come from?

Without being able to answer that question one might ask if these shareholdings were actual investments by Thomas Harrison or did they represent compensation for services rendered? It is tempting to put the latter construction on this. As indicated earlier, the business of the mines was taking up a lot of Thomas Harrison's time for no other compensation other than expenses. As land agent for the Pagets at Beaudesert he was probably paid something like £40 a year, a similar sum to that which he drew from the Radcliffe Trust and Earl Spencer. The fee served the function of a retainer for services which involved some regular duties and occasional periods of activity. From the correspondence of the period 1783-5 it does appear that Harrison was under additional pressure of work and at one point is employing his son to assist him. So it is perhaps not surprising that he also looked for other opportunities to make some extra money. Certainly during this period he became a shareholder in several associated companies.

In the Stanley Smelting Company the major shareholders were Uxbridge and Williams, but the smaller shareholders were all active functionaries in the setting up and running of the company, so it is reasonable to infer that they were rewarded with small shares that would one day compensate them for their extra efforts. The same interpretation can be placed on Harrison's shares in the Greenfield company, except that here Uxbridge was not a shareholder and it can only be deduced that these shares represented a reward from Williams for "services rendered". These services may have been in conflict with his nominal master Lord Uxbridge and therefore may raise a query about Harrison's integrity. In a rather rambling letter dated 11 May 1786, Harrison is full of apology to the Earl of Uxbridge, although the exact cause of the upset is not identified. The earl was annoyed with Harrison and Williams about something and one interpretation may be that he was unhappy with the way Harrison had represented his interests.

Thomas Harrison and the Canal Age

The final company, the Flint Coal Canal Company, is more of a puzzle. The company was set up in 1784, involving many of the players in these other companies. They did go as far as obtaining an Act of Parliament approving the canal in 1788, but the canal was never built. The only construction was a bridge over the Wepre river with a plaque bearing the names of the directors, strangely enough nowhere near the line of the proposed canal. The authorized capital was £20,000. Was this capital actually raised? Did anyone lose money? Did anyone make any money? What was the point?

At the time of his involvement with the Anglesey enterprises, between 1782 – 1786, Thomas Harrison was able to build Wolverton House at a cost of £1840. He was able to recover £500 from the Radcliffe Trust, but even so was a large amount of money for the age. And from what we might guess about his "regular" income this figure represents more than ten times that figure – a highly speculative amount in any age, even assuming that he could borrow the money.

It is tempting to conclude that the house was built from the proceeds of his activity in Anglesey during the period. The modernisation of the old farmhouse may have begun with modest intentions in 1782, but in the last two years of the building program he must have realised large tranches of money from his industrial shares that enabled him to build Wolverton's largest house. Such a conclusion can be drawn from the coincidence of the building of Wolverton House and his adventure in the copper mining industry.

Harrison and Williams may have been men cut from similar cloth: both were very bright, legally trained but with no great prospects in life other than what they could earn through their wits. Williams' father was a middle class landowner in Anglesey, but by no means rich. His son had legal training and was able to build a respectable practise in Anglesey. His first involvement in the copper business obviously inspired him to develop his deal-making skills in this industry and at one time he held monopoly control of all copper mining in Cornwall and Wales, as well as the related processing industries.

By comparison Harrison was a small player but he seems to have been astute enough to develop some wealth from his contacts. On the whole he appears to have held his own with Williams and emerged financially better

Manno's Manor

off from the experience, and the knowledge gained may have encouraged him to invest in other industrial enterprises, which he undoubtedly did.

A final comment about Williams may give us some taste of the character of the man he had to deal with:

> Let me advise you to be extremely cautious in your dealings with Williams. He is a perfect tyrant and not over tenacious of his word and will screw damned hard when he has got anybody in his vice.[11]

The Canal Comes to Wolverton

The late 18th century witnessed a spate of canal building across the country and the creation of these waterways was an important first step in England's industrial revolution. In 1790 some promoters planned a canal that would join the Oxford Canal at Braunston with the River Thames at Brentford. It was to be called the Grand Junction Canal - a name it bore until recent times when it was changed to the Grand Union Canal. The proposed new canal would cut through the northern part of the Wolverton Estate and the Radcliffe Trustees met on 14th June 1792 to consider the implications and came to a quick conclusion in support of the plan. It was the most momentous change to the landscape since the enclosures of the 16th century. I do not believe that they would have come to this conclusion without the confident leadership of their man on the spot, Thomas Harrison. A land agent of a more conservative cast of mind, such as Thomas Quartley, may well have advised against it rather than enthusiastically promoting the idea. The significance of this decision cannot be underestimated. The existence of the canal in 1837 must have been a deciding factor in settling the engine repair shop at Wolverton, and it is quite arguable that without the canal there would be no railway works and without the railway works there would have been no Milton Keynes.

They would not have considered the impact on the countryside since that was a concept unknown to 18th century people, but they did see the advantages of a canal to transport goods. The bisection of farms was a matter easily dealt with by the building of bridges. The canal was approved by Act of Parliament on 30th April 1793.

Thomas Harrison and the Canal Age

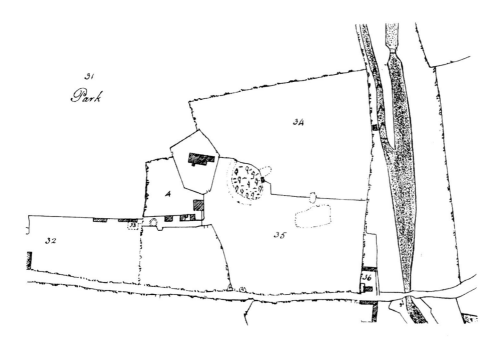

This 1804 map of Old Wolverton shows the lock channel as it once was.

Work began at both ends of the canal immediately but it was to be some years before the "navigators" came to the middle section in Wolverton. The greatest challenge at Wolverton, as was to be the case for the railway 40 years later, was the passage across the River Ouse. The original plan provided for four locks on the Southern bank and five locks on the Northern bank but in 1799 the engineer had second thoughts and proposed an aqueduct instead. However, because this project would add a further year of building they went ahead with temporary locks anyway. You can still find the remnants of these on the river bank.

The passage of a canal through Wolverton seems a small thing to us now, but the economic changes it brought to Wolverton were quite momentous. As I have already reported, the 1801 Census records Wolverton's population at 238; in 1831 this number had reached 417, almost double and without a steam engine in sight. Stony Stratford's population remained constant throughout the same period. This increase can only be attributed to the canal with its new wharf with jobs at the wharf and in the carting goods to and from. The Slated Row cottages date

Manno's Manor

from about 1820 and the very name indicates that probably for the first time roofs could be covered with imported slate from Wales, carried of course by canal.

With the locks in place the canal opened for traffic in the autumn of 1800. Work started on the aqueduct two years later. The contractor, interestingly enough, was Thomas Harrison himself. Harrison was not without previous experience in canal ventures although he had not been involved in any completed projects. He was not an entirely disinterested party in the coming of the canal to Wolverton. Harrison was inclined to spread his investments widely but he was not an investor (as far as we know) in the Grand Junction Canal, but it was as a building contractor that he won the contract for the construction of the aqueduct over the River Ouse. Today we might detect a whiff of conflict of interest, but the Trustees did not seem to notice, or at least not record any objections and had full confidence in Harrison in such matters. The Canal Company must have been of like mind because they did award him the contract. The aqueduct was built with three arches to support a wooden trunk which was lined with clay to prevent leaks - which it failed to do. The design was flawed. Boats began to use it in August 1805 but it was probably a perilous structure from the start. A few months later part of the embankment slipped. Repairs were effected but the Company Architect was not satisfied. Arguments about who was at fault went back and forth between Harrison and the Canal Company until February 1808 when the aqueduct spectacularly crashed overnight.

The lock-keeper at Cosgrove, a Mr. Cherry, was the first to notice the disaster at 11 pm that night and had the presence of mind to close the gates at his end and send out the alarm. Most Wolverton houses were high enough above the valley to be unaffected, but there was great consternation at the mills and at Stony Stratford about the prospect of flooding. Farmers also became anxious about their livestock in the meadows. That this happened in the middle of the night only aggravated the anxiety, but when daylight came, although the valley was in flood, it was no worse than a normal winter's flood and apparently livestock losses were minimal. In three days the water level subsided and even though an enormous quantity of earth had slipped into the river there was still an unblocked channel for the river course.

Thomas Harrison and the Canal Age

The consequences were huge, not only for the canal company, which was denied traffic until the aqueduct could be rebuilt but also to the famers and not least, the wharf workers and carters who probably lost income during this period.

Thomas Harrison insisted that he was blameless and the fault lay with the men who had built the aqueduct. The Canal Company were unconvinced and sued and took matters into their own hands. They built a temporary wooden trunk in April 1808 so that traffic could resume and commissioned a permanent structure. Stone piers were built and an iron trunk was ordered from the Ketley Iron Works in Shropshire to span the piers. This time they got it right, and in January 1811, the "Iron Trunk" was opened. It has now been in continuous service for over 200 years.

Harrison was taken to court and found liable despite his protests and damages were set at £9,262 - a considerable sum of money in those days, but one, which Harrison was readily able to pay. However, the shoddily built viaduct left at least one black mark against Harrison in what was otherwise a distinguished career.

The canal construction and the aqueduct was not without its consequences for the River Ouse and Wolverton. The Ouse was always liable to flooding after periods of heavy rainfall, and this is still the case today, but in the normal course of events the river would rise after heavy rain and then subside within a day or so. This normality was no longer observed in the post-Aqueduct period; more acres were flooded and the waters lingered for a longer time. After a particularly heavy rainfall in 1823 the flood spread wide over the lower reaches of the valley and even reached Wolverton House to a level of 17 inches above the floor. A civil engineer brought in some years later concluded that the aqueduct was partly to blame because it restricted the flow of water through the piers at high spate. It was not the only reason; the mill race was also a cause. The river was subsequently widened and deepened between the aqueduct and the mill.

The canal operators more than recovered their investment before railway competition ate into their profits, but canals continued to be of importance in the commercial transport of goods. Narrowboats, usually in pairs and often carrying coal, were still a regular feature in Wolverton in the 1950s, but by 1960 commercial traffic was gone and leisure craft were increasingly using the waterways.

A pair of working barges passing through Wolverton in the 1950s

There were quite important wharves at Old Stratford, by The Galleon at Wolverton and beside the New Inn at New Bradwell. Gradually these ceased to function. The presence of the canal and its links to the sea made it possible for the enterprising Edward Hayes to establish his boat building business at Stony Stratford. In some ways the construction of the canal prepared Wolverton folk for the greater changes which were to come 40 years later with the railway line, and it was in part due to the presence of the canal that the London and Birmingham Railway Company decided to build their engine repair shop at Wolverton.

Wolverton House

Thomas Harrison's surviving visible legacy to Wolverton is Wolverton House, which he built between 1782 and 1784.

The Jeffries Map of 1760 (page 223) shows farm buildings close to the present site of Wolverton House so we may assume that there was a pre-exisiting farm house on this site or thereabouts. Whether any of this was used in the construction of the new house we do not know.

By this time the Longueville manor house had gone and apart from some of the larger inns at Stony Stratford there were no houses of any

Thomas Harrison and the Canal Age

significance in Wolverton. Harrison's building project changed that. Even so, it was by no means a grand house and by comparison with many large manor houses was a modest building. Even compared to what we know about the Wittewronge mansion that his family used at Stantonbury it was small. However, it was spacious enough, with large rooms for the family and servants quarters in the attic. In 1784 it was also brand new.

Apart from providing a comfortable home for his family and servants the house signalled that Thomas Harrison had arrived. He was henceforth able to style himself Thomas Harrison of Wolverton and to all intents present the appearance of a member of the landed gentry.

The house must have been well built because it has stood the test of time. After his death in 1809 his son Richard continued to occupy the house with his widowed mother and own family and after Richard died, his widow and son Spencer remained as tenants until 1892, when Grace Harrison died. Spencer and his family then retired to the south coast.

Wolverton House Today

Manno's Manor

At this date the trustees were presented with a problem. The house was less attractive for the middle classes who preferred to live more conveniently in places like Stony Stratford and it was not desirable for wealthy industrialists who might prefer to build their own baronial pile on their own large estate. It was also slightly too grand for a farm tenant.

Some tenants were found for a period. Amongst early 20th century tenants was Dr Habgood, a Stony Stratford medical practitioner. His son John, who later became Archbishop of York, spent some of his boyhood in what he remembers as a very draughty house in Winter. The house by now was now separated from the farm and let as an independent dwelling.

After the war it was leased to Buckinghamshire County Council, who used it as a residence for Grammar School pupils whose parents were working overseas. They also used some of the buildings as offices and sometimes the house was used for residential courses. It was eventually sold after 1970 along with the sale of the whole estate to MKDC. Today the building is used as a restaurant.

Wolverton House from the west.

Thomas Harrison and the Canal Age

Thomas Harrison's will extended to several pages and over 4,000 words. He was able to make provision for various daughters and his grandchildren and indeed the poor of Wolverton and Stony Stratford, but the bulk of his inheritance was shared between his two surviving sons, John, from his first marriage, and Richard, from his second marriage. John's life and interests were in London and St. Albans, where he was at some time an alderman and mayor. Richard stayed in Wolverton and tok over his father's role as land agent to the Radcliffe Trust, a position he held until his own death in 1858.

During his life Thomas Harrison's business interests were extensive and possibly intricate and it is more than the scope of this chapter to cover them all, but we can note that when the Trustees had to sell off the inns in Stony Stratford to pay a land tax in 1802, Thomas Harrison was at hand to buy *The Bull* and a field known as Gardner's Close, which was where the school and St Mary's Church was later built. He also purchased Browne Willis's old Water Hall mansion at Bletchley. He then had it demolished, possibly with some development plans in mind. In the event death intervened and nothing was done until it was sold to Sir Herbert Leon who built Bletchley Park.

The Harrisons may have done very well out of their purchase of *The Bull*. This was, in those pre-railway days, a golden age for the coaching trade. However, Richard Harrison over-reached himself with the Stony Stratford bank, which he established with some other investors. It failed in 1820 and *The Bull* was put up for sale in 1821 so that he could meet his obligations. The Particulars and Conditions of Sale[12] describe nine bedrooms, a dining room, two parlours, a kitchen and wash house, a brewhouse, and of course good beer and wine cellars. The yard was even more extensive, with stabling for 70 horses, a coach house, a chaise shed, a blacksmith's shop, two straw houses, a coal house, three wells, water troughs and six acres of pasture.The property also included walled gardens and some rented properties in the court, which were described as "several genteel dwelling houses and comfortable cottages". It was a complete self-contained industry and at the time employed a staff of twenty.

This incomplete account about Thomas Harrison's life and activities revealsis a fascinating portrait of the kind of man who led progress in the latter half of the 18th century. As a land agent he was still very much

Manno's Manor

involved with the agricultural world which had dominated life for so many centuries, but at the beginning of the industrial revolution Thomas Harrison was one of those who understood the opportunities. He was able to comfortably carry his duties to various agricultural estates and shoulder new industrial opportunities as they came along, and, along the way, make a great deal of money.

Thomas Harrison has left more than a trace on the area but his lasting legacy will probably be his facilitation of the Grand Junction Canal. There is also, for now, Wolverton House.

---

1 Inner Temple admission registers. Admission date 25/11/1754; call date 12/2/1757. 3rd son of Sir Thomas Harrison, kt. This might be Sir Thomas Harrison 1701-65

2 George Lipscomb. The History and Antiquities of the County of Buckingham. London: J.W. Robins, 1847. Vol. IV, p. 345.

3 Helen Bamford, David Went & David McOmish. An Archaeological Survey of the Manor House and Gardens, Stantonbury, Milton Keynes. Records of Buckinghamshire, Vol. 45, p. 174.

4 George Lipscomb. History and Antiquities of Buckinghamshire. London, 1847. Vol. IV p.350.

5 Thomas Harrison. Mona Mine MS. University of Wales, Bangor: MS3544.

6 Ibid.

7 ibid.

8 Thomas Harrison. Memorandum dated 11 October 1785, Mona Mine MS. University of Wales, Bangor: MS 3485.

9 Thomas Harrison. Memorandum dated 31 March 1788, Mona Mine MS. University of Wales, Bangor: MS 3046.

10 Dorothy Bentley Smith. A Georgian Gent & Co.: The Life and Times of Charles Roe of Macclesfield. Landmark Publishing Ltd: 2005. P.473.

11 Letter from Thomas Wilson to James Watt, 15 September 1790.

12 1st June 1821

TEN

WOLVERTON BEFORE THE AGE OF STEAM

Roads, Inns and the Coaching Trade

When the 18th Century opened the people of England, although they did not know it at the time, were on the brink of a long period of rising prosperity. The religious strife which had dominated and undermined the previous century had reached a peace of sorts and the role of monarchy had been brought into some balance with the powers of Parliament. There was now time to focus attention on more mundane matters, not least of which was the appalling condition of the roads, which were, in many parts of the country, barely passable. Given the position of Wolverton and Stony Stratford on the Watling Street this was a matter of great importance.

As good a description as any of the parlous state of the roads was this account by an attendant of Prince George of Denmark, husband of Queen Anne, who travelled in 1702 from Windsor to Petworth to meet King Charles III of Spain, then on a state visit to England. The journey of 50 miles took 14 hours, less than walking pace, and is here described by one of his attendants.

"We set out at six in the morning by torchlight to go to Petworth and did not get out of our coaches (save only when we were overturned or stuck fast in the mire) till we arrived at our journey's end. 'Twas hard service for the Prince to sit fourteen hours in a coach that day without eating anything and passing through the worst ways I ever saw in my life. We were thrown but once indeed in going, but our coach, which was the leading one, and his Highness's body coach would have suffered very much if the nimble boors of Sussex had not frequently poised it or supported it with their shoulders from Godalming almost to Petworth; and the nearer we approached the Duke of Somerset's house the more inaccessible it seemed to be. The last nine miles of the way cost us six hours to conquer them; and indeed we had never done it if our good master had not, several times, lent us a pair of horses out of his own coaching whereby we were able to trace out the road for him."[1]

Manno's Manor

We can take this as typical. After an Act of Parliament in 1657 had established the office of postmaster general and a Royal Mail service, the average speed of travel was no better than 3 miles and hour. At first there was not, and could not be, a mail coach; the roads could not support such a method of delivery. Instead, a post boy, either riding a laden horse or leading a pack horse, trudged up and down the highways to deliver the mail packets. When a post office was established at Little Brickhill in 1687, this marked a full 12 hours journey time from London.

The old society, dominated by agriculture, was on the cusp of change, and would undergo a dramatic transformation in the 19th and 20th centuries, but in 1700, there was only a glimmer of the light of change on the horizon. It was enough for some people to pay attention. The demand for raw materials and manufactured goods was on the rise and the old seaways and riverways were no longer sufficient for satisfactory delivery. Mercantile interests were developing in parallel and these men required improved communication which could only come through an improved road system.

Medieval England had made do with the old Roman military roads and old ridgeways for cross country travel. Over the years new trackways had developed, some for through traffic and some for local farm traffic. The Thomas Jeffreys map of 1760 shows the pre-railway road system, probably much as it would have been found in 1700, except for a marked improvement in the quality of the road surface. On the map you can see all grades of roads in the Parish, from farm tracks, to cross-country roads and to the Watling Street as a principal highway.

It was the introduction of Turnpike Acts in the 18th century that resulted in huge improvements to road travel. Up to that time the responsibility had been laid upon the parish, which may have been effective enough for a local road running through the parish where there was obvious self interest in maintenance, but it was much harder to get cooperation for an arterial road like the Watling street, where small parishes, not unreasonably, could see no advantage in keeping up the road for travellers passing through. Government tried various coercive measures, with mixed results, but it was not until the Turnpike Acts allowed the collection of tolls to pay for the upkeep of roads that a systematic road maintenance scheme came into being.

Wolverton before the Age of Steam

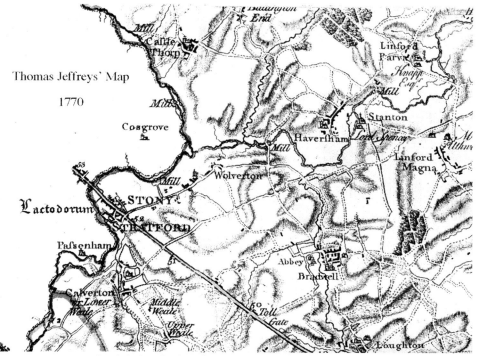

Roads before the Canal Age: 1770 Map by Thomas Jeffreys

The very first of these acts involved Stony Stratford. An act of 1707 formed a Turnpike trust for the section of road between Fornhill (near Hockliffe) and Stony Stratford (a distance of about 15 miles) and was steered through Parliament by Sir John Wittewronge, who owned the manor of Stantonbury. Wittewronge also held estates near Harpenden and had a vested interest in good communication between his two mansions but it says something for the vision of these men in that they were able to understand the importance of a good arterial road. In an age when travel might be measured in days the saving of half a day was considerable. Once the act had been passed, the commissioners, who included men like Browne Willis, the MP from Whaddon Hall, were able to borrow money at 4 per cent annual interest and rebuild and maintain the road to a standard. A scale of charges was set at each toll bar and the income raised was used to pay off the loan and invest further into the maintenance of the roads. We can look back with some surprise that the scheme was successful. There would have been much temptation for the less scrupulous to pocket the

Manno's Manor

proceeds and neglect the roads, but it seems, that across the country, various worthy gentlemen took their responsibilities seriously and through thousands of acts of Parliament in the succeeding years the road system was brought up-to-date. Stony Stratford benefited. As the 18th century progressed the engineering of roads improved, so that they became more stable with better drainage.

Toll rates were set to broadly reflect road usage. A coach drawn by four horses was charged 1 shilling, whereas a chaise drawn by a single horse paid only 6d. A horse and rider would only pay 1d. And a pack horse was charged only half that. There were some curious exceptions: a wagon would be charged 1 shilling except if it was laden with grain when the toll was only 6d. Smaller carts only paid 8d. As a rule, animals, which were expected to do less damage to the road, were charged much less. You could move a score of oxen for 6d and the same number of pigs for 3d. Twenty sheep or lambs were assessed at 1 penny.

Toll gates were erected at each end of the Wolverton manor - at the Stony Stratford bridge and at Two Mile Ash. Travellers would encounter another gate at Loughton and then at Fenny Stratford, so any journey that was not locally limited could become expensive.

Nevertheless, the system worked and a succession of Turnpike Acts in the eighteenth century eventually built a decent road system throughout the country. The Wolverton to Newport road was turnpiked with a toll gate close to Debb's Barn. Once this bar was set up all commercial movement between Wolverton and Stony Stratford (and there must have been a great deal) was subject to toll. Journeys from Wolverton to Cosgrove by road had to pay two tolls so there was a great incentive to use the track to Wolverton Mill and make the crossing there, toll free of course, which put a great strain on the track and the wooden bridge.

Other mechanical improvements followed the establishment of good road surfaces. Carriages could now be designed with lighter and narrower wheels which could travel at much greater speeds. Wider wheels, which had once been necessary to straddle the ruts in the road could now be dispensed with and by the end of the century the system of coaching inns with teams of fresh horses every twenty or so miles meant that average speeds of almost twelve miles per hour became standard on the principal routes.

Wolverton before the Age of Steam

The other technological improvement was the invention of sprung carriages. Earlier systems, at first developed in Hungary, suspended the carriage on an underframe over the axles with chains. This helped to absorb the shocks of riding on bumpy roads. Over time these chains were replaced with leather, and by the late 17th century these leather straps were held by C shaped springs made from laminated iron. Steel springs a century later made this ride even more comfortable. The twin developments of improved roads and lighter, more comfortable carriages, combined to improve road travel.

By the mid 18th century it was possible to travel from London to Manchester in 4½ days, at an average speed of 5 miles per hour. This gave added importance to Stony Stratford which was now conveniently a day from London and a day from Birmingham. The inns must have enjoyed their heyday in this period and they grew in size and number and the town prospered. Even though there were disastrous fires, particularly the one of 1742, the Inns quickly recovered their trade and the splendidly rebuilt facades of *The Cock, The Bull* and *The Swan* remain as evidence of their 18th century prosperity.

As the century progressed average speeds doubled and the road system became highly organised. Time was of the essence and "stages" were established along the road so that each coach could be supplied with a team of fresh horses. The journey could continue after a break of only minutes to the next stage. In some respects the ostlers in each innyard were organised like Formula 1 crew at a pit stop. The horses, once refreshed, fed and stabled, could then be teamed up on a returning coach.

The road system became even more sophisticated with the development of posting houses. These posting houses were originally established to carry the Royal Mail so that the post boy could pick up a new mount at each house and make speed to the next house. Before too long it occurred to travellers and innkeepers alike that the same system could be utilised by ordinary travellers. So travellers would in effect rent a horse for each stage of the journey.

Which brings us once again to the premier industry, apart from agriculture, of Wolverton and Stony Stratford, the coaching trade. Now that improved roads had placed Stony Stratford at a mere day's journey

Manno's Manor

from London, it assumed a greater importance. The inns which established themselves on both sides of the road can now occupy our attention.

The major inns established themselves on the east side, closer to the centre of the town. By the 18th century (and probably earlier) there were five large inns - *The Cock, The Bull, The Swan, The Red Lyon* and *The Horseshoe. The Cock* and *The Bull* are still in business today. *The Swan*, which had variants of this name, survives as an 18th century building at Numbers 94-96 High Street. *The Red Lyon* and *The Horseshoe* occupied the land on which St Paul's School was built in the late 19th century, although neither survived the advent of the railways.

The Cock may be the oldest and there is some circumstantial and some actual evidence to support this view as was discussed in an earlier chapter. It is interesting to note that throughout the centuries *The Cock Inn* does not get into financial difficulties, which would suggest that outright ownership of the land meant that they never had to find money for rent, or even taxes.

The other four inns leased their land from the manor. We do not know when these leases began and we can only deduce dates from records from the late 15th century. *The Swan* was a place of record in 1526 because it is next door to a property owned by Bradwell Priory. This would suggest an earlier establishment.

The Bull Inn makes its first recorded appearance in the Parish Registers in 1671, but a document of 1710 mentions that it had been leased for 80 years, which offers us a date of 1630 as a foundation. We do not know, and perhaps will never know, whether another inn with a different name occupied this site in earlier years. Since it rented land from the Radcliffe Trust we can get a clearer idea of the scale of the enterprise from the recorded rents it was paying, first to Sir Edward Longueville and then to the Radcliffe Trust. This document shows us that *The Bull* was renting about 50 acres from the Trust, and while nowhere near as big as the larger farms on the manor, which varied from 200 to 300 acres, appears to be a sizeable small holding and suggests a scale of food production that would be needed to satisfy their guests. The fields, parts of West Rylands and East Rylands and The Leys were all to be found between Stony Stratford and the later Wolverton House. In addition *The Bull* has a close (that is an enclosed field) of four acres at the back of the Inn. For this they paid the Trust £94

Wolverton before the Age of Steam

per annum. It was a large sum and compares with the three main farmers who were paying £270, £210 and £225 respectively. It is a measure of the demand for good pasture for horses and the ability of the inn trade to pay that these premium rates could be charged. In the 1713 *Particular of the Manor* a Mr. Sanders has *The Bull* and its related fields, although in the following year his name is crossed out and that of William Ayres written in. In the third survey of this set, about three or four years later, Ayres has a lease with 11 years to come, so he may have been given a 15 year lease.

The Horseshoe Inn had a lease of 74 acres in total in 1713, which would indicate a large establishment. In that year it was held by Matt Eyres and his mother for 40 years, with another 20 to come. The similarity between the names might suggest that William Ayres was from the same family. *The Horseshoe* was known as a wagon inn and tended to specialize in accommodation for wagoners and carters. It may have been the 18th century equivalent of a truck stop and it may also explain why it quickly went out of business in the 19th century with the development of canals and railways. Road haulage was not to make a comeback until the 1950s. *The Horseshoe* does not appear in Robson's 1839 directory.

The fifth great inn, the *Red Lyon* was next door to the *Horseshoe*. It was leasing, or had been leasing since 1709 36 acres, 30 of which were in Greenleys. With another 20 years to come on the lease. The Red Lyon had been mentioned in William Edy's will. There is also a meadow, described as Red Lyon Leyes "which may be built upon with advantage" that would indicate the establishment of the Red Lyon for a long time as it had given its name to a meadow - some 90 acres, a small farm.

There is some hint that the two neighbouring inns amalgamated in the latter half of the 18th century,because in the Charity accounts and the Constables book there is only the one entry for *The Lyon and Horseshoe*.

Naturally enough, there were and are, inns on the west side of the road. *The White Horse* at 49 and 51 High Street is first documented in 1540. *The George* dates from the 17th century and *The Cross Keys* first appears in the middle of the 16t[h] century. *The Talbot* may date from the 18th century and in the 17th century three new inns appear on the Market Square, *The Crown, The White Hart* and *The King's Head.* They were not unimportant coaching inns but they were never quite as large as their counterparts on

Manno's Manor

the east side. Since the focus of this book is the Wolverton manor, I will not go into detail here.

To complement this list there were a number of smaller inns about which we know very little. Some of the names are fleeting: *The Black Boy, The Rowbuck Inn, The Nag's Head, The Queen's Head, The Angel, The Gate, The Bell, The Crown.* They were all on the east side and it is possible that they were in some instances the same establishment under different names. Some, or perhaps all, may have been little more than alehouses. To this list we can add *The Rose and Crown* which came to attention in 1609 through Michael Hipwell's will. It was probably functioning in 1577 when Michael Hipwell is listed as an innholder on the east side and there is evidence that Hipwell's father owned some land in that part of Wolverton, but other than this the history of *The Rose and Crown* is as murky as the rest of the inns.

When we come into the railway age the situation changed dramatically. All of the inns went into decline and *The Bull*, like the others, must have suffered from this loss of trade. *The Cock* appears to have weathered the downturn rather better.

The 1841 Census shows *The Cock* kept by John Battams and his wife, with five staff.[2] The 1851 Census, which is a bit more specific, shows it in the hands of the widow Mary Chapman. Her staff include a barmaid, House Maid, Waitress, Kitchen Maid, Post Boy, Porter and an Ostler. She also had five guests staying there that evening. Yet next door, John Reeve the Grocer (who also had a branch at Wolverton) was also employing six live-in staff, and the detailed line says that he was employing 3 men and 1 boy indoors and 11 men and boys outdoors. From this evidence in 1851 the grocery was a bigger business than the coaching inn.

The Bull appears to have fallen on hard times after the coaching trade collapsed. In 1851 it records Henry Wilmin as the victualler with only two servants. In 1841 it was kept by Samuel and Sarah Rich. They had four daughters, aged between 3 and 14 living with them. There is no hint of staff or guests in either census. The picture is not dissimilar in 1861.

By the 19th century all of these inns were in private ownership. The Radcliffe Trust was subject to Land Tax but a new act in 1799 and later in 1802 allowed them to redeem their taxes with a lump sum payment. The lump sum payment would earn interest at 3%, which would in turn be applied against taxes. Accordingly they decided to sell some of their Stony Stratford properties, especially the inns, which were put up for auction. Their land agent, Thomas Harrison, who never appeared to be short of funds to invest in property, accordingly obliged and successfully bid on *The Bull*. From this time on the managers of these hotels were either tenants or employees, which may explain the turnover. Thomas Harrison and his son probably did well out of this establishment until the forced sale of 1821.

The High Street circa 1864

Despite this downturn, these three establishments have survived into the 21st century as hotels with impressive facades onto Stony Stratford High Street. Today it is no longer a busy thoroughfare as the A5 now bypasses Stony Stratford

Trades in Stony Stratford

In the early years of the 19th century Stony Stratford would be largely undistinguishable from other small market towns. The inns were dominant, and while one could find the full range of smaller tradesmen: to service the needs of daily life there was no manufacturing industry to distinguish it from the ubiquitous cottage industries that pervaded most small town and village life in these parts. Pigot's 1830 directory for Stony Stratford offers this assessment:

Manno's Manor

Lace is the manufacture of this place, nearly all of the lower class of females being engaged in its production; but its chief trade arises from its thoroughfare situation.

Lace making, like straw hat making, tailoring and dress-making, was literally a cottage industry. The lacemaking was undertaken by women working in their own homes. Manufacturers would organise the production and marketing and they too would work from their own homes. The lace makers were paid at a piece rate, and probably not very much.

Today, lace making appears to be a very genteel craft, the pictures of young girls and women sitting outside their cottages in the sun with their pillows conform to our romantic of a peaceful, rural English past. The reality of a lace maker's life in the 19th century was harsh. Lace makers worked at home, getting in as much as ten hours of lace making in, as well as running the household. Lace was made through a so-called 'putting-out system', meaning that lace dealers would supply lace makers with patterns and thread and then come back to buy the finished lace, deducting the price of the thread. Lace makers often worked for more than one dealer, but ultimately dealers had the upper hand in deciding how much a lace maker could get for her efforts. The existence of a lace maker and her family was often hand-to-mouth and many young women preferred to go into domestic service, rather than make lace.

There were four lace manufacturers at this time: John Loe, Robert Thomas Lyons, Josiah Michael Smith and William Talbot Wallis - all living on the High Street. The early 19th century may have represented the high point for lace manufacture. The development of machines in the Midlands gradually eroded the practice of hand lace making and the same Pigot directory in 1842 was to ruefully observe that lace-making "has greatly declined." In that year John Loe was still active, although now relocated to a back street and the only other lace maker was Amos Cowley of Old Stratford.

In every respect the town was thriving in 1830 with a population of 1499 reported in 1821, thus overwhelming the Wolverton Manor which was still reporting a small population. In addition to the inns and taverns already described the town had two wheelwrights on hand, three saddlers and harness makers and two veterinary surgeons. The inhabitants could draw upon the services of nine bakers, five butchers, three confectioners,

Wolverton before the Age of Steam

five grocers and four wine and spirit merchants. For their clothing they could find nine tailors, eight boot makers, six milliners and dress makers, two straw hat makers, two glovers and four linen and woollen drapers. Furniture and household needs could be satisfied by two cabinet makers, two basket makers, three tallow chandlers, three ironmongers and two coal merchants. Professional services came in the form of two branch banks, three attorneys, two auctioneers, two chemists and four surgeons, and, given Stony Stratford's 18th century history, six fire insurance agents. In addition the town had two maltsters, two watch and clock makers two millers, five painters, plumbers and glaziers. The town also had four stonemasons, and interestingly, two toy dealers. There was also a printer and bookseller on the high street.

There were also a surprising number of schools; five private schools, and the National School. The National School, with Henry Potter Malpas as its master was located in the High Street and included the old *Rose and Crown* which Michael Hipwell had bequeathed to the town as a Grammar school.

Markham's account of the school suggests that it was very poorly funded for most of the first 200 years and is critical of the lack of contribution from the community. There is a hint from Browne Willis, writing in 1753, that some of the funds from Hipwell's charities may have been embezzled. He was referring in particular to the Buckingham Gaol charity which was to be funded by *The George* and two adjoining houses, but whether this peculation extended to the *Rose and Crown* Charity we do not know. Michael Hipwell's conception of a self-sufficient enterprise did not live up to its full potential.

The other schools were a mix of Dame schools and "Ladies" and "Gentlemen's" schools largely designed with the intention of turning out people who could adopt the right etiquette and manners. One school that has earned some special mention was the Dancing Academy of Mr Joseph Hamblin on the corner of the Market Square and Mill Lane. He was such a personality that Charles Dickens, ever the careful observer of character, spotted him at the *Cock Inn* and used him as a model for Mr Turveydrop in his novel *Bleak House*. He left this description:

> He was a fat old gentleman with a false complexion and a wig. He had a fur collar, and a padded breast to his coat, which only wanted a

Manno's Manor

star or a broad blue ribbon to be complete. He was pinched in and swelled out, and got up, and strapped down, as much as he could possibly bear. He had such a neckcloth on that his chin and even his ears sunk into it, that it seemed as though he must inevitably double up if it were cast loose. He had, under his arm, a hat of great size and weight, and in his hand a pair of white gloves, with which he flapped it, as he stood poised on one leg in a high shouldered, round elbowed state of elegance not to be surpassed. He had a cane, he had an eye glass, he had a snuff box, he had rings, he had wristbands, he had everything but any touch of nature; he was not like youth, he was not like age, he was not like anything in the world but a model of Deportment.[3]

At the time Dickens saw him he must have been over 60. He had been in Stony Stratford since 1830 at least, possibly earlier. In the 1851 census he has 8 young girls, aged between 9 and 13, as boarders. One must assume that he took day students as well. He offers his occupation "Professor of Dancing" He had three other teachers at the school at that date so it must still have been a viable business. However, by 1861 Joseph Hamblin has passed on and so it seems has his school. His widow and daughter continued to live in part of the house with a cook.

Stony Stratford's Market Square in 1819

Wolverton before the Age of Steam

Most inns and alehouses were still brewing their own beer in the early 19th century. Larger inns had their own brewhouse; alehouses had more primitive facilities.

Beer doesn't (or at least didn't) travel well and until the invention of motorized vehicles could only be delivered by horse-drawn dray. Speeds of 3 to 4 miles per hour were a serious restriction on the range of delivery, so I imagine that access to Northampton or Bedford beers were out of the question in the 19th century, unless the railway was used.

Traditionally, ale houses brewed their own beer. Malt (the tricky ingredient) was obtained from a Maltster and from there on the fermentation process was fairly straightforward. I assume the quality of the product was highly variable. Breweries began to develop in the larger cities in the early 18th century and gradually spread to the provinces. There was a brewery in Newport Pagnell dating from 1780. It was not apparently very successful, undergoing a series of bankruptcies, but limped along through a series of different owners until it was bought by Charles Wells of Bedford in the 1920s, largely for the pubs associated with it. They closed it down.

There was a brewery in Stony Stratford, although little is known about it, that was purchased by the Phillips family in the 1850s and then known as The Britannia Brewery. The Phillips family had extensive brewing interests in Bicester, Monmouth, Coventry and Northampton (the Northampton Brewery Company). I cannot find any reference to a Brewery in Stony Stratford in the 1839 Trade Directory, although there are two Maltsters, William Golby on the High Street and Thomas Ward on Horse fair Green. In the 1842 Pigot Trade Directory, Thomas Carter of the High Street is listed as a Brewer. In 1854 the brewery is in the ownership of Revill and Thorn. There was also a Maltster and Brewer in Cosgrove, and it would have been possible (although I have no evidence of this) for barrels to be delivered by canal, even as far as the Black Horse.

The early trade directory also shows us that Stony Stratford was growing a middle class. Medical practitioners, lawyers were able to make a living here. And there were some specialized trades emerging, like watch and clock makers, which could only be supported by a community of a certain size. It is noteworthy too that the town had two chemists. In smaller and less prosperous places drugs and remedies were still administered by grocers.

233

Manno's Manor

Stony Stratford had by this time developed into the most significant town on the Buckinghamshire section of the Watling Street. This would change with the coming of the railway, which was at once the ruin and salvation of Stony Stratford. In 1831 it had a population almost four times that of Wolverton. By 1851, even though Stony Stratford's population also increased due to the railway works, it had been surpassed by Wolverton and by the end of the 19th century Wolverton was double the size of the old town.

A New Church for Wolverton

Meanwhile, change was afoot a mile away on the old manor of Wolverton. As we have seen the construction of the canal had a transforming effect on the economy and population of Wolverton. Now the church became the centre of everyone's attention.

When Henry Quartley arrived at Wolverton in 1794 the church was considered to be in a very poor state of repair, and, not having been high on the Trust's agenda for some years, was now in urgent need of attention. By this time the building and tower was over 400 years old. Thomas Harrison was asked to conduct a survey and estimate the cost of the work. However, Quartley, in contrast to the selfless Edmund Green his predecessor in the earlier part of the century, held the view that the vicarage, by that time about 70 years old, needed more urgent attention and persuaded the Trust to contribute £200 towards the cost of rectory repairs in 1796.

The church stayed off the agenda until 1802 when Harrison re-presented a plan for repairs. There was no immediate action as one of the trustees, the Earl of Aylesford, was interested in a grander design and for a few more years still the medieval church continued to satisfy. Aylesford, who brought some enthusiasm and experience of church building to the table, appears to have promoted the initiative and was asked by the board to develop plans for a new church. He discovered a young architect, the 36 year-old Henry Hakewill and brought him to a meeting of the Trustees on 27th May 1808. At this meeting the Trustees made a decision to procure plans and estimates and a year later Hakewill's plan and estimated cost of £3,742 17s. was given the green light.

An early drawing of the new church.

The design of the church was quite distinctive, and proved to be even more unusual in that few churches were built in this style after this date. Its Romanesque style with references to Norman architecture was in marked contrast to the old church and only had a brief fashion before 19th century church building returned to the English style. What can be said about Hakewill's architectural choice is that it was a deliberate reminder that this church is the oldest foundation on the Wolverton Manor and precedes by at least 200 years the development of Stony Stratford.

Hakewill's plan involved pulling down the old nave and chancel while retaining the structure of the tower. The tower now became the western entrance for the new church and was faced and decorated in the new style. The drawing above, dating from the 1840s, shows the new church in pristine condition.

The construction was a long one and the new building was finally completed in 1815 at almost double the first estimate. When all the bills were totalled and paid the Trust had spent £7,792 18s 7½d. As Lipscomb drily noted, "Few villages in England can boast of so splendid and costly a church as Wolverton."[4] One additional consequence of this rebuilding project was that the landscaping of the grounds around the church and rectory led to the filling of the ancient castle moat.

Manno's Manor

The retention of part of the old tower meant that a part of the older history of the building was preserved. Some of the older stone was used in the foundations and rubble walling, although all of the stone facing was from new quarries. As one might expect stone for the older building was sourced from the local quarry at Cosgrove. The better quality stone must have been carted from further afield. Some ashlar ironstone has been identified as coming from a quarry at Towcester. Northamptonshire quarries at Weldon, Clipsham and Helmdon appear to have provided the facing stone for the medieval church

The new canal made the transport of stone much easier and the architect was able to go further afield to quarries at Attleborough near Nuneaton and Bilston, near Northampton. Although stone was transported considerable distances during the medieval building period, the new transportation system made the carriage so much easier and faster. This was also a new age of iron manufacture and the windows were made by a company in which Thomas Harrison had an interest and were delivered by canal to the Old Wolverton wharf. Contrary to its external appearance the new building is brick-built but faced with stone from the midland quarries. The tower was preserved in its limestone form but faced with cut stone from the Attleborough quarry.

The interior of the new church is highly, and one might even say, extravagantly decorated. It is not hard to see where the money went.

Two hundred years later it still stands in its original setting, largely oblivious to the area's development over its lifespan. The unusual choice of a Romanesque architectural style also provides distinction. It is a small gem.

Tucker's Girl

We last looked at the Church Warden's Account Books at the beginning of the 18th Century. At the outset of the 19th Century little had changed. The sick and the poor and the needy were still the responsibility of the Parish. Occasionally people with means would make charitable donations such as Michael Hipwell's £5 in the 17th century and Thomas Harrison's £100 bequest for distribution amongst the poor 200 years later, but such instances were sporadic and hardly amounted to a system. The system that was in place was funded by rates levied upon those who could pay.

Wolverton before the Age of Steam

In 1834 the government passed the Poor Law Act which, for the first time took such responsibility from the Parish and created a larger administrative unit called a Poor Law Union. From this time forth Wolverton and Stony Stratford were in a district centred on Potterspury. The 1834 Act was a step towards a more uniform system.

Before I go on to this let us take one more look at the system administered by the Churchwardens.

Two of their number were appointed overseers for the year beginning in April. It appears that they divided the parish, which extended from Bradwell Brook in the east to Watling Street in the west, one administering the east side and another the western part. The overseers appear to come from the ranks of the larger farm tenants. The new overseers for 1809-10 are Robert Battams from Stacey Bushes Farm and William Wilkinson from Brick Kiln Farm. The rate, at 1/6d. in the Pound, was assessed only against land and property, so the farmers had a vested interest in the management of this money, which they appear to have managed very carefully, because there was usually each year returned a surplus of income over expenditure.

Here is the minute of the annual meeting of April 3rd 1809

Balance recorded of late overseers	£86 17s 9½d
do of John Tucker	£20 0s 0d
by 1/6 Rate	£271 11s 0d.
Total	£370 8s 9½d
Disbursements brought down	£290 0s 7d
Balance due to Parish	£ 80 8s 2½d

April 3rd 1809. At our annual meeting this day held we have perused the preceding accounts of Thos. Ratcliffe and John Brill and approve of the same and find due to the Parish Eighty Pounds eight shillings and two pence halfpenny which we Direct to be Paid to Robert Battams and Wm Wilkinson who were appointed to be overseers for the ensuing year.

A H Cathcart Curate
William Oliver
Thos. Ratcliffe
John Brill

Manno's Manor

John Tucker's contribution of £20 was an unusual payment. In the detail of the accounts its purpose becomes clear. On December 11th 1808 the following entry appears in the Churchwarden's Account Books:

Received of John Tucker on account of Mary Edmunds Child

£20 0s 0d.

This was the usual practice when a man responsible for getting an unmarried girl pregnant was assessed a fine to defray the cost to the Parish - in this case £20. Some months before this entries for payments to "Tucker's Girl" begin to appear, starting with a payment of 2/6d for one week on July 20th 1808. Thereafter, there are regular payments of 2/- a week, paid every fortnight, to *Tucker's Girl.*

Gradually we can piece together a story.

In September there is a payment of 4/- to the magistrates for a removal certificate and a few days later a payment of 6/6d to "a man to Convey Tucker's Girl to Marsh Gibbon out 2 days." The payments of 2/- a week continue and then on November 5th there is a payment to Bet Williams "for Tucker's Girl Towards her Months" - 10s. And again on November 19th another payment of 10s. "Paid Bet Williams on account of Tuckers Girls Month." She gets a similar payment on November 25th and December 3rd and on December 10th is give a further 2/6d for extra trouble. Weekly payments to *Tucker's Girl* continue to January 7th 1809. Thereafter, Mary Edmunds is entered under her own name and is paid £1 every 10 weeks (still at the 2s a week rate) for a year after this. I assume until the £20 is used up.

My reading of this is that the pregnancy of Mary Edmunds is first recognised and acknowledged in July. She is thereafter paid at a rate of 2s a week. The initial reaction must have been for her to move to Marsh Gibbon, presumably where she had relatives, but that she may have chosen to return. The removal certificate was required for movement from one parish to another at this time. Bet Williams was the midwife who was paid 10s. a week during *Tucker's Girl's* last month of confinement. Bet Williams appears in other unrelated entries, so is probably Wolverton's local midwife. It is interesting that Mary Edmunds is only described as *Tucker's Girl* until the child is actually born and John Tucker has made his payment of £20. I assume that if the pregnancy had not gone to term or the child

Wolverton before the Age of Steam

had not survived then John Tucker would not have been liable for the whole amount and Mary Edmunds would have remained anonymous. If no child survived birth then the stain of illegitimate birth would not attach itself to Mary Edmunds.

John Tucker was probably already married when he got Mary Edmunds pregnant, so she was effectively on her own. 2s a week amounted to bare subsistence and was the rate paid to the sick, so out of the £20 put up by John Tucker, she received about 20 months support after the other expenses were deducted. Options for girls in this situation were extremely limited. Support could either come from her immediate family or she could get married, if she could find a man to take her. I hope the Mary Edmunds story had a satisfactory outcome.

After the National Insurance Act was passed in 1948, benefits offices paid out sick benefits every two weeks. The Government were not reinventing the wheel but were continuing a much older tradition.

The Churchwarden Accounts for Holy Trinity show payments to the sick every two weeks. Judging by the names that are repeated most of these cases are for old people or those with long term illnesses. I doubt if a cold or a sniffle would have got much sympathy from the overseers. In any case, with payments of only 2 shillings a week, nobody would willingly wish to see their income cut by two-thirds or more

Here is a sample of entries for 1808:

Paid Wm Clark 2 weeks at 2/-	4s 0d.
Paid Wm Caves 2 weeks at 2/6	5s 0d
Paid Thos Cook 2 weeks at 1/-	2s 0d
Paid Wm Cross 2 weeks at 2/-	4s 0d
Paid F Arnold 2 weeks at 1/3	2s 6d
Paid Widow Wills extra 2 weeks at 2/-	4s 0d

and these amounts repeat every two weeks.

It is not clear why some were paid different amounts, although this would suggest that other factors were taken into account, such as age and household income. Most of these people were seriously ill as the payments

Manno's Manor

go on for some months. There are few, if any, examples to be found where someone appears on the books for a week or two and then restored to health, so as I remarked earlier, nobody took time off for minor complaints. The money was provided only to alleviate extreme hardship.

The Slow Decline of Farming

At the close of our period the prospects for farming might have looked brighter than they actually turned out. Looking back we can now say that the best years of agriculture were over by the time of the Napoleonic Wars. Food prices had risen, but rents had also risen by 14%. Grain prices reached their peak in 1812 and then began to fall and farmers everywhere struggled. Rent reductions of 10% were allowed between 1820-24 and again from 1829-36. Farm labourers wages fell and unemployment was high. Desperate people responded by burning hayricks and destroying farm machinery. Everyone suffered in one way or another. Richard Harrison, probably the wealthiest man on the manor, was a partner in the Stony Stratford Bank, which failed in 1820, and he was left with considerable debts. The decline continued throughout the 19th century.

In 1800 80% of the total population drew their income from agriculture. By the end of that century that figure might have been as low as 4%. The industrialisation of the country had been a complete revolution. Wolverton as we know was to derive direct benefits first from the canal and then from the railway of the country's new found wealth. But for that, as I observed at the beginning of this book, the 19th century would have witnessed the gradual depopulation of Wolverton and Stony Stratford.

The enclosures completed in the 17th century created five or six farms ranging from 200 to over 400 acres. By the 19th century this arrangement had settled to fewer but more sustainable farms. Manor Farm in the north, Stonebridge House in the east, Stacey Bushes in the south, a farm based on the brick yards along the Watling Street, and Wolverton House Farm. There were two smaller farms, Debbs Barn, near Stony Stratford and Wolverton Park Farm. Land formerly taken by the inns for pasture was no longer required after the coaching inn trade fell off after 1840 and was absorbed into the farms.

When a survey was conducted for the Trust in 1847 the two largest farms were Brick Kiln with 468 acres and Wolverton House Farm with 478

Wolverton before the Age of Steam

acres. Manor Farm had 323 acres under its control and Stacey Bushes 409 acres. Stonebridge House in the east had lost land to the railway and was left with 318 acres. Park farm was smaller at 150 acres and Debb's Farm had only 89 acres.

After this report Debb's Farm, which had been struggling under the last tenant John Whiting, was absorbed by the Wilkinsons and Park Farm was split between Manor Farm and Wolverton House Farm. Wolverton Park Farm house was then rented to J E McConnell, Superintendent of the Wolverton Railway Works.

Farming was also very hard in the last quarter of the 19th century. Cheap corn could now be imported from North America and frozen sheep and cattle could now be brought to England from Australia and New Zealand, again at lower prices. As a consequence the Trust had to reduce their rents by 10% and 20% in the 1880s. Conditions were not to get better for British farmers until after WW II.

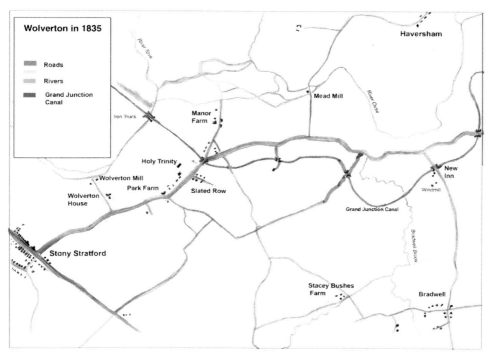

Wolverton before the railway

Manno's Manor

A new farm house and buildings for Stacey Bushes farm was constructed in 1848 on Stacey Hill. The old farm buildings by Bradwell Brook were demolished. The Battams family continued to farm there until 1888. It was farmed by John Richards until 1920 and thereafter by Edward Norman until 1937. He struggled during the depression. He was succeeded by a member of the Luckett clan until 1960 and in the last decade of its existence by B. .C Gurney.

Stonebridge House was also rebuilt in 1855 but continued under the tenancy of the Ratcliffe family until 1884. The Norman family occupied the farm until 1948. Then for 5 years it was let to Raymond Turney. The last tenant in its history was W. E. Gurney.

Manor Farm had similar longevity of tenure, coming into the 19th century with the Gleed family it then passed into the hands of a branch of the Wilkinson family, who thereafter farmed it until 1929. The Whiting family then took over the farm for the last 41 years of its life.

When Spencer Harrison gave up Wolverton House Farm in 1892, the Trust decided to separate Wolverton House from the farm and rent it as a large country house. In this year Warren Farm was created and the trust built a new farm house in the field that used to be known as the Warren. Henry Barrett was the first tenant and he remained there until his death in 1917. The Turney family then took over the tenancy, which they retained until 1970 when the entire estate was sold to Milton Keynes Development Corporation.

Brick Kiln Farm has been tenanted by the Wilkinson family since 1742. They were brick makers as well as farmers, as the name of the farm suggests, and this tradition continued into the 19th century. The Wilkinsons were there for several generations until the death of George William Wilkinson in 1893 at the relatively early age of 45. This was not the only surprise. Most people thought that he had substantial wealth, and were shocked to learn that he was in debt at his untimely death to the sum of £1,100.

The Trustees, themselves owed money, could not consider a further Wilkinson tenancy and this long period of family tenure came to an end. A man called I J Shirley took over in 1893 and farmed there until 1931. After this the Luckett family took on the farm until 1970.

Wolverton before the Age of Steam

Once established, tenant farmers, were usually able to pass on the farm tenancy to the next generation, and we can see this in the continuity of names over a 200 year period. The Ratcliffe family, for example had been on the estate since 1722, at Park Farm and Stonebridge House Farm. The Gleeds were established at Manor Farm and the Battams at Stacey Bushes Farm.

We can look back now and see that the coming of the Railways could not have been better timed in the case of Wolverton. Men who had been on borderline wages of 6s. a week, could now find work at Wolverton Station for 18s. a week. Had the London to Birmingham line gone through Buckingham, as first planned, Wolverton would have further declined, Stony Stratford, having lost the coaching trade, would have become equally poor, and I would not be writing this today.

A Cock and Bull Story

This first volume of the story of Wolverton, extending over a period of 1,000 years or more, comes to and end just before the thunder of a steam locomotive on rails broke the peace of the rural landscape forever.

The history I have presented lacks great historic incident but is remarkable for its largely uninterrupted prosperity. There were crop failures and serious outbreaks of plague and there was throughout this period poverty and hardship for some, but the majority could count themselves fortunate. Wolverton escaped the direct consequences of war. It was never the scene for any of England's civil war battles and was too central to the heartland of England to be subject to foreign invasion. For 1000 years Wolverton's residents were able to enjoy quiet prosperity.

Its location on the Watling Street helped Wolverton's economy. There were always other sources of income than simply the yield from crops and livestock. Later the introduction of the canal by itself doubled Wolverton's population. You can't help but wonder at Wolverton's luck. At the beginning of the industrial revolution in the 18th century, the improvement in roads and the development of canals brought newer forms of economic prosperity to Wolverton. In the 19th century, when Wolverton could have become another rural backwater, a series of accidental decisions brought a railway works to Wolverton and in the 20th century, at a time

Manno's Manor

when the railways were in terminal decline, a new city was created in North Bucks.

Even so, at the time of the arrival of the first steam train 175 years ago Wolverton village was still a small place and was probably quite unprepared for the next revolution. On September 16th 1838 Stony Stratford's inns were probably full and busy and looking forward to continuing prosperity. Many of Stony Stratford's residents probably walked to Wolverton Station the following day to greet this new phenomenon, the steam locomotive, making its first uninterrupted journey from London to Birmingham. They most likely cheered and applauded this new exciting development without even thinking about its future impact on Wolverton and Stony Stratford. That evening they returned home with the news and some men that evening were only too happy to recount the days events in both the Cock and the Bull to travellers who were still using that conventional means of transport.

One may imagine that as the evening wore on the tale-tellers in their cups embellished their account of the day's events. Did their listeners hear a Cock and Bull story?

The Cock and The Bull, both hotels today, are great survivors of the days of the coaching trade. Both inns in the centre of Stony Stratford were equivalent in size and amenities. Several of their rivals had fallen away and these two were supreme Were they likely candidates for the origin of the "Cock and Bull story"?

The phrase is said to have originated in Stony Stratford as a result of the rivalry between these two comparable establishments.

Rivalry and competition must have been at its keenest during the great coaching years but there is no reason to suppose that it had diminished by 1838. Local legend has it that the rivalry extended to the telling of traveller's tales, bragging rights going to the Inn that could boast the most entertaining tales. Naturally this encouraged the tellers of "tall tales" which may have started with a vestige of truth but ended with something so fanciful as to be implausible. Thus the phrase "Cock and Bull story" came to be applied to any story that you might doubt the truth of - "That's a bit of a Cock and Bull Story!"

Wolverton before the Age of Steam

However, you may treat this version of the origin of the phrase with some scepticism. Robert Burton writes in 1621 (a date that may pre-date The Bull) in his Anatomy of Melancholy:

"Some mens whole delight is to talk of a Cock and Bull over a pot."

And we have to take into account the American use of the word "bull", meaning rubbish or purely fanciful. Again we can't be too sure if this has an older meaning in the English language or if this may be a polite abbreviation of "bullshit".

Whereas, about the same time, the poet John Taylor is using the word "bull" to mean a joke or jest:

"Wit and Mirth ... Made up, and fashioned into Clinches, Bulls, Quirkes, Yerkes, Quips, and Jerkes."

The Cock has an older tradition in story telling and features in Chaucer and other medieval writers. Usually the tales were told in a comic tradition.

We can make the argument both ways. A Cock and Bull story could be an outlandish and funny story that comes from an older tradition of storytelling, or, it could have its origins in the two coaching inns in Stony Stratford. On the night of September 17th 1838 the buzz would have been about the events at Wolverton Station earlier that day. Was it a Cock story or a Bull story or both? Take your pick!

---

1 Rosamond Bayne-Powell. Travellers in Eighteenth Century England. 1951.
2 1830 1nd 1842 Pigot Directory shows Joseph Clare. 1839 Robson Directory G Harman. Guest refers to Battams and Co leasing the Engineer. Radcliffe Arms Congreve and Clare.
3 Bleak House,. 1852 Chapter 14 p 182
4 Lipscomb v 4 p 418.

Appendix I Wolverton at Domesday

A printed version of the Wolverton entry is reproduced here.

ᛗ Ipſe Maigno ten Wluerintone.ꝑ xx . hid ſe defd.

Tra . e . xx . car . In dnĩo . ix . hide . 7 ibi ſunt . v . car.
7 xxxii . uilti cũ . viii . bord hñt . x . car . 7 adhuc . v.
poſſunt fieri . Ibi . x . ſerui . 7 ii . molini de . xxxii . fol.
7 viii . den . Ptũ . ix . car . In totis ualent ual . xx . lib.
Qdo recep. xv . lib . T.R.E. xx . lib . Hoc ᛗ tenueꝛ
iii . teigni . Hoꝗ un Goduin hõ Heraldi . x . hid ha
buit . 7 alt Tori Huſcarle . R . E . habuit . vii . hid
7 dim . 7 iii . Aluric hõ Eddid reginæ . ii . hid 7 dim
habuit . Ipſi oms cui uolueꝛ uendere potueruɴ.

In translation it reads:

M Mainou holds WOLVERTON himself. It answers for 20 hides. Land for 20 ploughs; in lordship 9 hides; 5 ploughs there. 32 villagers with 8 smallholders have 10 ploughs; a further 5 possible. 10 slaves; 2 mills at 32s 8d; meadow for 9 ploughs. Total value £20; when acquired £15; before 1066 £20. Three thanes held this manor. One of them, Godwin, Earl Harold's man, had 10 hides; the second, Thori, one of King Edward's Guards, had 7 1/2 hides; the third, Aelfric, Queen Edith's man, had 2 1/2 hides; they could all sell to whom they would.

In 1086 there were 32 villagers and 8 smallholders, 10 slaves and two mills. In other words there are approximately 50 families living on the manor. This might translate into a population of 200-250, not much different, as we shall later see, from the population at the beginning of the Industrial revolution.

Manno's Manor

Appendix II The Estates of the Barony

Ellesborough

Ellesborough is now a small village south of Aylesbury. The township was quite extensive and after the conquest divided into three parts. Manno, Lord of Wolverton got one third of this, obviously quite cheaply as it was valued in 1086 at 2½ times what it was worth in 1066. It was probably subinfeudated quite early on, although we do not discover names until after 1166 when we know that William Brito held certain lands in Ellesborough from Hamo, Lord of Wolverton. The name suggests that this William was either a descendant of one of Manno's Breton knights or a junior member of his family. The land for half a knight's fee descended from William Brito until about 1261 or 1262 when it descended through the female line to John de Seyton of Maidwell in Northamptonshire. Thereafter it was known as Seyton's Manor. There was a further division of this estate at some time in the early fourteenth century when another manor emerges that has come down to history as Chequers, which is now used as a retreat for the Prime Minister. Chequers acquired its name from Helyas de Scaccario or "of the Exchequer" who held this part of the manor for a quarter knight's fee from the de Wolvertons.

The overlordship was retained by the De Wolvertons and their successors the de Longuevilles until at least 1636, when there is last any record of this. The whole business of knight fees or payment for service had been obsolete for centuries and whatever payment was involved must have been very small in comparison to the later value of the land and the power of the overlord to impose change was severely limited by this time.

Chalfont St Giles

As with Ellesborough Chalfont was subinfeudated to two of Manno's knights. The practice was one which made good sense to the overlord in the 11th century. The knights were experienced fighting men who could leap into the saddle at short notice to meet their commitments to their overlord and he to the king. All they needed was sufficient land to support their expensive warlike activities, so from the outset Manno had to parcel out much of his land to his followers in return for their guaranteed service. Over time this became less convenient for everybody. Knights were less

Appendices

willing to keep themselves in readiness and the call for service could usually be resolved through a payment which would allow for the cost of hiring a mercenary. There was probably some scope for the overlord to make a little bit of money on the deal as the cost of a mercenary might be less that the value of a knight's fee. Other ways of making money from the land was the practice of paying "relief" when the manor was inherited by a son. It was a sort of inheritance tax whereby the relief payment was set at a reasonable amount - possibly a year's income from the estate. In the economy of the 11th to the 14th centuries these practices worked well enough but after English kings found new ways of taxation to fund armies the apparatus of knight's fees fell into neglect and it became scarcely worth the legal cost to record the payment.

The Chalfont Manor covered almost 4,000 acres and was considered wealthy enough to be assessed at 2½ knight's fees. This is reflected in the division of the estate into three manors, Chalfont Bury, The Grove, and The Vache - the latter two taking their names after the dominant families from the earliest years. The Vache and the Grove families both perpetuated their lines for several centuries and gradually gained more control of their lands as the de Wolvertons declined. The last mention of any overlordship is in the 16th century. Chalfont Bury manor remained under the de Wolverton overlordship until 1349 when the estate was divided between the four daughters of Sir John de Wolverton who died in that year, most likely, given the date, of the plague.

Isenhampstead

This manor may have been part of the Chalfont estates of Manno for it does not get a mention until 1165 when we hear of Alexander de Isenhampstead who held it for a knight's fee. Within two generations the family had adopted the name of Cheyne and the manor was known as Isenhampstead Chenies and later simply Chenies. The Cheyne family appear to have been risk takers because on several occasions the manor was taken by the king for debts owing. But each time they seem to have recovered their position and various branches of the family extended their reach to other manors like Drayton Beauchamp, cogenhoe and the Grove. By the 16th century daughters of the Cheynes were marrying into the

Manno's Manor

Russell and Wriothesley families whose heirs subsequently became Dukes of Bedford and Earls of Southampton.

Drayton Beauchamp

Drayton and its adjoining small manor of Helesthorpe does not appear to have figured very strongly in the interest of the de Wolvertons, other than to collect the appropriate fees. The evidence from the Domesday survey suggests that these lands might have been severely devastated by the destructive progress of William's army in 1066. Helesthorpe was valued at £4 before the conquest and only 20 shillings when acquired. By 1086 the value had only appreciated to 40 shillings, half of its pre-Conquest value. Similarly drayton was valued at £5 before the Conquest and twenty years later was assessed at £4. One gets the sense that the barons were happy to let local interest squabble over the estate. In 1225 William de beauchamp occupied the manor but his right was contested by Roger de Drayton who claimed that his great grandfather Osbert once held the manor in the reign of Henry I. He lost the case and the Beauchamps continued their possession until 1312, when the estate was left to two daughters as co-heiresses. One of them, Alice, was abducted by "strangers" and murdered soon after the death of her father and her interest fell to her sister Elizabeth who was married to Ralph de Wedon. There were no suspects in the case and the matter was not pursued but at this distance in time it is tempting to put forward Cicero's famous argument *Cui bono* - who benefits? It would not be hard to conclude that Raplh de Wedon was behind this murky business. Ralph's troubles were not over, although he was never accused of complicity in the murder, because there were other claimants to the manor and the matter rumbled on in court until 1328.

Throughout all this the de Wolvertons appear to have taken a hands off approach.

In 1349 a new name enters the picture, William de Hynton, who claimed hereditary rights over the manor (how is not clear). He conveyed the manor to the Countess of Norfolk and her son, John de Cobham, granted the manor to the king in 1363. For what reason other than "because of the great love and good affection he had towards the Prince, eldest son of the King" is not clear. Once more the Wolverton interest (now

Appendices

held by the Longuevilles) appears to be marginal. Later the manor is granted to one of the members of the rising Cheyne family.

Aston Sandford

This is a small manor of mainly pasture land of 678 acres. Manno subinfeudated this manor quite early to Odo and he may have been the ancestor of those who later took the name of Sandford. It owed half a knight's fee to the Baron and was expected to contribute 10 shillings annually towards the guard of Northampton Castle. The de Sandfords presumably met their obligations without demur because the manor appears to have had a trouble-free history - at least as far as litigation goes.

Padbury

Nearer to Wolverton, Manno acquired several manors in North Bucks. Padbury at 2,000 acres and with a 20 hide assessment was almost as valuable as Wolverton and close enough to be managed directly. It remained under their direct control until the middle of the 14th century when various parts of the manor were sold off. This may have coincided with the minority of Ralph de Wolverton and the disappearance of the male line after the Black death of 1349.

One interesting character to acquire land here was Sir John Hawkwood, the famous mercenary or condottiere, who campaigned in Italy in the latter part of the 14th century. Hawkwood, who was the younger son of an Essex squire campaigned withEdward III in the 1340s, but like many was left without occupation or prospects when hostilities ceased after 1346. These men, no better than bandits at first, gained some credibility when they were hired by one of the Avignon Popes to defeat their enemies. Hawkwood, initially a junior commander, eventually became leader of the so-called White Company and variously hired his small army to contesting Italian States, mostly Florence and Milan. Although almost unknown in England, Hawkwood figures largely in Italian history of the 14th century and there is even a bronze mounted statue of him in Florence. He was well-rewarded for his services and set about acquiring properties in England to support him in his eventual retirement, which never came, as death took him in 1394. The manor was acquired in 1379 and indeed was inherited by his widow and son. Later in the 15th century it was sold to All Souls Colege Oxford.

Manno's Manor

Lamport

Lamport (sometime Landport or Langport) no longer exists as a place and in time became part of the great Stowe Estate. In 1066 it was assessed at 2½ hides and valued at 30s. It was held by Manno's man Gerard who may have been the ancestor of the Langport family who prospered here until the 15th century when Thomas de Langport left his estate to his two daughters. Part of the manor went to the Dayrell family and part to Thomas of Wykeham (probably Wicken).

Thornborough

Thornborough was another prosperous Ouse estate held by Berner from Manno. It was assessed at one knight's fee. The church at Thornborough was granted by baron Hamo of Wolverton to Luffield Priory in 1155. Further grants were made to the Priory which by 1279 held about one third of it. The priory was dissolved in 1494 ahead of the general dissolution and at that time the land went to the Abbot of Westminster. Edward VI granted this land to Sir Nicholas Throckmorton. Most of the rest of the manor was gifted to Biddlesdon Abbey by the de Fresne family who became the main tenants during the de Wolverton overlordship.

Wicken

Manno was given one part of the Wick manor, which eventually was known as Wick Hamon, subsequently Wickham and then Wicken. The land was directly administered from Wolverton until the middle of the 14th century when the surviving heirs to the de Wolverton estates, each sold their portion to Richard Woodville of Grafton, ancestor of Elizabeth Woodville who captivated Edward IV and thus became a progenitor of English monarchs.

Loughton

Loughton manor was divided in two by the time of the conquest, separated by Loughton Brook. One manor went to Walter Giffard, the other to Manno the Breton. Manno settled two knights on his manor upon acquisition but by the 12th century when Geoffrey de Loughton emerges, it appears to be in the hands of one family until 1461 when it was conveyed to trustees. The trustees transferred their rights to John edy, by that time

Appendices

prominent in Stony Stratford. There were family disputes about the rights to thae manor in the 16th century but the manor does appears to have remained with one branch or other of this family.

Stoke Hammond

Stoke, as it was originally, acquired its name from Hamon, the Baron of Wolverton, in the 12th century. The manor comprises about 1600 acres of mostly grazing land. The VCH described it over 100 years ago as "a somewhat scattered village.......with many half timber 17th-century cottages, some of which have thatched roofs." The village and the area still retains its rural character today even though it is on the edge of Milton Keynes. Manno kept this manor under his direct control, presumably with a steward to mange the estate which had hitherto been shared between eight thanes. This sort of division does suggest the idea of eight small holdings and this may have continued under the new barony, but with these small holders paying tithes to Manno. In 1247, William, the Baron, subinfeudated the manor to Alan son of Robert, although there are some documents suggesting that this may have happened earlier.

In the 14th century parts of the manor were granted to a member of the de Grey family and in time most of the manor was in the hands of the earl of Kent until the 16th century when it was sold.

Thenford

The village of Thenford is near Banbury in Oxfordshire and was always a small manor. It has little significant history after the conquest, at least in connection with Wolverton. It was most likely granted to one of Manno's followers and possibly because of its relative remoteness from the rest of the barony lost contact with the honour of Wolverton and was forgotten.

Maidwell

Maidwell was split into two manors, one of which was awarded to Manno. He in turn subinfeudated it to Berner, probably not the same Berner who was given Thornborough. Simon de Maidwell occurs in some deeds but eventually the manorial family took the name of Seyton which prevailed until the 18th century.

Manno's Manor

The Leicestershire Manors

Manno probably acquired these estates after 1075 when earl Ralph's son rebelled against William. Lutterworth was a significant manor. The early history of each is obscure. It is quite possible that they were subinfeudated to earl Ralph's Breton followers and that when Manno acquired them he took an oath of fealty from the incumbents and life continued much as before. The Verdon family emerge from Lutterworth in the Middle Ages and the Poultney family in Misterton.

The Domesday entries are as follows:

Mainou the Breton holds LUTTERWORTH from the King. 13 carucates of land. There were 9 ploughs. In lordship 3 ploughs; 2 male and 1 female slaves. 6 villagers with 7 smallholders; 12 Freemen have 4 ploughs. Meadow, 12 acres.

The value was and is £7. Earl Ralph held these 3 lands.

He also holds 2 carucates of land in MISTERTON. There were 2 ploughs. Now 1 Freeman with 1 smallholder has 1 plough there. The value was and is 20s. Earl Ralph held it.

He also holds 2 carucates of land in CATTHORPE. There were 2 ploughs. Now in lordship he has 1 1/2 ploughs. A mill at 2s.

The value was and is 20s. Earl Ralph held it.

Appendices

Appendix III Lords of the Manor

After 1066	Manno le Breton
C. 1114	Meinfelin
1155	Hamon
1184	Hamon son of Hamon
1198	William de Wolverton
1246	Alan de Wolverton
1250	John de Wolverton
1274	Sir John de Wolverton
1341	Sir John de Wolverton
1349	Ralph de Wolverton
1351	Divided between two daughters, Elizabeth and Margaret and their husbands.
1399	Sir John de Longueville
1439	Sir George de Longueville
1457	Richard de Longueville
14	Sir John de Longueville
1537	Arthur de Longueville
1556	Sir Henry de Longueville
1613	Sir Henry Longueville
	Sir Edward Longueville 1st baronet
1661	Sir Thomas Longueville 2nd baronet
1685	Si Edward Longueville 3rd baronet
1713	Dr John Radcliffe
1714	The Radcliffe Trust
1970	The Manor is sold to the Milton Keynes Development Corporation. *(Wolverton House, Wolverton Park and later Wolverton Mill were sold separately.)*

Manno's Manor

Appendix IV Vicars of Holy Trinity

This is the official succession, taken from Lipscomb's compilation. The list finishes in 1838, which is the close of this volume's history. Below I have added some notes about earlier clergymen taken from the Wolverton deeds.

1240 Alan
1260 Thomas
1260 William Bullingham
1274 Robert de Buckingham
1298 Ralph de Wolverton
1298 John de Ely
1334 Richard Ordwy
1361 Henry
1361 Adam Vincent de Caldecote
1370 John Waite
1371 John Syward
1390 John Napper
1394 Richard Dey
1404 Thomas Wychewode
1405 Robert Gornesthorpe
1405 John King
1411 Robert Bengrove
1417 William Dalby
1431 Thomas Legeley
1435 Richard Stacey
1438 Simon Fitzralph
1438 Nicholas Pardon
1447 Thomas Spencer
1452 Nicholas Pardon
1452 John Daventre
1457 William Camyle
1477 John Hancock
1517 William Herose
1543 John Rawlinson

Appendices

1546 George Turner
1587 Ralph Langford
1596 Robert Reynolds
1631 Thomas Pen
1645 Robert Ladbroke
1645 Gilbert Newton B.A.
1660 Robert Bostock B.A.
1661 Robert Duncumbe
1673 Alexander Featherstone M.A .
1684 Joseph Dogget M.A.
1686 Edward Chebsey
1702 Thomas Evans
1720 Edmund Green
1754 Edward Smith MA.
1782 Samuel Hale L.L.B.
1794 Henry Quartley
1838 Henry Reade Quartley M.A.

Further notes

I have also come across some references in the 13th century Wolverton deeds held in the Bodleian Library. These all relate to the the time when William FitzHamon was Baron, so as they are undated, they could relate to any time between 1220 and 1247.

Deed 49

William son of Hamon grants and confirms to William Capellanus of Wolverton with ½ virgate in Wolverton which Hugh Capellanus once held.

In another deed (244) he is a witness as William the vicar of Wullverton, and in another (474) the grant of a piece of land is described as between the land of Master William Vicar of Wlverton.

The deeds clearly describe William as Vicar of Wolverton and the first deed identifies a half-virgate of land (15 acres) which was probably assigned to support the vicar.

This would suggest a line of Hugh, followed by William, before Alan becomes the incumbent circa 1240.

Manno's Manor

For the most part these vicars maintained a living by having a piece of land attached to the church, usually known as glebe land, and through tithes - a fraction of the yield of the peasantry. Some of this was used to maintain the church and support the Priory. After the dissolution of the monasteries these practices continued until the church and vicarage came into the hands of the Longueville family in the 17th century. For about 100 years after that the income of the vicar was a matter of dispute until it was finally put to rest through a court hearing in 1805.

Appendices

Appendix V The Cock Inn

The Cock may be the earliest inn in medieval Stony Stratford, although the evidence for saying this is tenuous and best discussed here in an appendix.

Firstly, its location in the very centre of the town and the fact that it never appears in any of the manorial deeds from the 13th century onwards, suggests that this burgage plot was sold early.

Some have suggested that the Cok or Coccus family of the 14th century may have been associated with the Cock Inn. Let us examine that.

It is true that there are men and women with this name who appear in 13th and 14th century deeds. They variously bear the name Cocus, Coccus, Cok, le Cok and le Cooc. Could there be a connection? Is this a basis to date the Cock Inn earlier than the 16th century?

There are two things to say first: spelling was by no means as precise as it became in the age of print, and at the time that some names were written down surnames were only just beginning to emerge, and even there you could not find the hereditary consistency you might find today. William the Miller, for example, might have a son named John, who was later known as John of Cosgrove because he was born there.

The other problem is that these documents were written in a mixture of Latin, French and English, and it was really only in the 14th century that English words began to appear on official documents. Hitherto they had been mostly Latin with a mixture of French. The first uses of Cocus or Coccus are attempts to Latinize the name; later, French intrudes. We can put two interpretations on these surnames: they could either mean Cook or Cock.

Let's look at some transcripts of the surviving deeds:

The first group come from the lordship of William, son of Hamon, and can only be dated between 1214 and 1247 (the period that William was the lord) since the deeds themselves carry no dates. I have only included those parts which relate to those named Cocus or le Cok.

Deed 47 (undated, early 13th century)

> 6 half acres of land in Wolverton abutting on Watlingstrate between the land of Dom William son of Hamo and the land of Adam Coc

Deed 477 (undated, early 13th century)

Manno's Manor

Witness Richard Cocus of Wolverton

Deed 655 (dated 1252)

> John son of Alan of Wolverton agrees with Richard son of John of Wolverton and his wife Agnes, John grants (and here follows a list of properties with rents due - among them 3s on John Cocus's)

Deed 66 (mid 13th century)

> Richard Cocus witness

Deed 68 (mid 13th century)

> Richard Cocus witness

Deed 60 c 1300

> Richard Cocus witness

One deed identifies a ½ virgate (about 15 acres) used by Hugh Cocus and granted by William to his son Robert for customary use. Some payment would be made to the lord, although this is not mentioned here. Payment would be understood as by this date most of these land transactions had moved beyond direct military service to the lord; however, foreign service to the king is still a liability for the tenant. A later deed, describing another transaction, does incidentally mention that the land of Adam Cocus is on Watling Street. The relationship between Adam and Robert is not known. At the time of the first deed Robert has two daughters only. Did he have a son at a later date? Or is Adam a brother or cousin? Or indeed, was Adam a son of either Emma or Matilda who took the surname Coc? (If so this might be an argument for associating the name with the property, but we have no way of knowing.) Somewhat later Richard Cocus appears as a witness on some other deeds. The only thing we can infer from this is that Richard was an important enough figure to be a part of the courts where these transactions took place.

From this very slender evidence we can make the following inferences. The Cocus family was important enough in the 13th century for their land transactions to be documented. Some part of their land abutted Watling Street. That's about all we can say with certainty. There is a clear relationship between Hugh and Robert, but not between those two and Adam, Richard and John.

Henry Cok, witnessing the deed below and another of the same period, was possibly a serving priest at a chapel that pre-dated St Mary

Appendices

Magdalen, although there is no way of corroborating this. This does support the idea that the family were well connected in the district.

Deed 242 (late 13th century)

Witness Henry Cok, clerk

Another set of deeds survive from the early 14th century. The Latinised version of the name has gone, and if it is the same family, it is now Cok or le Cok or some variant.

Deed 78 1304

Nicholas Cok, son and heir of William Cok of Stonistratford releases to Robert de Hyntes of the same his claim on one acre of the meadow due Est of Wolverton above Heeforlong which is called Fourtyrodes. Of this, Robert has 2 parts by release from Nicholas and a third part Robert had by release from Agnes, widow of William Cok as dower.

Deed 130 c 1320

Richard de Houghton of Stonistratford grants and confirms to Biclas de Ardena and Dionysia his wife, 8 acres land in Wolverton; 2 acres are together at Depedene next land of Andrew le Cooc (and) of Geoffrey Hasteng; 2 acres abutt against Richard's headland next (unreadable); 1 acre called le Heydacre against which the aforesaid 2 acres abutt.

This set of documents does show us that the Cok family had land in Stony Stratford. This is also a period when Stony Stratford is beginning to emerge as a place separate from Wolverton; hence William Cok is identified as "of Stony Stratford." Although this deed refers to an acre in the east of Wolverton, the Coks clearly have their roots on the west side of the manor.

Deed 93 21st March 1331

Witness John le Cok

Deed 481 24th December 1331

Isable le Cok, widow of Thomas le Megre of Wolverton releases to Henry son of Anketil of Stoni Stratford junior all claims in 2 1/2 acres in Le Est field of Wolverton, which she obtained from her husnband as in the deed of feoffment of 5 Edward II

Manno's Manor

Deed 90 Tuesday after Michelmas 1331

John Auncell of Wolvertone grants and confirms to Thomas Oxe of the same and Agnes his wife 1 messuage with curtilage in Wolvertone and 2 selions adjoining next those of John le Cok. The messuage is between that of the grantors and that of John le Cok in le Est ende of Wolverton.

And these documents from 1331 again refer to some land in the east end of Wolverton.

On the basis of these scraps of evidence we can reasonably conclude that there was a family of this name of some prominence in Wolverton and most probably at the Stony Stratford end. Since they held land with some service attached it is also reasonable to say that the men were from a class of people who could, if pressed, do military service, or, better still, buy their way out of it. So it is likely that they enjoyed higher status than the average peasant.

There is an Alric the Cook who was granted Steeple Claydon by William I, then assessed at 20 hides, equivalent to Wolverton. There was also a Gilbert the Cook who held land from William in Northamptonshire. These were men of status, not men who stirred the broth in cauldrons, but men who organized and oversaw the kitchens. So the name Cook, often written as Cok, is one of the older surnames and not necessarily ascribed to mean kitchen workers.

This is not to say that the name was passed on from generation to generation. Sometimes they were - Butler and Chamberlain are good examples of this, but the practice was not universal. It is really not until the 13th century that some surnames begin to take root and not until the 14th century that they were required.

It is quite possible that the name originated locally. Hugh Cocus, or even his father, may have been the cook, that is the man who supervised the kitchens for the Baron of Wolverton. He was not a cook as such but a household knight who was given this management responsibility. In return for this service he was granted some land to support himself and his family. The Coks or Cooks may have sprung from these origins.

The suggestion that the name derives from the Cock Inn is plausible but equally difficult to substantiate. There is a man called Bules and le Bole

Appendices

(Bull) around in the 13th century and there is no evidence one way or another that he took his surname from the Bull Inn - if indeed it existed. It may be that the Cok family, with land abutting Watling Street, were in a position to exploit their location by building an inn or tavern and since they were a family of some status it is possible that their prosperity came from such income. It may well be that they called their inn the Cock and took their name from that, although I would be more convinced if the name were de Cok rather than le Cok.

The problem with both words is that they were both rendered in Middle English in the same way. Cock is latinized as coccus in most documents. Equally Cook is rendered in popular latin as cocus. So there is really no way for us to distinguish between the two after seven or eight centuries.

Another observation to make is that Cook is a very common surname and that Cock is extremely rare. There were only 729 people with the surname Cock in he last census - an imperceptible number. Not that this proves anything much but even if there were only this one Stony Stratford family bearing the name in 1300, one would expect many more after 30 generations. But there again, names do die out, or they get changed or modified. For example, the family who became the first earls of Southampton, changed their name from Writh to the rather more complex Wriothesley. Neither name today has survived as a surname.

The conclusion is that there is some linguistic evidence to make the connection between the Cock Inn and the family Cok, but no solid documentary evidence. We have two facts: there has been a Cock Inn in Stony Stratford for several centuries and there was a family named Cock or Cook living in the area in the 13th and 14th centuries. They may or may not have owned a hostelry, but it could have easily been called the Horseshoe or the Three Swans as The Cock. The apparent similarity of the names is not evidence of association.

Documentary evidence of the existence of the Cock Inn start to make their appearance in Chancery documents from 1500 to 1515, according to William Page in the VCH. I have not looked at these documents, but they would probably relate to taxes, which Henry VII was addicted to raising by any means.

Manno's Manor

The next piece of early documentary evidence is frankly controversial, and seems to stem from a footnote in George Lipscomb's History of Buckinghamshire, published in 1847. He wrote: "Mr. Serjeant Piggott willed in 1529, the the Town of Stoney Stratford should have his Inn there, called The Cock, towards the sustenation and reparation of the Bridges." (p.367) This information is re-presented and expanded upon by Sir Frank Markham in his *History of Stony Stratford*, but without any caveats. William Page, however, in the Victoria County History, does point out that there is no mention of The Cock or any bequest in Thomas Piggott's actual will, and concludes that there may have been a separate deed, now perhaps lost.

All of these conclusions may be correct, but these historians have arrived at these conclusions by inference rather than by evidence. Thomas Piggott did marry into the Edy family, who owned The Malletts and a fair amount of land abutting the Watling Street. It is a fair assumption that this included The Cock Inn, but their ownership is not documented.

Once again we have some scraps of factual evidence that may or may not be related and a lot of inferences that have been drawn from this to create a picture, which may or may not be reasonably accurate. Such are the pitfalls of history.

Appendices

Appendix VI Money

Monetary values are also an issue for the historian. Even in as short a period as my lifetime the purchasing power of a nominal pound has changed dramatically, and this coupled with the translation to decimal currency in 1971 makes it very difficult to render old values into a modern context. Some historians have tried to translate sums of money from an earlier age into present day values. While this approach may have its uses it tends to ignore other factors such as taxation and the fact that many parts of the economy in earlier times were cashless. For example, the medieval peasant earned very little actual money but part of his livelihood was covered by growing his own food and his house, such as it was, was mortgage free. He also lived in a low tax economy. The 17th century Vicar of Holy Trinity earned £50 per annum which made him one of the highest earners in the community. You could not say this today about C of E vicars who are paid much more modestly. Over this vast sweep of history monetary values have changed so much as to make comparison meaningless. In 1086 the entire manor was valued at £20. In 1714 the rent on the manor yielded £2,700. Today the land and properties are worth millions. Therefore I have approached this by simply stating the amounts of money as they were at the time and would suggest that the reader see these sums as relative to the age in which they are used.

The original penny was a silver coin which had the value of its silver content. The weight was eventually standardized by the crown so that 240 of these pennies made one pound in weight of silver. In the Middle Ages the penny could buy a lot, so it was worth while scoring it and breaking it in half for a half-penny, or into quarters to make "fourthings", or farthings as they were later known. In the Middle Ages the penny was largely the only coin in circulation, although some odd coins were introduced like the groat, the noble and the angel. Most accounting was expressed in Pounds, shillings and pence after being introduced by the Italian bankers in the

Manno's Manor

14th century, although the pound and shilling coins had to wait for the reign of Henry VII to be struck.

By the time this history reaches the 18th century the accounting of all disbursements is expressed as Pounds, shillings and pence, although the curious symbols "L" for pound and "d" for penny are a holdover from the Italian bankers who counted heir money in Livres, solidi, and denarii. The annual income from the Wolverton manor in 1713 was £2,187 2s. 4d. - a sum which is probably the equivalent of millions today. Shortly after 1066 Manno was able to buy the entire manor for £15. Monetary values are therefore relative to the times.

BIBLIOGRAPHY

Bailey, K.A. (2004). *Who was who and who became whom: Buckinghamshire Landowners 1066 and 1086*. Records of Buckinghamshire, Vol 44.

Bamford, Helen, Went, David & McOmish, David. *An Archaeological Survey of the Manor House and Gardens, Stantonbury, Milton Keynes*. Records of Buckinghamshire, Vol. 45.

Barber, R. (1994). *Henry Plantagenet* . Barnes Noble Books.

Barber, R. W. (1970). *The knight & chivalry*. Longmans.

Barker, J. (2006). *Agincourt. The King, the campaign, the battle*. Abacus.

Bartlett, R. (2002). *England Under the Norman and Angevin Kings, 1075-1225*. Oxford University Press, USA.

Baskerville, G. (1972). *English Monks and the Suppression of the Monasteries The Bedford Historical Series*. Jonathan Cape, London.

Bayne-Powell, Rosamond. (1951). *Travellers in Eighteenth Century England*.

Bentley Smith, Dorothy. (2005) *A Georgian Gent & Co.: The Life and Times of Charles Roe of Macclesfield*. Landmark Publishing Ltd.

Beresford, M. W., & Joseph, J. K. S. S. (1979). *Medieval England: An Aerial Survey*. (2nd ed.). Cambridge University Press.

Bishop, M. (1986). *The Middle Ages* (2nd ed.). Mariner Books.

Bradbury, J. (2005). *Stephen and Matilda*. The History Press.

Briggs, A. (1986). *A Social History of England* . Penguin (Non-Classics).

Britnell, R. H. *The Origins of Stony Stratford*. Records of Bucks. Vol XX Part 3, 1977.

Brushe, John. *Holy Trinity, Wolverton, Buckinghamshire*.

Buckinghamshire in the 1760s and 1820s: the county maps of Jefferys & Bryant. (2000).

Butler, L. H., & Given-Wilson, C. (1980). *Medieval Monasteries of Great Britain*. Michael Joseph.

Cantor, N. F. (1992). *Inventing the Middle Ages*. Lutterworth Press.

Castor, H. (2005). *Blood and Roses: The Paston Family and the Wars of the Roses* . Faber & Faber.

Castor, H. (2010). *She-Wolves: The women who ruled England* . Faber & Faber.

Clark, G. N. (1963). *The Later Stuarts 1660-1714*. OUP Oxford.

Curry, A. (2006). *Agincourt: A New History*. Tempus.

Manno's Manor

D'Aubigne, J. H. M. (2008). *History of the Reformation in the Sixteenth Century*. Powder Springs Press.

Davies, G. (1963). *The Early Stuarts 1603-1660*. OUP Oxford.

Delaney, F. (1989). *The Celts* . Hunter Publishing inc.

Dickens, Charles. (1852) *Bleak House*.

Dyer, C. (2003). *Making a Living in the Middle Ages: The People of Britain 850-1520* . Yale University Press.

Elvey, G.R. *Luffield Priory Charters, Parts I and II*. Buckinghamshire Record Office.

English Heritage. *Stony Stratford: Historic Town Assessment. Draft Report*.

English Heritage. *Wolverton and New Bradwell: Historic Town Assessment. Draft Report*.

Evans, J. (1998). *Flowering of the Middle Ages*. Thames & Hudson.

Fenn, J., & Ramsay, A. (2011). *Paston letters: original letters, written during the reigns of Henry VI, Edward IV, and Richard III by various persons of rank or consequence; history ; with notes historical and explanation*. Nabu Press.

Fleming, R. (2011). *Britain After Rome*. Penguin Global.

Gies, F., & Gies, J. (1991). *Life in a Medieval Village*. Harper Perennial.

Gottfried, R. S. (1986). *The Black Death* (New Ed ed.). Papermac.

Guest, I. (1991). *Dr. John Radcliffe and His Trust*. The Radcliffe Trust.

Guy, J. (1990). *Tudor England*. Oxford University Press, USA.

Hackwood, F. (1985). *Inns, Ales and Drinking Customs of Old England*. Bracken Books.

Hassell, J. (1819). *A Tour of the Grand Junction Canal*. Islington

Hobbes, Thomas. (1651). *Leviathan*.

Hollister, C. W., & Frost, A. C. (2003). *Henry I*. Yale University Press.

Hoskins, W. G. (1977). *Making of the English Landscape* (Revised ed.). Hodder & Stoughton Ltd.

Huizinga, J. (1968). *The Waning of the Middle Ages*. Peregrine.

Hutchinson, R. (2008). *Thomas Cromwell*. Phoenix.

Hyde, Francis E., Markham, S. F. (2002). *A History of Stony Stratford: And the Immediate Vicinity*. Wolverton & District Archaeological Society.

Hyde, Francis E. (1948). *A Short History of Wolverton*. Wolverton.

Jack, Harry. *Locomotives of the LNWR Southern Division*. RCTS 2001. p. 26.

Jacob, E. F. (1961). *The Fifteenth Century, 1399-1485*. Oxford University Press, USA.

Bibliography

Jones, D. (2010). *Summer of Blood: The Peasants' Revolt of 1381*. UK General Books.

Jones, T. (2005). *Terry Jones' Medieval Lives*. BBC Books.

Kennett, White. (1695) *Parochial Antiquities attempted in the history of Ambrosden, Burcester* Vol 1, p 24. .

Leland, J., & Chandler, a. J. H. (1998). *John Leland's Itinerary: Travels in Tudor England*. Sutton Publishing Ltd.

Lipscomb, G. (1847). *The History and Antiquities of the County of Buckingham, Vol. IV.*

Mackie, J. D. (1952). *The Earlier Tudors, 1485-1558*. Oxford University Press, USA.

Markham, S. F. (1986). *The History of Milton Keynes and District: Up to 1830 v. 1*. Wolverton & District Archaeological Society.

Markham, S. F. (1986). *The History of Milton Keynes and District: v. 2* . Wolverton & District Archaeological Society.

McKisack, M. (1959). *The Fourteenth Century, 1307-1399* . Oxford University Press, USA.

Miles, D. (2006). *The Tribes of Britain*. Phoenix.

Miller, E., & Hatcher, J. (1978). *Medieval England: Rural Society and Economic Change 1086*. Pearson.

Mortimer, I. (2009). *The Time Traveller's Guide to Medieval England: A Handbook for Visitors to the Fourteenth Century*.

Myres, J. N. L., & Clark, S. G. (1986). *The English Settlements*. Clarendon Press, Oxford.

Newby, H. (1988). *Country Life: A Social History of Rural England*. Cardinal Books.

Page, William, ed. (1923). *Victoria County History: Buckinghamshire.*

Penn, T. (2011). *Winter King: The Dawn of Tudor England* . Allen Lane.

Platt, C. (1979). *The Atlas of Mediaeval Man*. Macmillan.

Poole, A. L. (1963). *From Domesday Book to Magna Carta 1087-1216*. OUP Oxford.

Power, E. (1963). *Medieval People*. Rowman Littlefield.

Powicke, S. M. (1963). *The Thirteenth Century 1216-1307*. OUP Oxford.

Pryor, F. (2006). *Britain BC: Life in Britain and Ireland before the Romans*. Harper Collins UK.

Manno's Manor

Pryor, F. (2007). *Britain in the Middle Ages: An Archaeological History.* HarperCollins UK.

Purkiss, D. (2007). *The English Civil War: A People's History.* Harper Perennial.

Ratcliff, O. (1900). *The History and Antiquities of the Newport Hundreds.* Cowper Press: Olney.

Rivet, A. L. F., & Smith, C. (1979). *Place Names of Roman Britain.* Batsford Ltd.

Roberts, J. (2011). *Guide to Scripts Used in English Writings up to 1500.* British Library.

Ross, C. (1983). *Edward IV.* Methuen.

Salway, P. (1984). *Roman Britain. The Oxford History of England, Vol Ia.* Clarendon Press.

Seward, D. (1983). *Richard III: England's Black Legend.* Littlehampton Book Services Ltd.

Sheahan, James Joseph. (1862) *History and Topography of Buckinghamshire.* London

Sidney Smith.(1851) *Rides on Railways.*

Stenton, Sir F. M. (1970). *Anglo-Saxon England.* OUP Oxford.

Stonor-Saunders, F. (2004). *Hawkwood.* Faber & Faber.

Sykes, B. (2006). *Blood of the Isles.* Bantam Press.

Tinniswood, A. (2008). *The Verneys: A True Story of Love, War and Madness in Seventeenth-Century England.* Vintage Books.

Toulmin Smith, Lucy. *The Itinerary of John Leland in or about the Years 1535-1543, Vol II.*

Tuchman, B. W. (1979). *A Distant Mirror: The Calamitous 14th Century.* Macmillan.

Warren, W. L. (1998). *King John.* Yale University Press.

Warren, W. L. (2000). *Henry II.* Yale University Press.

Watson, J. S. (1963). *The Reign of George III: 1760-1815.* OUP Oxford.

Webb, D. (2001). *Pilgrimage in Medieval England .* Hambledon & London.

Wickham, C. (2010). *The Inheritance of Rome: A History of Europe from 400 to 1000 .* Penguin Books.

Williams, B. (1963). *The Whig Supremacy 1714-1760.* Oxford (at the Clarendon Press).

Bibliography

Williams, R.J. & Zeepvat, R. J. (1993). *Bancroft - a late Bronze Age/Iron Age Settlement, Roman Villa and Temple Mausoleum.* Buckinghamshire Archaeological Society, Monograph, Series 7.

Wilson, D. M. (1976). *Archaeology of Anglo-Saxon England* . Methuen.

Wolffe, B. (2001). *Henry VI.* Yale University Press.

Wood, M. (1981). *English Mediaeval House.* Ferndale editions.

Wood, M. (1982). *In Search of the Dark Ages.* BBC Books.

Wood, M. (1988). *Domesday: A Search for the Roots of England.* Guild Publishing, London.

Woods, W. (1976). *England in the Age of Chaucer.* Stein & Day Pub.

Wotton, T., Kimber, E., & Johnson, R. A. (1771). *The Baronetage of England: Containing a Genealogical and Historical Account of All the English Baronets Now Existing. Illustrated with Their Coats of Arms. To which is Added an Account of Such Nova Scotia Baronets as are of English Families; and a Dictionary of Heraldry. by E. Kimber and R. Johnson, Volume 3.* London.

Yarwood, D. (1985). *The Architecture of Britain.* Harper Collins.

Zeepvat, R.J. (1991). *The Milton Keynes Project.* Records of Buckinghamshire, Vol. 33.

Ziegler, P. (1991). *The Black Death.* Alan Sutton Publishing.

Manuscript Sources

Bodleian Library: Radcliffe Deed Deposit.

Badminton: Archives of the Duke of Beaufort

Buckinghamshire Records Office: Various papers relating to Wolverton and Stony Stratford.

Nottinghamshire Records Office: Archives of the Duke of Portland.

University of Wales, Bangor: Mona Mine MSS.

Public Record Office: London and Birmingham Railway Archives

Manno's Manor

Acknowledgements

A book such as this does not come to life unassisted.

The pioneering history of Wolverton was produced by George Lipscomb in 1847. This was followed by the Victoria County History, edited by William Page in 1923. Both have thoroughly mined the state documents for references to Wolverton and Stony Stratford. I am also indebted to F.E. Hyde and Sir S.F. Markham for their published works on local history in the mid 20th century. I would have made little progress without the pioneering work of the Wolverton and District Archaeological Society in the 1950s which was continued professionally by the Milton Keynes Archaeology Unit in the last quarter of the 20th century.

I have drawn heavily on the work of Dr. Ivor Guest for information about Dr. John Radcliffe and the Trust that bears his name. His book has provided me with very useful pointers to primary documents which I have been able to access. Thanks are also due to The Radcliffe Trust who have kindly given me permission to access, and in some cases copy, their documents on deposit at the Bodleian Library.

The staff at the Bodleian Library have been unfailingly professional and helpful during the many hours spent in their reading rooms. The same can be said of the staff at the Buckinghamshire County Archive and at the Milton Keynes Library.

I wish to thank Matthew Nayler for directing my attention to Thomas Harrison's activities in Anglesey and Karen Roman who has shared with me a lot of information about her ancestor, Thomas Harrison. June Watson was also instrumental in clearing up a reported error in Richard Harrison's age.

In the progress of this book Robert Ayers has been unfailingly helpful with his wisdom and advice and I would also like to thank Christopher Gleadell who has from time to time been able to contribute from his deep knowledge of the Wolverton area.

And finally, and literally too numerous to mention by name, are the contributors to the Wolverton Facebook pages and my Wolverton Past Blog who have in countless small ways acted as a corrective to my thinking and added new insights.

INDEX OF PERSONS

A

Aelfric, Thane of Wolverton 31–33, 49, 247

Azur Rufus 46

B

Basing, Adam 59

Basset, Egelina 73

Basset, Gilbert 73

Battams, John 228

Battams, Robert 237

Battams, Thomas 188

Battison, John 172, 176, 181–182, 192, 197

Bayly, Henry 206–207

Bayly, Sir Nicholas 205–206

Beatrice, wife of Meinfelin 52

Beaumont, Sir George 173, 175, 197, 192

Bernerus son of Azur 46

Bisi a thane of Calverton 76

Bostock, Robert 147

Brill, John 237

Brittain, James 177

Bromley, William 162, 173, 197, 192

Burgred of Olney 33

Bury, Edward 6

C

Carey, Catharine 157

Carne, Christopher 149–151

Carter, Christopher 173–175, 192

Chapman, Mary 228

Cheyne, John 129

Cheyne, Sir John 60

Cogenhoe, Agnes 60

Cogenhoe, William 60

Cole, William viii, 110–111, 164

Cotton, Elizabeth 157

Creed, Richard 5

Crispin, Miles 61

D

Dawes, John 206, 209

de Albini, William 56

de Arderne, Nicholas 83

de Bello Campo, Peverel 45–46

de Bello Campo, Stephanus 45–46

de Bolbec, Hugh 76

de Bolbec, Isabella 76

de Bolbec, Walter 73

de Bossu, Robert 54, 143

de Calverton, John 74, 79, 119

de Cogenhoe, William 124

de Courtney, Reginald 73

de Freine, Henry 46–47

de Loughton, Bartholemew 45–47, 115, 252

de Louth, Roger 124

de Stoke, Owen 46–47

de Wolverton, Alan 56

de Wolverton, Cecilia 59

de Wolverton, Elizabeth 59

de Wolverton, Joan 59

de Wolverton, Margery 59

de Wolverton, Ralph (d. 1351) 59

de Wolverton, Sarah 59

de Wolverton, Sir John (d. 1274) 59

de Wolverton, Sir John (d. 1342) 59

de Wolverton, Sir John (d. 1349) 59

de Wolverton, William 56–57

Manno's Manor

de Wolverton. Constance 59
Drayson, Catharine 203
Duncumbe, Robert 147
Durham, Samuel 89
Durham, Thomas 189
Durrant, Thomas 192

E

Earl of Aylesford 234
Earl of Uxbridge 205-210
Earl Spencer 201-202, 205, 210
Edmunds, Mary 238-239
Edward the Atheling 49
Edy, John 75, 131, 156
Edy, William 227
Escourt, Edmond 188
Evans, Thomas 147, 186, 257

F

Furtho, Edward 157
Furtho, Thomas 149

G

Galfridi, William son of 46
Gascoigne, Sir Nicholas 157
Giffard, Walter 61, 65, 122, 252
Gill, George 182, 197, 182-183, 185
Gleed, Thomas 188
Godfrey, Dorothy 163
Godwin, Thane of Wolverton 31-33, 49, 247
Grant, William 183
Green, Edmund 186-188, 234, 257
Grosmont, Henry Duke of Lancaster 64

H

Hakewill, Henry 196, 234-235
Hamblin, Joseph 231

Hamon, son of Hamon 54
Hamon, son of Meinfelin 9, 40, 43, 46-47, 51, 54-56, 73, 84, 124, 252-253, 255, 257, 259
Harding, William 177
Hardwick, Phillip 6
Harold, King of England 32
Harrison, John 183, 201, 207
Harrison, Richard 209, 219
Harrison, Spencer 242
Harrison, Thomas 182-183, 188, 193, 199-201, 220, 201-207, 220, 209-212, 214-217, 219-220, 229, 234, 236, 272
Hassell, J.C. 1, 10, 9
Hastings, John 132
Hawise, wife of William de Wolverton 57
Hawkwood, Sir John 65, 251
Hayle, John 132-133
Hearne, Thomas 160
Henry I, King of England 39
Henry III, King of England 56-57, 74, 137
Henry VI, King of England 137
Henson, George 189
Hewes, John 124
Hinders, John 149
Hipwell, Michael 156, 228, 231
Hughes, Michael 209
Hughes, Rev. Edward 205-206, 209
Hunt, Joan 60, 124, 127
Hunt, John 60

I

Imworth, Richard 124

Isenhamstede, Alexander de 46–47

J

Jones, Edward 209
Judith, Countess of Northumbria 33

L

Ladbroke, Robert 147
Langford, Ralph 146
le Coc, Adam 64
le Grik, William 115
le Warner, John 134
Leland, John 141, 160
Leofwin Oara 49
Leofwin of Nuneham 49
Longueville, Arthur 129
Longueville, George (d. 1499) 129
Longueville, Margaret 152
Longueville, Marie 163
Longueville, Sir Edward (1604-1661) 157, 159

Perry, William 180
Pryor, Charles 182

Q

Quartley, Henry 187–188, 234, 257
Quartley, Thomas 183, 212

R

Radcliffe, Dr. John 163–165, 168–169, 171, 255
Ralph, Earl of East Anglia 37, 40
Ratcliffe, Thomas 181, 188
Rich, Samuel and Sarah 228
Richard III, King of England 138
Roe, Charles 207, 220, 267
Roger of Ivry 61
Rook, Simon 134

Rowse, Thomas 143

S

Savage, Alice 133
Savage, Richard 132
Scott, Robert 180, 191
Scott, Thomas 177
Simon son of Berner 46
Smith, Edward 187, 257
Smith, Henry 190
Smith, Sidney 8, 10, 8, 270
Snowe, Richard 145
Stephenson, Joseph 183
Stephenson, Robert 5–6
Swannell, William 177

T

Thori, Thane of Wolverton 31–33, 49, 247
Trusbut, Agatha 55–56
Trusbut, Sir William 55
Tucker, John 237–239
Turner, George 146

V

Vacca, Warnerus de 43, 46–47
Verdone, Bertram de 46
Vis de Lou (Videloue), John 64
Vis de Lou, Geoffrey 62
Vis de Lou, Roger 46, 62–63
Vis de Lou, William iii, 60–61, 64, 156

W

Wake, Hugh 59
Wall, Thomas 188
Walsingham, Sir Francis 145
Waltheof, Earl of Northumbria 49
Weight, George 7
Wilkinson, John 209

Manno's Manor

Wilkinson, William 188
William de Warenne 52
William I, King of England 29, 38, 262
William Rufus, King of England 39
Williams, Thomas 205-206, 208-209
Willis, Browne viii, 80, 111, 139, 185, 219, 223, 231
Wilmin, Henry 228

Winemar the Fleming 61
Wittewronge, Sir John 201-202, 223
Wodell, Richard 177, 181, 191
Wodell, Thomas 181-182
Woodville, Elizabeth 135-137, 252
Wulfhere 25-26, 35, 26-27, 32, 91
Wulfward White 33

INDEX OF PLACES

A

Anglesey 205-206, 208, 211, 272
Ardwell Fields 99, 177
Aspley 163
Aston Sandford 40, 251
Aylesbury 5, 30, 40, 164, 248

B

Banbury 5, 40, 253
Bancroft 12, 17, 19-20, 23-24
Barr Close 97, 149
Barr Piece 97, 149, 177
Beachampton 69, 131
Beaudesert, Staffordshire 205-206, 210
Bedford 109, 233, 250
Berkshire 62, 157
Birmingham 5, 10, 5-7, 199, 216, 225, 243-244
Bletchley Park viii, 219
Brackley 5
Bradwell Brook 4, 11, 17, 20, 95, 101, 107, 155, 177, 199, 237, 242
Bradwell Priory 54, 57, 62, 87, 95, 107, 110, 129, 141, 144
Braunston 212

Brentford 212
Brick Kiln Farm 155, 177, 237, 242
Brill 81, 237
Brittany 37-38, 40
Brook Field 18, 177, 181
Buckingham viii, 5, 25, 30, 40, 69, 75, 93, 127, 131, 138, 156, 163, 165, 220, 231, 243, 256
Buckinghamshire 4-5, 8, 12, 35, 19, 29-30, 33, 37-39, 42-43, 49, 51-52, 54, 60, 65, 109, 119, 127, 143, 159, 199, 220, 218, 234, 264, 267, 272

C

Calverton 4, 11, 13, 26, 30, 67, 69-70, 73-79, 85, 94-95, 119, 115, 131, 151
Carshalton, Surrey 172
Castlethorpe 33, 70
Catthorpe 40
Cerrig y Bledda mine 208
Chalfont St Giles 40, 59, 124, 129
Chenies 43, 60, 129, 249
Chester 206
Chicksand Priory 74, 144-145
Clifton Reynes 56

Cogenhoe Manor 60
Colt's Holm 98
Cosgrove 2, 20, 70, 105, 131, 157, 214, 224, 233, 236, 259
Cowfair 77

D

Dean's Close 97
Debb's Hook 98-99
Drayton Beauchamp 40, 249-250
Dunsley 42

E

Ellesborough 40, 42, 248

F

Fenny Stratford 19, 60, 67, 124, 224
Fiddler's Butts 99
Flintshire 209
Fornhill 223
Fritwell, Oxfordshire 163
Fuller's Slade 9, 13, 72, 83, 94, 177
Furtho 75, 149-150, 157
Furzes 99, 149, 154, 177
Fyfield, Hampshire 55

G

Gayhurst 146
Geddington 80
Godalming 221
Grafton 135, 159, 252
Grange 23, 106, 144
Greenleys 9, 94, 99, 177, 227

H

Hanslope 33, 61, 123
Hardingstone 80
Haversham 20, 26, 69-70, 111, 131-132, 199
Helsthorpe 40, 42

Hertfordshire 38-39, 80, 157, 201-202
High Park 199
Higham Ferrers 109
Hockliffe 223
Holy Trinity 38, 89, 99, 110-111, 119, 112, 142-143, 146, 189, 196, 205, 239, 265, 267
Horsefair 77

I

Icknield Way 42
Ipswich 93
Isenhampstead 43, 60, 249

K

Kent's Hook 98-99

L

Lactodoro 19, 67-68
Lamport 40, 42, 45, 252
Lavendon 33, 49
Leicestershire 38-40, 45, 254
Linces 98
Linford 70, 151
Little Billing 60, 122-124, 127, 160
Little Brickhill 68, 222
London 5, 10, 5-7, 11, 42, 68, 70, 80, 93, 118, 135, 137-138, 170, 172, 181, 190, 196, 201, 220, 205-206, 208-209, 216, 219, 222, 225-226, 243-244
Loughton 11, 26, 30-31, 40, 42, 45-47, 63, 75, 115, 131, 151, 224, 252
Low Park 99, 177
Lower Slade 97, 177
Ludkin's Closes 99
Ludlow 138

Manno's Manor

Luffield Priory 54, 57, 89, 143–144, 252

Lutterworth 40, 254

M

Magiovinto 19, 67–68

Maidwell 40, 42, 45, 248, 253

Manor Farm 12, 20, 23–24, 133, 144, 155, 177, 181, 240–243

Market Harborough 40

Market Square 73, 77, 85, 227, 231–232

Marron Field 97–98

Mead Mill 107, 131–132, 180

Mill Lane 77, 231

Milton Keynes ix, 10, 3–4, 35, 168, 180, 196, 220, 212, 242, 253, 267

Misterton 40, 254

Morter Pitts 99

N

Newport Hundreds viii, 30

Newport Pagnell viii, 20, 30, 70, 75, 93, 101, 119, 191, 199, 202, 224, 233

Northampton 40, 47, 59, 69, 80, 109, 123, 138, 146, 184, 233, 236, 251

Northamptonshire 33, 39–40, 45, 54, 60, 62, 80, 109, 123, 127, 154, 157, 201, 203, 236, 248, 262

O

Olney viii, 33, 119

Orton Longueville 121–123

Orton Waterville 121

Overton, Huntingdonshire 121–122

Oxford 5, 35, 71, 76, 85, 108, 133, 143, 146, 165–168, 170, 172, 185, 187, 212, 251

Oxfordshire 29, 49, 163, 253

P

Padbury 40, 42, 100, 124, 132, 251

Passenham 25, 68, 75, 131

Petworth 221

Portfield Way 101

Q

Quinton 172

R

Radcliffe Infirmary, Oxford 165–167

Radcliffe Library, Oxford 165–166, 187–188

Radcliffe Observatory, Oxford 165, 167–168

River Ouse ix, 4, 30, 70, 107, 117, 149, 181, 185, 213–215

Roger's Holm 97

Russell Street 77

Rylands 97, 177, 226

S

Seckloe 3, 34, 50

Severidge 66, 98, 177

Shenley 75

Simpson 49

Snellshall Priory 62, 145

Southampton ii, 93, 250, 263

St Albans 68, 136, 201

St Helens 209

St Mary Magdalen 60, 76, 79, 83, 85, 146, 260

St. Giles 185

Stacey Bushes 117, 149, 177, 237, 240-243

Stantonbury 30, 70, 131, 187-188, 201-202, 220, 202-203, 217, 223, 267

Stoke Hammond 40, 54, 62, 253

Stonebridge House Farm 155, 177, 180, 240-243

Stony Stratford viii-ix, 1, 4-6, 9, 15, 35, 51, 63-64, 67-70, 89, 70-73, 89, 74-84, 86-88, 91, 96-97, 101, 111-118, 130-132, 134-136, 138-139, 142-143, 149, 151-153, 156, 167, 173-176, 180-182, 184-186, 195, 199, 209, 213-214, 216, 218-219, 221, 223-225, 229, 231-235, 237, 240, 243-245, 253, 259, 261-264, 267, 272

Swansea 207, 209

T

Tattenhoe 145

Terle Mill 132-133

Thenford 40, 45, 253

Thornborough 32-33, 40, 45, 47, 54, 63, 143-144, 252-253

Thornton 69

Towcester 19, 67-68, 236

Tring 42

Two Mile Ash 11, 224

U

Upper Hey 98

W

Wakefield, Yorkshire 169

Wallingford 42

Waltham, Herts. 80

Water Hall viii, 219

Watling Street ix, 4, 11-13, 19, 39, 62, 67, 70-76, 78, 83-85, 94, 97, 109, 112, 115, 118, 130, 148, 152, 154-156, 167, 176-177, 180, 199, 205, 221-222, 234, 237, 240, 243, 260, 263-264

Wavendon 49

Wepre, Flintshire 209, 211

West Mill 101, 132, 180

Whaddon Hall viii, 223

Whittlewood Forest 54-55, 135

Wicken 40, 45, 54-55, 84, 124, 132, 183, 188, 252

Wiltshire 94

Winchester 109

Windsor 221

Wingrave 40

Wolverton i, iii, vii-ix, 1-9, 11-15, 35, 15-17, 20, 23-26, 35, 26-27, 29-34, 37-40, 43, 45, 47-51, 66, 55, 57, 59-65, 67-79, 83-85, 87-88, 91, 93-97, 99-103, 105, 107-110, 119, 113-119, 121-122, 124, 127, 129-134, 141-149, 151-157, 160, 163-165, 167-168, 171-173, 176-177, 197, 180-181, 185-186, 188-189, 191-193, 195-196, 199-201, 203-205, 209, 211-221, 224-226, 228, 230, 234-238, 240-245, 247-253, 255-257, 259-262, 267, 272

Wolverton House 155, 193, 211, 215-218, 220, 226, 240-242

Wolverton Park 15, 99, 155, 177, 240-241

Manno's Manor

Wolverton Turn 12, 15, 35, 15, 24, 26, 35, 26, 94

Wroxeter 11, 68

MAGIC FLUTE PUBLICATIONS

Previously Published

The Lost Streets of Wolverton   Bryan Dunleavy

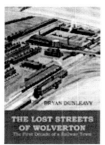

This book tells the story of the creation of England's first company railway town, almost 175 years ago. It describes the decisions which led to its location, the ad hoc planning which led to this new community and its growth and development in its first decade. The works, the housing, the shops and most of the amenities have since disappeared as a consequence of new development and the book is a valuable reconstruction of the early town from preserved documents and reports.

ISBN 978-1-909054-004   PRICE £10

I Grew Up in Wolverton

Conversations and memories

Ruth Edwards

A compilation of Facebook conversations about growing up in Wolverton covering the second half of the 20th century.

ISBN 978-1-909054-035   PRICE £10

282